Also by Richard W. Kropf

Teilhard, Scripture, and Revelation

Evil and Evolution

A THEODICY

Richard W. Kropf

RUTHERFORD ● MADISON ● TEANECK
FAIRLEIGH DICKINSON UNIVERSITY PRESS
LONDON AND TORONTO: ASSOCIATED UNIVERSITY PRESSES

Associated University Presses
440 Forsgate Drive
Cranbury, N. J. 08512

Associated University Presses
25 Sicilian Avenue
London WC1A 2QH, England

Associated University Presses
2133 Royal Windsor Drive
Unit 1
Mississauga, Ontario
Canada L5J 1K5

Library of Congress Cataloging in Publication Data

Kropf, Richard W., 1932–
  Evil and evolution.

  Bibliography: p.
  Includes index.
  1. Good and evil.   2. Theodicy.   I. Title.
BJ1401.K74   1983   231'.8   81-72041
ISBN 0-8386-3157-6

Printed in the United States of America

In Memory of
Margaret Norlin Foley
(1926–1979)
who fought "the good fight"

Contents

Preface

This book is concerned with theodicy, that is to say, with that part of theology dealing with God's justice. As such, it is a book that is involved with the long-standing problem of evil in the world and, in being so, continues a tradition that, at least in Western literature, goes back as far as the Bible.

Why then another attempt at this inexhaustible and apparently insoluble subject? For if it is true, as has been more than once said, that the ultimate test of any theology is to be found in its attempt to deal with evil, then I think it must also be said that on that account all theologies have more or less failed. What hope can there be that this attempt will prove any more successful?

The answer, I believe, must lie first of all in the analysis of the overall problem itself, on both the theoretical and the practical level. On the theoretical level the matter seems to be most complex, particularly when seen as a series of separate yet interconnected problems. For example, while sin may appear to be easily explained by human freedom, factors such as the presumed all-powerfulness, omniscience, and the total goodness of God throw this explanation into question. At the very least it appears to contain serious contradictions. At the same time, such an approach appears to shed no light on the reason for the occurrence of so-called natural disasters, or if it attempts to do so, is apt to end up in labeling them as "acts of God" in the most objectionable sense.

On the practical level, however, the matter is more straightforward: it is simply that sin, suffering, and death, experienced by us as evils, touch us too closely to be explained away by purely intellectual solutions, particularly any that would invoke the unfathomed workings of a good God. Such attempts, as we know too well, may just as likely end up in the rejection of God altogether. Here the inadequacies of the theories are translated into practice and the ultimate test for theology becomes the moment of truth for faith.

The complexity of the problem, however, may not really be so impossible as it sometimes appears. This is not to imply that any solution is quite simple; in fact, it is probably safe to say that the major reason for the failure of most theodicies is that they proposed a solution that simplified the problem by ultimately rejecting one or another of the stubborn factors that seemed to block the way to an easy solution.

These basic factors or elements that have to be kept in mind are four: first, the reality of God and the goodness generally attributed to such a supreme being; second, the reality of evil itself; third, the reality of the world in which both good and evil are found; and fourth, the reality of human freedom and responsibility. A solution that in any way eliminates any of these realities is, to my mind, no solution at all—certainly not a comprehensive theodicy in any satisfactory sense of the word.

While the major part of this book will be taken up with a discussion of each of these four major subjects (with a chapter or more given to each), what is more important is the attempt to constantly relate them, each to the other, within each chapter. Thus, beginning with a well-laid foundation, an analysis of the problem as such, I have tried to avoid the appearance of simply throwing together four "pre-fab" walls on which to tack a roof of sorts, but rather have attempted to work more like a mason, who even while working on one wall, adds a course or two of bricks along the others. In that way, I hope something of the completed structure can be seen at each stage of the project.

The reason for this procedure is important, both for the author and for the reader. For my part, the key to the whole problem is the process of evolution. Taken in isolation from each other, each of the four realities on which I focus is unintelligible apart from the others, even God, at least from the aspect of theodicy, for it must deal with God primarily in terms of the creator's relationship to the world, and that in its entirety. Again the object is comprehensiveness. A partial solution is of little help for a global problem.

For the reader this procedure may be even more important. This book was not written primarily for the academic who is adept at isolating a single subject for exhaustive analysis while at the same time able to keep all the other aspects of reality from getting lost.

Rather I had in mind primarily the busy "professionals," those deeply involved in helping others cope with the process of living—psychotherapists, medical personnel, counsellors of various types. If my procedure seems to be sometimes a bit repetitious on the one hand, and to strain forward toward a synthesis on the other, it is because I have been deeply concerned to treat this very difficult subject in a way that is not only comprehensive but comprehensible.

***

For anyone writing today, especially in the area of theology, sexism in language has become an occupational hazard of the highest degree. Anthropomorphism of a particularly patriarchal form seems to plague Western theology, but few feel that a shift to a predominantly matriarchal expression would improve matters theologically nor do editors (many of them female) show much patience for the contorted constructions involved in attempts to avoid the use of personal pronouns in reference to God. Certainly, a neuterized form cannot be deemed to be adequate at all for a God who is understood to be eminently personal. Conscious of all these difficulties, while I am not content to wash my hands of the subject, I must nevertheless stand by the limitations of my work in this regard.

***

While I have drawn from the thought of many who have pondered this subject, I am most indebted to the work of M. B. Ahern, whose concise book *The Problem of Evil* begins the bibliography, and whose analysis of the complex aspects of the problem to a large extent determined the structure of the present work. I likewise owe a special debt to David Ray Griffin, whose exhaustive introduction to and clear exposition of a Whiteheadian approach to the question is contained in his *God, Power and Evil: A Process Theodicy*. Nevertheless, my principal indebtedness is to the memory of Pierre Teilhard de Chardin (1881–1955). Although this is not a book on Teilhard or his system of thought, I could hardly have written it without the help and inspiration drawn from long years of study of his thought. In particular, it was his conviction that truth, wherever it is found, is marked by the triple qualitites of coherence, fecundity, and psychological dynamism, that has motivated me to attempt this book. Most specifically, it has been the fecundity of Teilhard's thought itself, the power of his evolutionary paradigm to generate new insights into our view of the universe, that has brought me to a renewed hope of finding some new coherence in treating theodicy from this approach. I hope that out of this attempt will also come renewed ambition not just to bear with the evils that afflict us but also to do all that is possible to overcome them.

Among those who deserve special credit for their help in the preparation of this book I want to especially thank Sr. Dorothy Smith, S.S.J., of Nazareth College in Michigan, for structural and stylistic advice, Dr. Raimundo Panikkar of the University of California (Santa Barbara) for his comments on my treatment of Oriental philosophies in chapter 4, and Dr. Robert Francoeur of Fairleigh Dickinson University for his particular aid in dealing with matters of biology and genetics in chapter 6. Hilary Callaghan must be given a "devil's advocate" award for her sometimes heartless pruning of my excess verbiage, and Pam Lourim given the prize reserved for cryptographers for her labors to render the results into a finished typescript. Special thanks, too, are due to Mathilde Finch for final editing and to both Dr. Ewert Cousins of Fordham University and Donald Kraus of the Seabury Press, whose advice and encouragement helped greatly to see to this book's publication.

Last but not least, I want to thank the many friends who patiently read through and discussed with me various parts of the original draft, sharing with me their own reactions to it in the light of their own sorrows and joys. Among them are George Zabelka, Chuck and Brigit Geroux, Donna Kustusch, and Gretchen Sullivan, and foremost among them was my father, Richard B. Kropf. Although these persons have been very special to me and contributed greatly to the formulation and reformulation of my own thought, they have, most of all, served as the more articulate voice for those others for whom this book has been written.

Evil and Evolution

1

Problems, Mysteries, and Truth

> if the sufferings of children go to swell the sum of sufferings which was necessary to pay for truth, then I protest that the truth is not worth such a price.
> —Feodor Dostoyevsky
> *The Brothers Karamazov*

The truth against which Dostoyevsky's character Ivan Karamazov protests is most difficult. At its core is the riddle that has plagued human belief and trust in God from the very beginning. From the earliest cave-wall attempts to ward off the unseen spirits that disturbed the order of nature to the anguished cries of those who died from, or even survived, the agonies and outrages of totalitarian labor and death camps, the protest has constantly been raised: "Oh God, how could you?" or "Oh God, why me?"

The first and most obvious truth that must concern us is the fact of evil. Yet for many, stunned by this truth, the existence of God is not so obvious. Thus Ivan Karamazov, the archetypal unbeliever, confronts his younger brother, Aloysha, the would-be priest, with the undeniable fact of evil in the face of the hidden God.

For Ivan, given the catastrophes of nature and the atrocities of humankind, the truth was unacceptable. Had Dostoyevsky only lived to even begin to imagine Dachau or Auschwitz after his own exile in Siberia, or even to see the ruins of Hiroshima and Nagasaki, belief in a God who would allow such things to happen might be more difficult if not impossible. Surely the confrontation with the truth presents us with a problem and, beyond that, a mystery.

A. Problem and Mystery

"What is truth?" To Pontius Pilate's scoffing question Jesus remained silent. For Socrates truth was the conformity of the mind to what really is—the accurate grasp by the human intelligence, as far as possible, of reality. Jesus had already told Pilate the truth and Pilate was not interested. Pilate thought that his power came from Rome, even though this was only superficially true. Perplexed by the problem of what to do with this man who stood meekly before him, whom he himself had declared innocent, Pilate yielded to political expediency, first sentencing him to scourging, and then, finally, to death. Thus for Pilate the truth was a problem.

For those who call themselves Christians, this man Jesus was, and is, the truth. This truth is (as Peter attested him to be) "the Author of Life" who had to die before the truth could make us free. And therein lies the mystery.

A problem, according to the philosopher Gabriel Marcel, can be pondered, analyzed, and eventually solved. But a mystery, a true mystery, can only be lived.[1] Problems confront us as immediate and apparent contradictions or dilemmas, while mysteries are, by definition, hidden and unyielding to logical analysis. The truth that Pilate could not grasp, and that the elder Karamazov (who stands for the unbelieving side of us all) refused to accept, is such a mystery. Approached merely as an isolated problem, any answer to the question of evil runs the danger of compounding the very evil that supposedly is to be explained. Thus in treating the Jews as a social problem (which indeed Christians had long made it to be) Hitler supplied an "ultimate solution" that compounded the evil of anti-Semitism to a degree scarcely imaginable. The price of ignoring the mystery of God's first chosen people remains disaster for Jew and Gentile alike. No amount of problem-solving can dissolve a true mystery; the so-called problem of God remains unsolvable in the face of evil only for those who, like Ivan Karamazov, refuse to enter fully into the mystery of God's life— and death.

But there is another danger here, and that is the one of "mystification," a danger that Ivan rightly protests. To *mystify* is to attempt to make a mystery out of what is basically a problem by failing to use the evidence and logic that may be available to clarify an issue and resolve it. That this often occurs is understandable, but it is never helpful, is generally misleading, and in the end obscures the true mysteries in life. Yet this is just what has often happened in dealing with the question of evil. Most primitive tribes, even in our own day, ascribe all death and sickness, and even old age in some cases, to malevolent spirits. So too in our own history—witness our own tradition's story of Eve and the Serpent!

Yet if there has always been an inclination to thus mystify the problem of evil, there have often been efforts to demystify the problem as well. One tribe in present-day Papua (New Guinea), seeks to solve the problems caused by the lack of knowledge and understanding of disease, old age, and death, by holding a ritual trial each time someone falls ill and dies. In this way they attempt to fix the blame on some member of the tribe or anyone who conceivably might have caused this person's death. In a society where head-hunting only recently ceased, such logic is not altogether faulty, for many deaths were the result of murder.

Similarly, in the Old Testament Book of Job, we are presented with a dramatic encounter in which Satan makes a deal with God to allow him to inflict on God's good servent Job a series of disasters in order to test his fidelity to God. Three well-meaning friends who come to console him in the midst of his woes attempt to solve the problem by accusing Job of wrongdoing—anything, even something he cannot remember. Through all this Job's wife, taking what might be called the "Ivan Karamazov approach," suggests that Job "curse God" and drop dead! Curiously, later translators and manuscript copyists, shocked by this attitude, changed her words to "bless God and die"—thus attempting to give a supposedly more religious interpretation of what Job should do.

But we must not smile too much at these halting attempts to explain the problem of evil. They are attempts, however crude, to demystify the question. There may very well be, as the psychiatrist-philosopher Carl Jung has pointed out, a dark or "shadow" side of God that accounts for the evil in the universe.[2] The Book of Job, even when tampered with, seems to have at least confronted what our Western religious tradition has otherwise failed to even recognize.

Thus Dostoyevsky and the original author of Job have each made their point, which is the real blasphemy that an overly facile mystification of evil presents. To ascribe evil directly to a God whom we claim to be all good and powerful is not only a seeming contradiction of logic as well as an insult to such a God, but also the surest way to legitimately question whether such a God could possibly exist. Should we, like Job, refuse to be consoled by easy and even seemingly logical answers and be ready to bow down before the true mystery—the unfathomable mystery of God? Or should we take the advice given by Job's wife? We shall see more of what Dostoyevsky's Ivan has to say, but for the moment let it be clearly understood that the unnecessary mystification of the problem of evil solves nothing and only does violence to the true mystery of God.

Yet the question must be posed: Does the attempt to solve the problems surrounding the existence of evil really remove the mystery? For example, if an innocent child dies due to a senseless mistake in a hospital, does it help or hinder human understanding and acceptance of a fact that cannot be changed (a dead child) to ascribe blame to human failure (a hospital employee careless about antiseptic procedure), or to malevolent agents (somebody with a grudge against the parents or child), or simply to nature (a microbe going about its parasitic life cycle)?

Now the possibility is that one or any combination of these factors could be responsible for the child's death. Yet does it do any good to engage in such detective work as long as we persist in adding to all these possible causes the idea that "God wanted a new little soul for heaven?" Would not this pious rationalization be the worst mystification of all? Yet if we truly believe that God is the creator of all natural processes and of all the agents (human or otherwise) that played a part in this child's death, do we not find ourselves forced to admit that there is at least a certain permissive will of God which, although it may not have ordered any of these things to happen, nevertheless allowed them to? If so, we seem in some way logical when we blame God.

Personally, I think there is enough mystery in God without adding to that mystery those problems of evil which are apparently solvable. To mystify evil is to come perilously close to glorifying it—to worshiping it in place of God. Not too many years ago a nurse who went to a Central American country to assist some missionaries was warned by the padres not to go near a certain mountain village because the Indians there had decided to worship thirteen devils. One would suspect, knowing the disease-ridden and poverty-striken conditions of these mountain tribesmen, that the easy answers so long repeated about suffering according to God's permissive will had finally backfired. In their simple minds, Ivan Karamazov's faith-shattering protest had found a primordial answer. For them a good God was not in control; the devils were. "Prostrate yourself before me and it shall all be yours" (Luke 4:7).

Must we give up and worship the thirteen devils whose captain Jesus refused to serve? No! Countless generations of Christians have believed what Jesus in his desert fast already knew—that the "mystery" of evil is a false god who is powerless before the mystery of the true and only God.

> I watched Satan fall from the sky like lightning. . . See what I have done, I have given you power to tread on snakes and scorpions and on all forces of the enemy, and nothing shall ever injure you. (Luke 10:18–19)

Is it possible, then, that the "mystery of evil" is a pseudo-mystery, one destined to fall from its dazzling place of cosmic enthronement in human minds? Dare we hope that, like venomous snakes and scorpions, evil will be rendered harmless in the end? Christian faith answers this question and tells us that ultimately this will be so.

In the meantime, can this false mystery be unmasked for what it is? Is it not a problem not unlike those which evaded primitive peoples' attempts to make sense of them, yet which seem ludicrous today, were it not for the suffering such ignorance perpetuates? I, for one, think so.

The reason for my confidence is that I believe that Christ came to destroy all superstition. Superstition is more than belief in magic or spells, astrology or any other fatalistic resignation to the forces of nature. At its heart, superstition is the misplacement of faith, the centering of our trust or fears in supposed powers that "stand over" (from the Latin, *super-stare*) or against our efforts to become what we are capable of being. To grant evil the crowning title of "mystery" without qualification is to superstitiously place it on a par with God.

B. The "Problems" of Evil

If we insist that evil is a problem rather than a mystery, it should be evident by now that a major reason proffered for the supposed mystery is that there is no single problem involved. Rather there is a whole complex of intertwined *problems.*

When, for example, Dostoyevsky's Ivan protests that he cannot accept the fact of a single innocent child's suffering being in any way compatible with the designs of a good and loving God, what is he in fact saying? Is it that he finds the existence of an all-good creator incompatible with any evil whatsoever? Or is he saying that only certain kinds of evil are incomprehensible, such as natural disasters, perhaps, or human cruelty, to mention two very different sorts of evil? Or is he speaking specifically about a single instance of human outrage that seems to have no plausible purpose in the vast scheme of things? While a careful reading of this "Rebellion" (the title of this chapter of Dostoyevsky's book) would indicate that he is attempting to speak for all the frustration and anger of the human race, still, is not the very passion of this passage a witness to that kind of confusion, or mystification, which a mingling of the various problems causes?

The first problem, that of the coexistence of God with any evil in the universe, seems upon closer examination to cause Ivan Karamazov no great difficulty. Dostoyevsky's Ivan seems willing to admit that in creating free creatures God is necessarily opening the door to the existence of some evil. Yet, as we shall see (in the next chapter), even on this level the problem of any kind of evil in the world raises profound questions, ones that threaten the concept of God as we have been generally taught to think of him. Given the fact of evil, can God really be all-powerful or all-good? Could it be that God is the despot, the executioner, or the impostor that the outraged philosopher Nietzsche said he is? Is not a good God who creates a universe with any kind of evil in it a contradiction in terms?

Suppose we conclude that the existence of a good God is in some way compatible with or allows for some evil, at least temporarily, in the universe. If so, what kinds of evils might be understandable? To probe this second question we have to consider more deeply the nature of evil and its varieties: moral, physical, and psychological. We shall have to consider whether or not some of these kinds of evil make sense, perhaps for the sake of a higher good—something that even Ivan Karamazov seems reluctantly willing to admit.

Even at that more specific level we are only talking in the realm of theory unless we get down to the concrete instances. It is here that we will have to confront all the seemingly senseless and brutal evils visited upon the innocents of creation, and it is here, with Ivan Karamazov, that we may find ourselves at wit's, and perhaps at faith's, end. For despite the abstract conclusions concerning God and good or evil as such, and despite the distinctions between the specific kinds of evil, we are still faced with the incessant question of Why?—why this little child? Why these innocent thousands or millions or more? To what possible good? These are the questions, the outrages, that "cry to heaven for vengeance." Yet no answers seem to appear.

This last problem, involving countless concrete instances of the suffering of the innocent, the problem that the English theologian John Hick has termed, with characteristic understatement, "excessive pain and suffering," remains *the* final problem of evil. Even if some evil should prove compatible with the existence of God—specifically those evils which seem necessary for the appearance of a higher good—still there remain countless examples in which no good purpose seems to be served. Even a single instance of such evil should outrage our sense of justice.

Thus Dostoyevsky's Ivan speaks of "the sum of suffering" and yet, as will be seen, he bases his sense of outrage on the occurrence of even one innocent child's suffering. This may be a ploy. The innocent child, to the degree it is really innocent of all sense of guilt or is without any conscious fear of death, suffers much like the simple beast, uncomprehendingly, dumbly. Rather, we suffer more for its sake, out of compassion—suffering with and for it.

Some, among them C. S. Lewis, would argue that such compassionate suffering, at least on a collective level, is nonsense. Any one person can suffer only so much pain. Beyond that, the individual organism and psyche apparently lapse into insensibility. Thus Lewis in his *The Problem of Pain*, argues that there can be no such thing as "the unimaginable sum of human misery," nor any "such thing as a (collective) sum of misery, for no one suffers it . . . the addition of a million fellow sufferers adds no more pain" (pp. 115–16). (One wonders if Lewis could have written this had he foreseen Auschwitz and the other death camps that added millions more!)

Despite the logical tightness of Lewis's argument, it presents little comfort to the human sense of justice or compassion. There is a certain universally shared sense of outrage at what appears to be the senseless suffering of a few innocent individuals, but proportionately more outrage over the undeserved suffering of millions upon millions. When Ivan Karamazov protests the suffering of even one innocent child, he is protesting, rightly or wrongly, the suffering of all innocents.

In the face of all this, logic apparently fails, not only in our inability to formulate the question in terms that adequately grasp what we sense is true, but even more in our failure to see any possibility of justice in God's ways. One is tempted to side with the Ivan Karamazovs and the Nietzsches of the world. Maybe at this point we suspect that Job's wife was right and that we should take her advice to curse God and drop dead!

Instead, like Job, we protest. If Job, in his presumed innocence, seems too good to be true, it is because he is a symbol of universal man. Not that we each presume our own innocence, but as Paul Ricoeur points out, Job's self-assured sinlessness forms an essential part of the story if it is to come to grips with the apparent senselessness of suffering. The agnostic Ivan Karamazov may well know himself to be guilty and deserving of punishment. But his urbane and cultured sensitivity rebels at the apparent senselessness and enormity of suffering in general. He secretly mourns his own impotence in the face of evil. Thus, if we cannot claim complete innocence ourselves, we use the obvious innocents in the world as symbols of the irrational side of our own suffering. Focusing on this apparent irrationality, we tend to feel justified in side-stepping the confrontation with that ultimate mystery which lies at the heart of the universe—and God.

C. The Heart of the Problem

"If only the universe had a heart!" This anguished cry of the French existentialist Albert Camus somehow sums up all the protest, frustration, and seeming hopelessness of the human condition in the face of what often appears to be overwhelming evil. Beyond all the refinements of metaphysics, the careful considerations of the distinctions among kinds of evil, or the concrete instances of human suffering, there lies a juncture or coming together of all the problems of evil in a single baffling question: Does existence in fact have any meaning beyond the feeble meanings that we ourselves give it? For Camus, this question lies at the core of all human anguish. For some, this meaning or "heart" is God; but for others it is simply ourselves, existing alone as rational, reflective beings in the universe. Over against us stands the universe itself and the evil that, to our eyes, appears to permeate every level of its existence.

The heart of the problem of evil is not one single thing, and yet, if it could be named, it would be this heartlessness—this cruelty that we not only visit upon ourselves but that is inflicted upon us by all the forces that combine to generate the universe. The question does not concern itself simply with God as opposed to evil. Nor is it limited, despite what Camus may have thought, to ourselves as confronting a universe that gives us existence for a moment and then would snuff it out. The heart of the problem combines all of these.

If there is no God, how are we to conceive of any ultimate good or evil? To whom are we to protest? If there is no real, lasting evil, what can we protest? If we do not really exist as rational and especially as free beings, then what is the point of our protest? Without this freedom, could anything we say or even think have any significance? As for the universe, although it certainly exists, what is its point, its meaning? Of what value are its successes and failures except as they somehow reflect a purpose or aim inherent in the very structure of existence itself? The heart of the universe, if there is such, must be found at the conjunction of these questions, and the heart of the problem of evil, as well as the key to any unlocking of it, will be found there.

Therefore it must be said from the outset that four critical factors will be presumed to exist fully as they have generally been understood: first, the existence of a personal God who is the creator of all; second, the existence of evil as a tragic reality; third, the existence of human beings as free and responsible agents; and fourth, the existence of the universe as a dynamic, evolving reality with its own laws of growth and development.

My repeated insistence on the full reality of these four pivotal elements may seem like an exercise in the obvious. It is not. As we shall see, too many easy solutions to the problem of evil have been offered at the price of eliminating one or another of these critical factors. In some ways they are like the four cardinal points of the compass. If a traveler merely wants to go to some specific place, he needs only to orient himself in the direction desired. This, however, being a journey of exploration, a sure sense of every major direction is needed.

To begin any exploration of theodicy we must, like Job, first take our stance, confronting God. Like the polar star, God lies completely beyond us in many ways, transcendent in respect to this world in his "otherness." True, theology also holds him to be the immanent ground of our existence, but like the ground beneath our feet, this aspect of God taken alone gives us no sure direction or sense of where we are going unless, in the distance, there is a point that still lies beyond us. Any theodicy, indeed any theology, that loses sight of this transcendent otherness of God loses, at the same time, any sense of movement or dynamism. A completely immanent God is too easily identified with whatever exists and in whatever manner it exists. In such a situation, the question of justice in theodicy becomes meaningless, for mere existence has little or nothing to say about the concepts of good or evil. Without a better "beyond," an absolute good that beckons us, there is little point in speaking of "worse" or "worst." In this sense, Dostoyevsky's statement that "Without God, anything is possible" had perhaps been better translated "Without God, anything goes!" It may be said that "Man is the measure of all things," but without the image of God man has also lost the standard of measuring what he himself could be.

At the same time, on our left (our sinister side, so to speak) we must take into account the actual reality of evil. Far too many theodicies, Christian ones in particular, have succumbed to the temptation to optimistically write off the existence of evil as inconsequential or at least a temporary thing in view of the ultimate victory of Christ. This may not be the same as trivializing evil, as some critics of Christianity have claimed, any more than the doctrine of Original Sin can be rightly seen, in a balanced Christian perspective, as a totally pessimistic view of the overall human condition. Still, to characterize that sin as a "happy fault" (as does the Easter Liturgy—because it "merited" so great a Redeemer) or to rapturously exclaim "Sin must needs be, but all shall be well," as did the thirteenth-century mystic Dame Juliana of Norwich, can be misleading. Such expressions lead many people to conclude that Christianity sees evil merely as a passing phenomenon against the backdrop of eternity, either discounting the enormity of evil or else glorifying it as a means to a higher end. Nothing, I think, could be farther from the truth.

In much the same way, a major part of the landscape of theodicy becomes distorted or even totally ignored when the fact of human freedom or responsibility is denied. This tendency has very ancient roots, going back to the materialism of some of the Greek philosophers, and even has its counterpart in some Christian theologies of predestination and total human depravity. Today, however, the denial of human freedom enters modern consciousness mostly through the tenets of scientific materialism and behavioristic psychology. While such views do not necessarily ignore the facts of pain and suffering in the world, they are correlative, in a way, to the denial of genuine evil. Without human responsibility, can we rightly speak of *evil?* Perhaps we might speak of discomfort, anguish, cruelty, or sadism, but the concept of evil requires something more. Even the notion of divine justice itself, as protested by Ivan Karamazov, presupposes that suffering is in some way, or at least ought to be, deserved as a punishment. When humans are not on trial then, God should be. If God alone is on trial, on what basis do we, if we bear no responsibility, assume that there is any such thing as responsibility (in the moral sense) in the first place? Who are we to judge?

Ethical and metaphysical questions like these might well leave one doubting God's goodness or even his existence, and confused about the meaning of evil, or about our existence as thinking and willing human beings. Traditional theodicy has, I believe, floundered, not on what it has denied, but on what it has failed to sufficiently consider. We have assumed that the structure of the universe was well enough understood to be taken for granted. No one was tempted to deny what he could see beneath his own feet. One could deny God because God was the least seen. One could deny evil because *evil* might be simply a concept expressing a limited point of view. One could deny human freedom as a more or less universal self-delusion. But the world itself could not so easily be denied. Even when the apparent reality of the world was denied by some ancient philosophies and religions, it was to explain how the world was not what it seemed to be, not to deny that in some form it existed. For them, it was not the world that was so much the problem as the evil that was seen as existing in the world. If the reality of the world could be explained away, then so might evil.

We are, however, the self-proclaimed realists of the modern Western world. We have believed that our feet have been firmly planted on the ground, even when dealing with theological subjects. Yet we have all too often forgotten to look down or even beneath the surface of things. Like the Antarctic continent, the last to be explored, the bedrock foundations of our physical origins lay concealed beneath an unyielding ice cap of centuries upon centuries of accumulated obscurity. As long as humans have existed upon the earth, we have remained for the most part content to live within the temperate zones of our familiar existence while directing our more ambitious urges toward the world beyond. There seemed no conceivable reason for even mapping, much less digging into that forbidding continent of the remote past.

Did not all creation come from nothing? Did not human free-

dom have its origin in God? As for evil, did that not also arise
(inexplicably perhaps, but nevertheless ultimately) despite God's
good intentions? The few who questioned generally looked in the
wrong direction, too often asking why? and for what purpose?
before first observing the "how" or the manner by which things
came to be.

Why did this so consistently happen down through the ages?
Was it that the subject was considered to be beneath us? Was it
because we simply did not have the tools to extract the accurate
information? Or was it, as it still is for many, because of some
great fright or shock that might be felt?

Evolution is a threatening word for many, particularly the
religious-minded. It conjures up fleeting visions of primeval chaos,
catastrophic upheavals, extinct and long forgotten species, ape-
men and missing links. Yet if the world, as it really is and not just
as we would like to imagine it, is a major element in our picture of
theodicy, then it may just be that evolution itself will turn out to
be the real missing link. Just as the general theory of biological
evolution has become the working model for the major part of
modern scientific endeavor, so too I believe, as did Teilhard de
Chardin, that any area of human thought, be it sociology, psychology, history, even philosophy or theology, must take the evolutionary structure of our world and our development into
consideration. Theology depends on philosophy, if not for its total
content, at least for its language and thought forms, but philosophy depends on cosmology (its overall world view) for its initial
grasp of and insight into reality. Without an accurate assessment of
nature as it really is, philosophy and theology run the danger of
existing in a vacuum of unreality. This is even more true of theodicy, which is forced to deal not just with the spiritual world of
divine-human interaction, but with the elemental realities of the
universe as well.

When I speak of the knowledge of evolution as a prime necessity for a comprehensive approach to theodicy, I am not according
it this place in a half-hearted or grudging way. It is not a case of
being obliged to let modern science have its say while hoping that
it will not upset things. On the contrary, I see it as an asset. It is
true that studies dealing with God's justice have kept multitudes of
theologians occupied (if not always gainfully so) during the great
spans of time before the emergence of modern evolutionary
theory. Yet the concept of evolution, of a slow, progressive development of one thing out of another, from a lower form to a

higher, is not new. It was given a biological interpretation as long ago as ancient Greece. The evolutionary concept of progress even comes into play in some vague way in traditional theodicy—for example, when it was claimed that evil could exist for the sake of a greater good. What really is new is that we have begun to understand the physical mechanisms of evolution and have been able to apply the basic philosophical concept of evolution to the facts of biological science. The result has not been simply a novel hypothesis to provide a plausible explanation for the assembled records of the past (such as the evidence amassed by paleontology) or for the laboratory-proved facts of biological sciences (such as genetics and microbiology). The result has been much more far-reaching. In the past many appeals were made to the creative designs of God, even when no one pretended to comprehend them. Philosophers had long conceived idealized orders or degrees of being, but with little result in an actual understanding of nature. Finally, with the aid of evolutionary theory a way was found in which the observable facts of nature not only began to coalesce into a unified picture and to provide, on this basis, a predictable course of new discoveries, but also began to open up a new vision of all reality.

The result has been nothing less than a total revolution in human thought. Like the Rosetta Stone, which unlocked the secrets of an ancient world whose mute monuments had puzzled successive civilizations, the knowledge of biological evolution has provided a key to unlock the secrets of reality, including the problem of evil, on a much broader scale. The theological or philosophical explorer could perceive evils as immobile immensities looming up before him like the ancient Sphinxes and pyramids in the desert wastes. But he could not begin to fully comprehend their meaning. Much of what he saw seemed to make sense, but much else seemed senseless, excessive, and enigmatic. Only with the new discovery of an ancient language could the past then speak not only of the past but of the present and future as well.

In devoting as much space as I have done to an evolutionary view of the world I am not trying to claim that the final answer to the problem of evil has been found. If I have insisted that evolution in some way belongs to the heart of the problem of evil, I do not mean to imply that through it alone the evil in the universe can be explained away or that the problem of evil's real existence is thereby solved. In some ways a universe in evolution is much more heartless than one seen as coming ready-made from God—even from an angry God! An evolutionary view, while explaining much, also complicates things, not only in our attempts to clarify what is evil or to understand the scope and significance of human freedom, but also to comprehend the very nature of God. Yet despite all this I am firmly convinced that, in plunging to the depths of the heart of the problem of evil, we shall also find what Camus could not—that the universe does, for all its seeming brutality, have "a heart!" This truth does, indeed, demand its price in suffering; but what price can be placed upon a heart?

Notes

1. Marcel, it should be noted, insists in his later work, *Tragic Wisdom and Beyond* (*Pour une sagesse tragique,* translated by Stephen Jolin and Peter McCormick, Evanston, Ill.: Northwestern University Press, 1973) that evil remains a mystery and not merely a problem because "All explanation fails. . . ." No doubt evil has to be lived through, explained or not: but so does life itself, or, again, human nature, which Marcel termed *problématique.* However, that *all* explanation fails I do not admit—at least not yet!

2. Although I do not entirely agree with his theological conclusions and especially with his tendency to selectively emphasize certain New Testament passages to support them, I heartily recommend John A. Sanford's recent work *Evil: The Shadow Side of Reality* (New York: Crossroad Publishing, 1981) for its excellent treatment of the Jungian approach to the problem. Even Sanford, however, has reservations about Jung's advocacy of a shadow side of God. See also Michael Galligan's excellent little book *God and Evil* (New York: Paulist Press, 1976) for his comments on Jung's view (pp. 57–60).

2
Almighty Goodness

Either God cannot abolish evil or He will not: if He cannot, He is not all powerful; if He will not, then He is not all good.

This unsettling statement, attributed to St. Augustine, succinctly states the basic question, or the general abstract problem, of evil. God's power and his goodness! Few doubt that these two qualities should belong preeminently to God. Yet, in the face of evil, are these not the first attributes of God that we begin to question?

Elie Wiesel, a modern Jewish writer, relates in his autobiographical account, *Night,* how, as he and his father were interned by the Nazis, he never once doubted God's existence. Nor initially did he doubt God's power; that was to come later. But after his horrifying exposure to the vast death camp of Auschwitz, he began to doubt, and still does question, the goodness of God.

Many thinkers, shocked by these and other atrocities, have not only questioned God's goodness and his presumed omnipotence, but also his very existence. Stubborn in their questioning and relentless in their doubts, they conclude that a God whose power falters or whose goodness is limited is no God at all. Such a God is dead—in name as well as in fact. The question arises, however, as to whether these two notions, of unlimited power and goodness, are necessarily inseparable from the idea of God.

A. God Almighty

The traditional Western concept of God sees him as almighty or omnipotent. "He has made the heavens and earth and all that dwell in them." Christians share this conviction with their Jewish cousins in the biblical faith. So too cries the Muslim: "Allah akbar!"—God is great. There appears little room for doubt. Does not the very concept of God imply that everything has its origin in him? Especially in the exalted language of philosophy and theology, this rootedness of all existence in God, who is described alternately as the Prime Mover (Aristotle), Pure Act (Aquinas), Being as Such (Augustine), and the Ground of Being (Tillich), or in countless variations on the same themes, is constant. All seem to stress that everything, without exception, has its origin in God and depends on his power for existence.

Without exception? Yes, and this is the apparent root of the problem. Evil can be no exception. However you may describe or define evil, there could be no evil if there was no creation. So God seems to be ultimately responsible not only for good but for evil as well. No doubt this is the way it looks at first glance. (Nonexistence itself as evil is another question.)

There are other ways around this problem. The ancient Babylonians and the Persians after them attempted to solve the problem by supposing there are two gods, one good, the other bad. One then simply divided the world into two parts: the spiritual, good world and the material, bad world. Each had its own creator. A pragmatic solution, and one that seemed to answer every question except the big one: could either god really be God in the face of another having its origin elsewhere? Such a solution leaves much to be desired. No doubt the writer of Genesis thought so. For him, God made everything, without exception, and "God saw that it was good." So for Western man the issue seemed to be settled, at least in principle, even if in practice the logic of this strict monotheism may sometimes have led to doubt about God's justice.

Other, more subtle suggestions have been made. Could God, though Creator of all, not have unlimited power over all things? As has so often been pointed out, even God cannot make square circles. Must not God be constrained by the logic of his own creation? Yet, I would suspect that if it were logically possible to have square circles, there would be little doubt in the uncritical believer's mind that this too would be within the power of God. Thus God's power can be understood (according to M. B. Ahern in *The Problem of Evil*, p. 14) to consist in "the possibility of bringing about anything that is logically possible for a being of unlimited power to bring about."

This logic of language, however, may raise more difficulties than it can solve. Suppose God started something he could not handle. Could it be that God created a process that got out of hand, like Frankenstein's monster or the computerized space ship in the movie *2001*, which turned on its human crew and began to do them in, one by one? It is precisely because our idea of God's omnipotence would be severely compromised by the idea of a runaway creation that the concept of God's omniscience or all-knowingness is generally understood to belong to the fullness of his power.

However, far from being a complete answer, the idea of God's omniscience presents another whole set of problems, especially when it is meant to convey the idea that God not only knows all the possibilities but also all the probabilities and even all future actualities! It may be argued whether or not such foreknowledge (and the additional problem of predestination that it raises) is a product of biblical religion or of Greek philosophical speculation about what people understand to be biblical religion. Yet, literally read, the Bible does seem to attest to such divine foreknowledge, as in Psalm 139, ". . . my days listed and determined, even before the first of them occurred." What then? How can we be free agents?

Despite the difficulties this foreknowledge raises, a truly personal, knowing, and willing God who is at the same time omnipotent would logically seem to have this power. For if God is the source of all existence and time as we know it, he also *exists* (stands outside of) independent of time. "There is no future thing for God," said Maritain. Thus there can be no surprises for God—only for us, it would seem!

Several things should be said regarding this delicate matter. The first is that we should be aware of the Hebraic tendency to conceive all significant events as preordained events, preexisting and fully formed in the mind of God. Thus typically, in later Jewish thought, the Torah or Law of God as an expression of God's wisdom is seen as preexisting from all eternity. So too with many other concepts in the Bible.

Second, we must also be aware, despite the aforementioned tendency, that the ability to foretell the future, often displayed by the biblical prophets as an authenticating sign of their mission as God's spokesmen, is nevertheless a distinctively prophetic type of prognostication. It is almost always conditional, indicating what the outcome of human decision and a certain course of action will most surely be, and it is almost never fatalistic, thus leaving a way out for a change of heart. This remains clear despite the tendency of Hebrew thought to skip over intermediary causes (as when the Scriptures speak of God's hardening people's hearts, meaning that God has allowed them to become stubborn in their ways). This distinctively prophetic type of foreknowledge has often become drastically changed and absolutized in later apocalyptic literature, where the events of history are depicted as entirely preordained. This change reflects a period of history when believers who existed as a scattered underground no longer had any control of their social destiny and could only make individual moral decisions in the face of overwhelming political events. Both of these later thought patterns, coupled with mythological conceptions of Fate drawn from ancient Greece and elsewhere, have probably resulted in the tendency to overliteralize our reading of biblical reference to God's foreknowledge, and a corresponding tendency to make a theological absolute out of the concept of predestination.

On the other hand, it must be admitted that the pure logic of the situation where God is seen as the origin of all existence would also demand a certain foreknowledge of at least the possible outcome of his actions. Added to this is the realization that in a world where human "think tanks" are employed to analyze the present and prognosticate the future, we can hardly imagine a God worth worshiping who does not only know all the possibilities but also all the probabilities. Even the philosopher, A. N. Whitehead, who denied God's knowledge of the future in the usual sense, seems to have admitted this much.[1]

When it comes to future actualities, however, this matter of the omniscience of God, coupled with the doctrine of the basic dependence of all creatures on God, has occasioned endless and, it would appear, almost fruitless debate. Whether it is viewed on the natural level of providence over nature or the supernatural level of God's redeeming grace and its effect on free will, there seems to be no clear answer to this problem.

It is all too clear, however, that a serious problem remains for theodicy. In defending human responsibility, even a partial fore-knowledge on God's part of the possible courses of action that a human may take would seem to lay the ultimate responsibility at the feet of God. Witness, for example, the scriptural remarks about Judas Iscariot and his betrayal of Christ.

In them there appear to be two contrasting interpretations of God's foreknowledge, and, by implication, his power. In one pair (John 13:18 and Acts 1:16f) God's foreknowledge is seen as a kind of predestination that makes the event have to be (in fulfillment of an interpretation of Psalm 41:9), while in Matthew (26:24) and Mark (14:21) we find that the stress appears to be on the tragic choice and the fate of the man who would carry out the betrayal (". . . better for that man if he had never been born"). Unless we read too much into Jesus' remark, the note of bitter regret might indicate that even God's power is limited by the freedom he gives his creatures. But would not foreknowledge of the outcome necessarily imply compliance on God's part—at least in the chain of events that led up to the existence of this free agent in the first place?

It would seem then that any view of God's power that includes even a limited foreknowledge of future possibilities puts us in the position of laying the ultimate responsibility of having started all things, good and evil, at God's feet. Presumably, then, God had good reason, a higher good in mind. Nevertheless, if even limited power and knowledge would make God responsible for some of the evil in the world, then complete omnipotence and perfect foresight would make God all the more responsible for the eventual existence of evil. So Augustine's logic (and that of his adversaries whose logic he sums up) seems, up to this point, flawless. Thus we must confront the question: can such an almighty God, who does not or will not prevent evil, be all good?

B. God and Good

If the concept of power has long been identified with God, so has the concept of the highest good. Names for this supreme being differ and have different linguistic origins, yet the close association between *God* and *good* persists—in their Germanic root the two words are identical! So strong is this identification of God with ultimate goodness that Jesus refused to allow himself to be called "Good Master" and insisted that "God alone is good!" When trying to describe the ultimate principle of the universe without using *Theos* ("divinity"—the word that the Greeks too readily applied to their mythological heroes), Plato simply turned to the Good, the Beautiful, the True.

In the face of this constant association of the good in its highest form with God, is it possible to define *good* in any fully satisfactory way? Many have tried, equating goodness with harmony, love, creativity, fulfillment, happiness, and even "being" itself. Each of these attempts has its merits and special nuances, yet each falls short. Is it not because they are trying to describe the indescribable, to contain the uncontainable, the ultimate, the nature of God himself?

Even so—even more so—how can evil then be compatible with good, particularly with the ultimate good that we understand to be God?

In the discussion of God's power and the problem of evil we came to the conclusion that power in itself, even unlimited power, did not necessarily rule out responsibility for or even a certain justification for allowing evil to occur for the sake of a greater good. So we have already assumed that good admits of some relativity—that while many things are good, some are better, and at least one is best. If this is true in any given class or category (at least we assume that a blue-ribbon first-prize winner has outclassed all its competitors, even the better ones), can it not also be true regarding all creation, and even more of the Creator in respect to creation? Was not this behind Jesus' remark: "God alone is good?" For while creation is good (and Jesus himself was outstandingly good), God as such, the incomparably holy, stands apart from or is utterly transcendent in respect to all created goodness or holiness.[2]

Even granting this important distinction, why consider anything to be evil at all in a world that is basically good? If everything is good, how can there be any real evil? Is it not just a question of lesser goods? There seems no doubt about it. Considering things simply as they exist, they all seem good in one way or another. I may think that mosquitoes are no good whatsoever, but as an organism displaying beauty (at least to other mosquitoes), efficiency (few airplane designers have done as well), harmony, persistence, and so on, a mosquito is a wonder of creation and, in that sense, good. Yet I think that we all have some problem in following the biblical writers and the philosophers on this point, particularly when it comes to the relationship between the mosquito and our tender skin. To us, or at least in respect to us, the mosquito is a plague that seems to serve no good purpose.

So let us try again. Let us take soda pop, or, if we prefer, have a beer. They seem good. They taste good. We believe that they are good—but only up to a certain point. Even too much Pabst's Blue Ribbon can make us unharmoniously tipsy, sick, or worse. So we can very much experience evil in the midst of what is otherwise good. Because of the evil that can occur, some would thereby attempt to abolish these "goods"; at one time it was "demon rum," then it was sugar, and now sugar substitutes in our soda pop!

Certainly there are much more serious parallels to these rather light-hearted examples, and we must move on to consider the real tragedies in life. But it should be obvious by now that we are speaking about a hierarchy or scale of good in that which is imperfect. Thus the insistence of Jesus that God alone, in the perfect sense, is good only underscores the relativity of all other goods.

This should bring us immediately to another aspect of the compatibility of divine perfection with the imperfect goodness of the world. During the Middle Ages one of the big questions of the time was whether or not God could have created a better world. At first glance this sort of debate might be dismissed as being in the same class of idle speculation as the question of how many angels could dance on the head of a pin. It is not. While "the best possible world" debate might appear to have been as inconclusive as the one about the angels, the stakes were extremely high. What the question amounts to is an attempt to reconcile the goodness of God with a less than perfect world, indeed, with a world that contains real evils.

While medieval theologians remained divided on the question, one thing was clear. A world that contains free beings is going to have flaws due to human error, no matter how well the rest of creation may have been put together. The possibility, indeed the inevitability, of human flaws and their consequences is the price that God is willing to pay to share the universe with free creatures something like himself. As the later philosopher Leibnitz was to put it, the best possible world is not necessarily a perfect world! It all depends on your (and in this case God's) purposes.

This insight should not really surprise us. Think what the alternative might be. For example, a few years ago some clever wag got the idea of marketing pet rocks, very successfully selling them to people who appreciated both the humor and the logic of their "advantages." After all, they are economical (at least before they started selling them), do not require feeding, are well behaved (never need housebreaking), and seldom, if ever, run away from home. They can not even be easily stolen if massive enough. They are practically immortal! However, more seriously, they leave something to be desired as pets. They cannot respond, move about at will, play, return affection, learn tricks, or actively perform other useful functions, all traits that we look for in our domesticated animals that we keep for our use and enjoyment. So it is with God's creation. God could have endowed the human species with much the same stable qualities that belong to a pet rock. Or God might even have given us the mobility of a dog or cat, and perhaps the instincts that make these animals to some degree independent; but God chose to do more. In the same way as a person who substitutes a pet for a child or for another human being, God would be settling for a creature incapable of the higher perfection that can be ours despite the risk of human misbehavior. God's presumed foreknowledge of man's wrongdoings did not stop him. In a profound sense, at least in the created realm, "the perfect is the enemy of the good!" Of course, it all depends on what is meant by *perfect*. A static and guaranteed "good," at least in the case of creation, it is not.

For most people, however, this obvious answer failed to answer the question, at least with regard to the "lower-than-human" levels of creation. Why could there not exist a better possible world, one without earthquakes, floods, diseases, and similar disasters? Apart from these apparent flaws, did not God allow even the goodness of his "subhuman" creation to be subverted by human freedom? Could there not be a freedom in which sin was an impossibility (like that which many theologians claim the saints enjoy in heaven)? Added to these questions was the speculation as to how one would recognize a perfect world when he saw one, assuming that God alone is perfect enough to be the judge. So the famous debate, in the course of raising many questions, seems to have solved none of them. Certainly one can think of a better world—one without natural disasters, and even possibly without sin, but thinking about it and the possibility of its existence might be two very different things. In what does this difference lie?

To some this difference really comes down to the gap between the "ideal" and the "real" world, while to others it merely reflects the incomparable distance between God and creation, despite the goodness of the former. Having granted all this, we still need to ask why the chasm between the ideal and the real worlds is so great? Or put another way, why does there seem to be such a gap between God's goodness and his power?

C. God and the Evolution of Good

To answer this question, which concerns the difference between what we imagine and what would actually be the best possible world, we must take a closer look at the results of this famous debate. For those who, like Leibnitz, would answer that this is the best possible world, it would rightly seem that God's perfect omnipotence and goodness are nevertheless limited by what is best for creation (as well as for God's purposes). But suppose one holds that there could be a better world. After all, such a world need not remain entirely imaginary. Does not the human race, with its technology, art, and even religion, attempt to make the world operate more smoothly and predictably, show more beauty and harmony, and enjoy more peace, prosperity, and fulfillment? Would not this be a sign of something? Is it not a vision of a world progressing from good, through better, to the best?

What I am saying here is that the answer to the question as to whether this is the best possible world is both yes and no. Now if this seems like double-talk (and in some ways it is), it is probably because the question has been phrased wrongly in the first place. Notice how the question asked if this world *is* the best possible world, or, in another form, whether or not God could have made or created a better world. Both forms of the question imply that God has finished the act of creation. Consequently, most of the traditional answers imply that the act of creation, properly speaking (that is, making something out of nothing or "first creation," as the medieval philosophers and theologians put it), is over and done with. What remains to be accomplished is whatever God, the laws of nature, or human beings do with this creation—this subsequent development termed "second creation" or only a kind of "creation," improperly speaking.

This is a very useful distinction, despite its quaint language, for what the medieval scholastics were hinting at is that the act of creation in a broader sense is not completely finished. Seen from this perspective, the word *possible* in the phrase "best possible world" becomes all-important. Are we talking about the best possible world *then* (back when creation was started), *now* (as we experience it), or *when* (sometime in the far-off future)?

This should not surprise us. Creation is an elusive subject to discuss. Even in the Book of Genesis we find some hesitation on how to express the concept, having two versions right within the beginning chapters. In chapter 1 (the more recent version, according to scholars) God is described as creating the universe from a "formless void"[3] in stages over six days. Each stage seems to be the product of a separate act of God, which, although it builds upon each prior stage, stresses God's spontaneous creative novelty. Humans, in this version, appear as the final installment in an organized, comprehensive whole, and all is good, and, in the end, "very good." But in the second chapter (the older story, beginning with verse 4b) all these initial stages are passed over, or at least taken for granted; they are treated only as prerequisites to the major creation of man and woman. Yet even this crowning work is paradoxically only a "second creation" (in the scholastic sense) inasmuch as the "slime of the earth," from which Man's body is fashioned, is already there—a point further emphasized in mankind's Hebrew name Adam as supposedly derived from the earth, the *adamah*, from which he is taken, and to which he will, ultimately, return.

This human-centered second story, while it also undoubtedly considers the whole work of creation as good, not only does not choose to picture creation in successively ordered stages, but in one aspect almost reverses the order of the first story. The trees and their fruit, the animals and the like, appear after man and woman as if in response to their needs. Most important there appears the sinister possibility of their misuse, and, as we shall soon see, the impending doom of the first sin. Thus, while some like to see in the first story the hint of an evolutionary plan, even while stressing God's initiatives, it is really the second story, with its depiction of human creation involving lower forms of existence and its emphasis (in chapter 3) on the human fall from a paradisal bliss, that seems to stress the ambiguous and unpredictable results of a second creation, with humanity's part in it leading to disastrous results. What are we to make of all of this?

St. Augustine pondered this problem of the *how* of God's creative activity long before the scholastics made their subtle distinctions. For Augustine it seemed obvious that the initial "something from nothing" aspect of God's creative activity was instantaneous, for before there was something there could be no time at all, time depending on the existence of things whose movement and growth can be measured. On the other hand, taking his cue not only from the Bible, whose "six days" he saw as symbolic, but also from nature as we see it around us, he concluded that what God had created instantaneously nevertheless contained within it certain *rationes seminales,* or developmental potentialities. These would, in time, unfold, much as acorns develop into oaks, to reveal the fullness of their nature.

What I am recounting here is not meant to claim that Augustine was an evolutionist, at least in any modern sense of the term. Even less do I wish to imply that the Bible was intended to contain, even in a vague form, a kind of evolutionary doctrine of creation. The Bible, it must be said again and again, teaches no particular kind of scientific theory. "The Scriptures" said a very wise Cardinal after the fiasco of the Galilean controversy, "were written to tell us how to go to heaven, not to tell us how the heavens go!" If that principle, translated more or less loosely from the Latin pun, applies to astronomy, it applies to biology also. What is certain is that the Bible, for its own specifically religious purposes, teaches in the language and story forms that made the most sense to the people of a particular time and culture. We, in the context of our own time and culture, must reinterpret it to extract its basic message for human salvation. Otherwise we run the real risk of confusing ancient language with timeless truth or even of losing sight of the truth in a welter of arguments about scientific theories that are basically irrelevant to the Bible's main purpose.

Nevertheless, if we combine the two creation stories and overlook their differences, much as the ancient editor(s) of the Book of Genesis did, we can make several observations. The first is that creation is, initially, out of nothing (a "formless void"). Second, within the process of creation there is a certain ordering that, if not in precise chronological stages, is at least a kind of order logically directed by the divine mind for the benefit of humankind. Third, we are definitely told that this creation is essentially good. Finally (as we shall soon see), we are told that certain modifications will have come about, partly as a result of human decisions and partly as a result of God's reaction to these human decisions.

If looked at from these biblical perspectives, as well as from the viewpoint of such ancient theologians as Augustine and a host of others trained in the traditions of classical philosophy and science, a total picture emerges of a creation that, at least in the broad sense, seems to be a kind of ongoing cooperative enterprise of God, humans, and even nature itself.

Now let us compare these observations to a more modern scientific view of the creative process, or as science prefers to term it, *evolution*. According to the august body of scientists and philosophers assembled for the Darwin Centennial Celebration held at the University of Chicago in 1959,

Evolution is definable in general terms as a one-way irreversible process in time, which during its course generates novelty, diversity, and higher levels of organization. It operates in all sectors of the

phenomenal universe but has been most fully described and analyzed in the biological sector.[4]

Putting aside for the time being the more controversial question as to whether or not this distinguished group was in fact
correct (at least in terms of the scientific evidence), let us simply
focus on what we might call the philosophical presuppositions and
beliefs contained in this all-inclusive statement.

First, while this assembly made no general metaphysical or
strictly philosophical judgment as to the ultimate goodness of what
they were describing, still the whole statement is shot through
with the dynamic of comparative values—from the unstated qualities of sameness, lack of variety, and low levels of complexity to
the "novelty," "diversity," and "higher . . . organization" found in
the more developed forms of life. All this implies a certain
significant value (may we say "goodness?") attached to the transformation from lower levels of existence to higher, from instinctive, determined organisms to those having greater freedom, from
mere quantity to higher quality—in a single phrase, from good to
better. Might one also presume, from the general drift of their
statement, the possibility of a *best?*

Perhaps this is to read too much into their statement, presum-
ing value judgments they did not intend. However, in light of their
statement, based on their reconstruction of the past plus an apparent faith in future, I do not think so, for they have pronounced this
process to be "irreversible" and "one-way" in time. This statement
would seem to say that, despite apparent setbacks and various
losses that have occurred within the process (for example, extinct
species, evolutionary throwbacks, etc.), on the whole, evolution
moves forward.

Even without the benefit of our own judgments about what is
good, better, or best in all of this, much that these presumably
hard-nosed and objective scientists had to say is astounding. For
without using the word, they seem to be assuring us that the final
outcome of evolution will be such that even the losses will not
cancel out that unnamed element of advance that is inherent in the
process—which is to say *progress.* Without a doubt, their claim of
"irreversibility" for the evolutionary process, particularly in view
of what our nuclear scientists have cooked up in their laboratories,
borders on being a pure act of faith, at least for the prospects of
continued evolution on this planet. It is more than even the Bible
would propose for belief. In view of its theological implications,
the importance of this statement is immense.

How so? Perhaps I am jumping the gun in raising such questions, for there is no point in reexamining the whole area of theodicy unless there is something new that might provide the key to certain problems. Let us suppose, for the sake of discussion, that the kind of evolutionary thinking that the assembled followers of Darwin represent is in fact, and not just in theory, the whole pattern of God's creative action and not just a hypothetical description of biological, or even cosmic, transformism. What theological possibilities might be seen?

Many, to be sure; but among them a major consequence of this assumption would be a reexamination of the tension between God's transcendence and God's immanence. Much of our problem in reconciling the existence of God with the existence of evil does not lie in our Western tendency to see God as completely transcendent to or "other" than his creation, as has often been implied by those exponents of what they believe to be an Oriental theme of God's immanence or presence with a corresponding acceptance of what is only apparently evil within creation. On the contrary, perhaps evil, or what we take to be evil, especially in the course of natural events, exists primarily because creation, understood as an evolutionary process, necessarily begins with forms of existence that are as totally unlike God as possible. This would not deny God's immanence or presence within the working of the process, but rather offer a new, dynamic understanding of what Thomas Aquinas said long ago: that the basic reason for God's immanence within creation (sustaining things' existence and providentially guiding them toward their fulfillment) is to be found precisely in his total "otherness" from them as the transcendent cause of their existence. In terms of good and evil, this would mean that created things, at least in their primitive evolutionary beginnings, would be at the same time as totally unlike God and as imperfect as could be imagined!

What then about the basic goodness of things and ourselves as existing in the image and likeness of God? How could these biblical affirmations be interpreted in such case? Again, if we were to see God's creative activity as an evolutionary process, is it not possible that this image and likeness is more what God intends us to become rather than what we actually are? Or could it be that God saw everything to be good because he has a good end in mind? If so, moral evil and natural imperfections are to be expected rather than wondered at. In addition, as we shall see, any process capable of greater perfection is accompanied by equal if not even greater possibility of error and defect!

Beyond these possible reinterpretations of the relationship of God to a universe and a still-evolving humanity, we might also confront another question, that posed by the concept of metaphysical evil. Is it better to be or not to be, as Hamlet's famous question goes. Is existence itself good, and nonexistence evil? To many this seems an idle question, one not worth serious consideration among the other more pressing practical problems of evil. Yet, is it not the basic question? If it is not pondered much (except perhaps by philosophers and those who contemplate suicide), is it not because we generally take the goodness of existence or being alive for granted? So perhaps we have settled the hypothetical question. We exist, we live, and we usually plan on living as long as possible— given half a chance at making our existence satisfactory. Yet if we were to put this same question to God (not that God could queston his own existence—he has no choice, given that God is *being as such*), does God really have any choice but to bring a creation into being?

Traditionally, the answer has generally been yes, that God did have such a choice; he could have elected to remain in solitary splendor. Perhaps it is necessary to say such things to emphasize his supreme transcendence and the gratuity, the utter "giftedness," of creation. Yet it is even more obvious that God did not choose isolation, and we assume that his choice has some vital connection with his nature, his urge to share existence, something that in turn we assume is good. How can we explain this "compulsion" of God?

Here, of course, we are confronted with the nature of God as love or self-giving. It is here that the God of the philosophers (and, we might add, the God of the theologians who feel constrained to adhere strictly to the language of philosophy) seems to fall so short of the God of the prophets. Perhaps to speak of love and the impulse to share that it implies is bad form for a philosophy or theology that is sworn at all costs to preserve the strict line of demarcation between the absolute being of God and the complete dependence of creation on his supremely free decision to create. Yet if the Apostle John did not hesitate to tell us that God is love, should we hesitate to speak of the urge or impulse to share through a self-giving act of creation that is the very nature of love, even if that impulse finds itself constrained to suffer the consequences that such self-giving entails? Perhaps the word *suffer* is too strong here, surely overstepping the bounds of what it is generally thought permissible to say about a transcendent God. Nevertheless, even if human language fails us, we must try to comprehend the tremendous consequences that the act of creation entails, not only for us, the creatures, but also for God, who creates.

This is doubly true when we speak of creation by way of evolution. If we can dare say that God is compelled to create by the nature of his being as love, and if we likewise conclude that to be is better than not to be or that creation is necessarily good, then what must we say about evolution? If creation is to some degree a necessity for God as an expression of his goodness, then the same might be said about the evident manner by which God created. May we not assume that if there was a better way for God to create than through evolution, with all its pains and joys, its catastrophes and triumphs, its display of human wickedness and holiness, God would have found this better way?

This brings us back, at last, to the famous debate about the best possible world. In view of what we have considered, we might not only agree with Leibnitz that we have the best possible world, but even go a bit farther and this time agree with C. S. Lewis and conclude that we have "the *only* possible world!" (*The Problem of Pain*, p. 35). Yet, if we are to take the relationship between God and a world in evolution seriously, then we must also add that the world is not yet what God or we fully intend it to be. If people have somehow imagined better possible worlds without sin or suffering, we may be assured that God has thought of such worlds long before. However, reality must, for the time being, be something else.

Perhaps we have overstepped the bounds of a completely trusting faith. What right, asked Jeremiah (and Paul after him), does the pot have to question the potter? Still, was not Augustine's rigid logic about God's seeming to be neither all powerful nor all good an even more devastating doubt? Yet Augustine remained a giant of faith, a man who believed that, despite all appearances, God can and will bring forth greater good to overwhelm all evil. We may not entirely agree with Augustine's interpretation of precisely how this is to come about. Still, I would be willing to believe with him, and, from the perspective of an evolutionary view of nature perhaps even more than he did, that when it comes to a manifestation of God's power and goodness there is much more to be discovered than has yet been revealed.

Notes

1. Whitehead's "persuasive" view of God's causality, which is a major part of the process described in his *Process and Reality* (New York: Harper & Row, 1961), of course involves God in his consequent nature as the pole of all future possibilities. However, insofar as God "persuades" these possibilities toward an ethical and aesthetically desirable outcome, God would certainly appear to have a good idea of the probabilities of success as well. But as David R. Griffin points out in his *Process Christology* (Philadelphia: Westminster Press, 1973 p. 186) strict divine knowledge of the future in the classical theological sense is an impossibility for God, inasmuch as the future, in the process view, is still indeterminate. Such divine foreknowledge would be, according to Griffin, in the same catagory as those things which theologians have always agreed are impossible in principle, hence also impossible for God.

2. Jesus' seeming rejection of the title "Good Master" (see Mark 10:17–18 and Luke 18:18–19; cf. Matthew 19:17) was, of course, predicated upon the strong association of "goodness" with "holiness." In Hebrew, to be good, *tov,* in the most eminent degree was to be necessarily sacred or holy, *kadosh,* which in turn carried the connotation of being separate (in the ritual sense of being set apart from the profane) and hence, ultimately, transcendent. Jesus' demurral of goodness is akin to Isaiah's declaration of God's triple holiness, i.e., holy to the superlative degree. (See Isaiah 6:3.)

3. I have followed here (as in the case of most of my biblical citations) the translation directly from the original languages given in *The Jerusalem Bible* (edited by Alexander Jones, Garden City, N.Y.: Doubleday, 1966) which incorporates the excellent notes originally published in *La Bible de Jerusalem* edited by Père Roland de Vaux, O.P. and published by Les Éditions du Cerf, Paris, in the one-volume edition of 1961. The "tōhù wā bōhû" of the Hebrew literally rendered means "trackless waste and emptiness" according to the above. Cf. *The Jerusalem Bible,* p. 15, note 6.

4. I have presented this quotation not as *the* "definitive" or only definition of evolution. I offer it, however, as typical of a large segment of scientific opinion on the subject. Undoubtedly many others will quarrel with such a broad description, particularly with its implications of a kind of direction to the process. For a detailed critique of the kind of thinking displayed here, the reader is directed particularly to T. A. Goudge, *The Ascent of Life: A Philosophical Study of the Theory of Evolution* (Toronto: University of Toronto Press, 1961) or, for more of a defense, to George Gaylord Simpson, *This View of Life* (New York: Harcourt Brace and World, 1964). While both books may be somewhat dated in terms of the most recent developments in evolutionary theory, their treatment of the philosophical aspects of the evidence and its ramifications remain perennially relevant.

3
The Shape of Evil

The belief in a supernatural source of evil is not necessary; men alone are quite capable of every wickedness.
—Joseph Conrad

Conrad's bold statement, on the face of it, would make this chapter unnecessary, but there is more to it than meets the eye. Mankind's "Heart of Darkness" may very well be capable of every kind of wickedness, yet mankind senses that the extent of evil often exceeds merely human capacities. How can this be? The problem is much more complicated than the mere fact of evil alone.

The problem of evil, as we have seen, is really a series of connected problems. The most fundamental of these has been bound up with misunderstandings about what is meant by the power and the goodness of God. Too often these divine attributes, taken simplistically and uncritically, have failed to take into account what real goodness in God, translated into love for his creation, really means. Only when God's power is seen in conjunction with a self-giving love manifested in the creation of free and loving creatures like himself, is any reconciliation of the idea of an all-powerful and all-good God with the existence of evil possible—indeed, not only possible but altogether necessary. Without the possibility and even the probability of evil there can be no creation at all!

Such a general statement can only be a beginning, the first step in a theoretical probe, so to speak. We have to be more specific. What kinds of evil can God allow? That God can, and must, allow the possibility of the occurrence of sin in free creatures seems logical enough, but how about death, sickness, or natural disasters? How can these fit in?

In dealing with this second, more specific, stage of the question, it is essential to first describe clearly, even if rather abstractly, just what kinds of evils there are, and what makes one kind different from another. Are all of our supposed "evils" really evil? We might even ask just what is meant by *evil* in the first place. How can we define evil? Is not evil, like good, self-evident? Perhaps; but observe what happened to our notions of "power" and "goodness" when we examined them more carefully. They turned out to take too much (or too little) for granted. So, too, in the case of evil. There can be no general description or definition until we take a closer look at the kinds of things humanity has called evil. We have not really analyzed what it is that makes people see certain kinds of things or happenings as "evils." Nor have we really looked to see how much these things vary and yet are all lumped together into a single concept. Added to this investigation into the *kinds* and *nature* of evil, we should try to gain some insight into the "genesis" of evil. Only when we have done all this can we begin to deal clearly with the concrete instances of evil in our lives.

So we must begin at the beginning, with the earliest myths about evil, and see where they take us.

A. The Myths of Evil

Closely akin to Joseph Conrad's observation, yet bolder still, is Dostoyevsky's (again in the person of Ivan Karamazov) paradox, that "if the devil doesn't exist, but man has created him, he has created him in his own image and likeness!" How true this is! Whenever humanity tries to find some kind of explanation for the existence of evil, that solution invariably mirrors humanity itself. Human explanations of evil inevitably end by restating the problem, blaming someone else—God, Satan, the first man, or first people—but in the end describing ourselves. What then is accomplished by such an investigation of myth? Do we not arrive at a dead end, or end up going in circles? So it might seem—but let us see.

Myth has been somewhat fancifully defined as "truth that never happened." By this is meant that myth is a way of symbolizing a profound and existential truth. While it can be described as a simile in the form of narrative, it is not really concerned with history or the way things came about so much as with describing the way things are. Yet if this is so, why the story element, why the pseudo-historical dramatic form? Why the "once upon a time" quality that makes it appear as if it was a moment in history? Paul Ricoeur, in his analysis in *The Symbolism of Evil*, enumerates three very important reasons for this. First, the story must point to a universal condition, and to do so must trace this condition back to the origin of things, to a point of common ancestry. Second, it must, through its "in the beginning" quality, include all time, for what better way is there to say that this is the way things are than to point back to the way things seem to have been from time immemorial? Thus "in the beginning" stands for all time, from beginning to end. Third, the dramatic story must reveal the struggle that exists within us between the ideal (the way things ought to be) and the real (the way things are). For this last purpose the most natural and effective form is the dramatic story, one that tells of a "before"—a kind of primal condition before history—and an "after"—the condition that we experience now. But as we shall see, the ideal quality of this "before" may also stand for something else, not only for what might have been, but also for what might someday be.

Ricoeur's analysis, I think, not only reflects three major functions of myth, but also, in doing so, helps us to see how each of the three major myths concerning evil (and a fourth variation of one) in turn tend to emphasize one or another of these functions. For while Ricoeur insists that they are neither history nor explanations of evil, I believe nevertheless, that they will turn out to be seen not just as three distinct variations of a general statement about evil, but as three separate statements about three basic types of evil: cosmic disorder, human suffering, and sin. Depending on the major preoccupation of a people, the prevailing myth will tend to focus on only one major type of evil. But, because the prevailing myth cannot entirely ignore the other types of evil, it will be forced to compromise, dealing with these by incorporating them as minor themes. Very often the result turns out to be inadequate, showing gaps in logic and, in the end, too often spreading the seeds of doubt and the eventual loss of faith.

The remedy for this is not, as some foolishly think, to abandon all myth and advance to purely scientific analysis. Myth, as Ricoeur has shown us, is a form of science, a mode of knowledge in its own right, perhaps the only way of knowing or reflectively experiencing the total dimensions of existential truth. If each of the classical myths of evil should prove somewhat inadequate by itself, the best course of action is still to let each speak for itself, for each can fill the gaps in the others if allowed to express its truth in its own unique way.

1. The Fall

The biblical story of the Fall of Man, which Ricoeur terms "The Adamic myth,"[1] is the account of evil best known to modern Western society. In it we see what seems to be primarily an account of moral evil or sin—the willful turning away from God by the first man and woman, whose names in Hebrew (*'ādām* = mankind; *'av* = mother)[2] symbolize the whole human race. In this account of moral evil, death and suffering are secondary; they are only a consequence of sin. There is no such thing as a cosmic evil, except a brief nod to a primeval chaos or formless void in the first of the two creation accounts; all has been quickly brought into order by God and all is good. There is no mention of suffering or death, except by way of warning, and until the first couple ignores this warning, all is paradise. So what possible reason could there be for humans wanting to sin or even being tempted to transgress?

The traditional commentators all point to pride as the cause of the transgression. Yet how do we make any sense of this pride, as merely wanting to eat from the tree of knowledge, when Adam already has knowledge of everything useful to know, even to the point of naming (which is to say, to have a controlling knowledge over) all the creatures of the earth?

Accordingly, we must look for a deeper pride—the prideful ambition of wanting to be as gods, equal to the creator himself. As Eric Fromm has pointed out, it is not that God doesn't want to have humans who would be in some way "as gods." In fact, to have them thus share in the work of creation is precisely what God had in mind. Rather, the sin of humanity was in thinking that it could change the rules of the game, becoming instantaneously equal to God through an assertion of its own will in opposition to the order (or should I say process?) initiated by God.

But still, how do we account for such overreaching ambition in the midst of paradisal bliss? Such pride may be quite understandable in moderns, who seem all too often persuaded of their godlike powers, and that apparently without any outside help. But for ancient man, especially for a humanity that saw itself initially blessed with every bliss that one could hope for, this kind of pride seems hard to fathom.

The ancient storyteller may have had similar misgivings and so he introduces another element (although not too convincingly)—that of deception. The Man pleads that he was beguiled by the Woman, while she, in turn, blames her misdeed on the Serpent, the Tempter, whom later biblical books will name Satan, "the Father of Lies."

Why all this buck-passing? Is it not because the truth seems so obvious as to make the substance of the lie incomprehensible? Certainly there must be under the innocuous symbol of a forbidden fruit, some profound disorder, one that is so far reaching that the biblical author could only point to a diabolic origin for such great human disorder. Mere disobedience, even to a divine command, is forgivable. But the sway of the lie, the continual delusion, is something else.

Martin Buber has helped to isolate the uniquely human character of the lie in contrast to all other forms of evil. Every evil that we know is, in fact, but a ramification of or an intensification of some other phenomenon that we find already present in the subhuman world. Suffering, death, even most moral evils, are the consequences of unchecked and intensified occurrences and drives found within nature. But the lie, the outright affront against the very nature of things—only humans at their very worst can conceive this. Alongside the outrageous perversion of the lie, all forms of protective camouflage, or even the illusion of a fruit appearing as the elixir of immortality, seem innocuous or even ridiculous. The outright lie defies all description. While unique to humans in the world of nature, yet it appears as something almost superhuman, a parody of the truth that is God himself! It demands a diabolic figure, a symbol even bigger than mere human life.

Yet the figure of the Serpent/Tempter really solves very little. If it epitomizes the degree of the perversion of the truth that was involved in the human race's rebellion against God, it nevertheless also emphasizes the basic problem of theodicy—the ultimate responsibility of the creator for all that exists, and with that, for evil as well as good. The later identification of this tempter with Satan, the archdevil, the leader of those spirits who refused to serve God in an earlier, prehuman rebellion (as depicted in the Book of Revelation), only pushes the basic difficulty farther back in time, or to before all time—somewhat the opposite of another explanation hinted in Genesis, the fleeting references to the Sons of God who

intermarried with the daughters of men to produce the race of the
Nephilim, or evil giants. None of these stories really explains anything, if by *explanation* we mean a solution to the problem of the
origin of evil in respect to an all-good creator. We have been
warned, however, not to look primarily for explanations in such
myths, but instead for deeper insights into the real state of things.

If, then, we ignore or at least resist the tendency to seek such
explanations of the origins of evil and simply let the story of the
Fall speak in its own symbolic language, certain truths will emerge,
some with more clarity than others. Most obvious is the universal
character of the catastrophe. There is no question of only a part of
the human race being affected. Adam and Eve stand as prototypes
of the whole human race, and although there may be conflicting
opinions as to whether their sinfulness is transmitted to the rest of
the human species (in fact, Judaism holds no such doctrine of
Original Sin in this sense), still the basic meaning of the story as
universally applicable to all humans, past, present, and future, is
readily understood, even by nonbiblical religious traditions. In
this sense, the question of the historical accuracy of the story is
beside the point. It is not really concerned about the historical
origins of sin (or suffering and death, for that matter) but rather
about the condition of humanity in its existential experience.

Likewise, in terms of the contrast between the ideal and the
real, between the vision of paradise and the picture of humanity
driven out to the East of Eden, we have no discussion of geogra-
phy but instead a graphic reminder of the gap between what we are
and what we imagine we could or should have been—or even a
vision of what we are yet to be! In this sense paradise represents
not so much a place or even a state of existence as it does a state of
mind.

These self-evident points of the story are not much different
from those in any other myth about evil and the human race. But
what this story depicts, perhaps more deftly than any other, is the
interior struggle of "everyman" not so much with God, nor even
with the devil, but with himself. It is here that the lie enters the
picture, not so much from outside as from within. If the bold-
faced lie of the Tempter to Eve, or even more, Adam's gullibility in
believing his wife, does not ring true, might this not be deliberately
a cue to look more deeply? Certainly there is pride involved, but it
is not so much the rebellious pride of wanting to dethrone God as a
stupid pride of thinking that we can outguess or do better than
God in providing for ourselves. Socrates once observed that no

one does evil for its own sake. We seek only the good. But we err in mistaking limited goods, bits, and pieces—perhaps even apples—for the ultimate good. If the story of a snake and a forbidden fruit appears a trifle naive, it may only be evidence of a superficial reading. Might not the biblical author have been trying to make the point that moral evil is rarely malicious in its intentions? It is more likely to spring from a kind of stupidity, but it turns out to be a foolishness that is truly diabolic in its devastation of human happiness. Although the stated motive for such brash disobedience— to become "as gods, knowing both good and evil"—seems plausible to us, the Biblical writer was not attempting to indicate that ignorance is bliss. Rather, he was demonstrating that a trusting innocence that accepts things as God intended them to be is, in itself, the realization of paradise!

Before we turn to the other great myths of evil, one final remark regarding the Adamic myth should be made. Does not the story still try to historically explain death and suffering as consequences of sin? Again, superficially, this may seem true and so understood caused little problem for a pre-Scientific Age. Yet I doubt that a mere explanation of the origins of such natural phenomena was the author's real intent. Did he really believe that a sinless existence would be without death, work, or occasional discomfort? This seems, unless we are being too subtle, a bit farfetched. Again, if we are to understand the language of myth not in terms of explanation but in terms of factual, existential statements about life, then a much more obvious meaning comes to mind. It is not that death, work, and pain suddenly come upon a scene where they were unknown, but it is rather, through mankind's foolish and overreaching pride that they become known in a new and ominous, disheartening, way. Death is now experienced as dying, and all that that implies for an ego-conscious being. Simple work now becomes toil, survival entails suffering, and even the birth of new life is fraught with pain.

If I have added what may seem to be a new twist in our understanding of the Fall (especially on this last point), it is not to try to rescue it from its inadequacies as a statement, much less as an explanation, of all evil in the world. It has been rather to try to bring to the fore what this story has done better than all the others, that is, to emphasize the moral disorder that sin has visited upon the universe. When we turn again to the subject of human freedom and sin, we shall find that Genesis will have even more to say. Sin is not, however, the only disorder to be found in the universe. For the full recognition of this fact we must turn to another myth, one from which even the biblical author was forced to borrow.

2. The Chaos of the Gods

The Primeval Chaos theme, expressed in what is probably the oldest type of creation story, has many variations. One version, the most philosophical in outlook, sees the act of creation itself as a kind of a divine fall, while another, more primitive version sees the created world as both the battleground and the product of a war between the gods. If the idea of multiple or opposed gods seems strange to us, we must remember that polytheistic thinking looks not so much for explanations regarding the origin of things (although apparent explanations form part of the story) as for comprehensible ideas about the behavior of what we would term the forces of nature. Gods or divinities were seen as the personification of such forces as the earth and its fertility, the wind, the storms, the sky, the sun and moon, and the rest of the heavenly bodies. While these all seemed to be harmoniously related, nevertheless the harmony existed as an uneasy truce between opposing forces. Occasionally, conflict broke out again, the moon seeming to swallow the sun at times of eclipse, the seasons encroaching upon each other, floods inundating the land, the earth itself sometimes shaking in terror. All these experiences bespoke primeval chaos reflecting a war among the gods themselves.

When the biblical authors expropriated certain elements of this primitive cosmology, they reorganized them under a single God who makes everything good. Yet the formless void still lurks in the background, put in order and held in check by the creator, but still waiting to reassert itself as pain, suffering, and death. Although it may be true that for the author of the third chapter of Genesis it is the first human sin, not a rival god, that breaks the primeval harmony, still it is out of this same void—"the slime of the earth" from which they have taken their existence—that their punishments arise.

However, there may be still another element found in the two-god version of the chaos myths that has influenced the biblical story of the Creation and Fall. Significantly, the archaic Indo-European word root for gods or powers of the spirit world is *div* or *dev*—even today we have the word *divinity*, as well as the Hindu term *deva* (for the general term *god*)—and we also have the term *devil*! If we follow this clue there seems to be no question about it; Jewish, Christian, and even Muslim theology have all identified the Tempter of the Genesis story with this figure who assumes the role of an anti-god, a false divinity that, although held in check by God, is nevertheless present in creation, ready to tempt mankind and to form a sinister league with the destructive forces of plague, famine, war, and other disasters. Later passages in the Bible would identify these evil powers with the angels who had become devils through their rebellion against God before the rest of creation took place (another story of distinctively Babylonian origin). Meanwhile various Gnostic theories would recast them as any number of powers or semi-divine forces that both link creation with and divide it from God.

Would it be too rash to credit these ancient myths and theological world systems with a deeper and more realistic understanding of a still untamed and chaotic side of creation? Do not the brute elements of the universe, the catastrophic upheavals of nature, the earthquakes, floods, droughts, and pestilences still break loose with devastating regularity? The simple paradise of Genesis seems too good to have ever been true, even before the first sin.

It may very well be the weak point of the chaos myths to have shifted the burden of evil too directly from humanity to God, or to the gods, both good and bad. In the light of the threat of modern doomsday weapons to wipe out all life on this planet, the ancient curses of natural disaster seem to pale into relative insignificance. Yet these myths, in spite of all their primitive and grotesque fantasy, do retain a certain power and persuasive hold over the human subconscious. It is as if all the human malevolence possible still pales into relative insignificance beside the horrors that nature can still unleash, or even more, that mankind can cause with nature's powers. Compared to such total disasters, it is as if the very worst of human sins (taken strictly in terms of their psychological content) are like the temper tantrums of a small child. They seem to have very little permanent effect—at least until that child can reach out and press the small button that will blow us all into kingdom come! Thus despite the fact that the author of the biblical story correctly pictured human malice as being at the core of our existential experience of evil, even he was compelled to allude to a more sinister force, a nonhuman propensity toward a chaos that is inexplicably contained within the outer shell of order and goodness—a certain diabolical disorder that can shatter the divinely given harmony.

A great deal more could be said in support of this group of

chaos myths. The whole idea of creation as a fall from divine simplicity, for example, has something in common with what was said in the previous chapter about the price that God had to pay for creation. It also could be seen as a counterbalance to our Western and biblically inspired tendency to overlook the "shadow" or "dark" side of God, but that subject is perhaps best left to another place. What is most evident, however, for modern evolution-consicous humanity, is the affinity such myths may have with our realization that the universe has emerged with what harmony it does possess only at the cost of great struggle and almost continuous upheaval. What we read as an ordered balance of nature is more like a truce that descends on a battlefield after most of the combatants have been killed or maimed. The progress of evolution has not been a steady march toward victory but more like Mao-tse Tung's strategy of "three steps forward then two to the rear," an erratic advance-and-retreat pattern that has carried us thus far, but more by inches than by strides.

If much has been made in this discussion about elements in the biblical story that may be traceable to the chaos myths, it is not simply to reveal problems that the writers found in some of their literary sources and then tried to correct because of obvious theological difficulties. If the biblical account of the first sin can be understood more fully only in light of the ancient stories it may very well have intended to contradict, so too the chaos stories need to be corrected or completed by the biblical view. Neither the chaos nor the Adamic myths were meant to be taken in any modern evolutionary sense. However, if we are to reinterpret them in any way that makes sense in our present mental climate, we must realize that it is not only the devil that humanity fashions in its own image and likeness, but its gods as well. If we find ourselves survivors, if not entirely victors, in this disaster-stricken landscape of evolution, we must realize that all the chaos is far from over. We can, through one more outburst of malice, or even through one more slip of Adam-and-Eve-like miscalculation multiplied on a megatonic scale, return our whole planet to the chaos from which it came. If the myth of the chaos of the gods had any validity in the past, its significance for the present has grown immensely. Having "become like gods" ourselves, much as the Tempter promised, we now toy with the very real possibility of a *Götterdämmerung*, a twilight of the gods far more lethal than ever imagined in the Germanic version of the legend. The death that the Tempter claimed would never be ours has become, in us, a godlike power to reduce ourselves and the world to ashes.

Even if the chaos myths need the corrections offered by the Bible, they contribute, on their own, one important insight that we can not afford to overlook. However it came about, chaos did not enter upon the scene only with the arrival of the human species. Chaos, and the struggle to overcome it, have been part and parcel of the whole process of creation from the very start. Human wrongdoing is, from this perspective, just one more instance of the general tendency of nature to regress to its primitive state. This is not to downgrade the special significance of human malice or failure, but simply to see sin within a cosmic context. From this viewpoint there is nothing new under the sun—only a new depth of degradation relative to a new height from which nature could fall.

3. Man as "The Tragic Hero"

Of the three basic myth forms we have been considering, the Greek motif of the tragic hero may have been originally (according to Ricoeur) derived from later additions to the stories of the primeval chaos. Nevertheless it definitely takes us a step farther in our understanding of the essence and varieties of evil. Whereas the biblical story of the Fall focuses on sin as the key to all evil, and the ancient myths of the chaos concentrate on the cosmic, physical manifestations of disorder, the myth of the tragic hero is preoccupied with the human and specifically psychological consequences of suffering and death.

Whatever lives must also die—"You are dust and to dust you shall return." Not only is death a condition universally afflicting life, but life is built upon death. Life itself depends on the death of that which nourishes and makes room for us. The story of life is that of a vast *invisible pyramid* (to use Loren Eiseley's phrase) in which one form of life has evolved upon and at the expense of other, lower forms. Even genetically speaking, evolution of newer forms of life depends, almost intrinsically, on the eclipse of and, very often, the destruction of the forms of life that have come before. If species evolve, it is only because individuals die.

Yet mankind would be different. Humans, according to the late biologist Theodosius Dobzhansky, are the only species that can reflect on their own death. While every other living type instinctively seeks to grow and preserve its life, still its individuals die dumbly and unreflectively without any perceptible regret. Humans have never quite accepted this. Humans always, in one way or another, attempt to become immortal, whether in the "spirit," in their children, in their reputations, or in the landmarks (even their tombstones) they leave behind. While death itself may not be cheated (even by those "crynologists" who would have themselves frozen, to be unthawed in a more long-lived age), the human type at least seeks to deprive death of its final significance and thus rob it of its power over the human spirit.

The ancient Greeks, in particular, developed this conscious- ness to a high art. The essence of the tragic is that humans, despite all their desire for deathlessness, must submit to death. Despite its universality, death is different for mankind. Only humans can suffer in this sense, for it is not the physical fact of death that sets humanity apart, but rather the psychological agony of knowing that we human beings must die. Surely here there must be some explanation.

The Greek tragic myth states this most starkly. Man, the "Promethean," would be like the gods and steal the "fire" of their immortality. Godlike in all but this, mankind would wrest away this privilege of divinity, but the gods are jealous and, driven by their own fates, are cruel. Behind the Greek myth stands the suspi- cion, even the conviction, that the divine and demonic are one and the same. What the ancient "chaos" myths divide into opposing forces, and the Adamic story identifies as a malicious rebel in creation, the Greek tragedy unites, and humanity is fated to be in eternal and futile opposition to the gods, who seem not to care.

If they do care, the gods manifest only a cruelly detached interest in mankind's struggle, which they then punish. No mere man may overstep his mortal bounds, yet no man worthy of the name would be *merely* man. Like Icarus, the heroic man will always fashion wings to soar to heaven; also like that first would- be astronaut, he finds, to his horror, the feathers of his ambitions coming unstuck as he attempts to beat his way toward the undying heat of the sun.

Human suffering, then, is born from death and yet it is much more than death. It is dying that is the punishment. But punish- ment for what? For pride? Yes, but for the pride of trying to be more than human, for having that *hubris*, that ambition to evade the fate of death. For that pride man must die twice; not just once in his body, but again in his mind.

It is in this ironic note that the force of this myth is found. In some way we might say that this myth represents the Greek golden mean between the impersonal fatalism of the chaos myths (where in one ancient version death is but the natural state of a material world created from the slain corpse of the evil god!) and the seeming capriciousness of death in the biblical account, although this other tendency is exaggerated even more in a later Babylonian myth where the hero, Gilgamesh, failing to slay the powers of death, has the plant of immortality stolen from him.

True, there is a kind of noble irony in the biblical story itself, where Adam, no longer innocent of good and evil, now knows what God knows and thus finds his way barred from the paradise where the tree of life could have been his forever. For him there is left the sweat and toil of wresting his bread from the earth and, for his wife, the pain of childbearing, and, at the end, for both of them and for their children, the grave. But if the biblical account is in some ways more tragic for its depiction of a death that did not have to be, it is flawed in its failure to come to grips with the necessity and inevitability of death in the natural scheme of things. That is to say, at least in terms of the world as we find it, the Greeks were more realistic.

Thus, setting aside the hope of immortality contained within the biblical story, the tragic theme of the ancient Greeks comes closest to the core of the problem as we experience it in merely human terms. The disorder inherent in the order of creation and the death that must accompany life are "givens," against which there seems no possible appeal.

It is not just in this element of inevitability, however, that the Greek hero embodies the highest tragedy. It is in his free but doomed protest against this fate. As J.-P. Sartre has succinctly put it, we are "condemned to be free." This freedom, rather than leading to some final liberation, only tempts us with the illusion of immortality. The "punishment" of human suffering and death turns out in the end to be nothing more than the refusal to admit that we are merely human.

As for the gods of these tragic myths, they prove themselves to be, despite their immortality, even worse than humans. Their cold detachment from the human plight interspersed with fits of cruel revenge eventually made them, in the eyes of Socrates, worthy of only scorn and contempt.

In these themes there is really nothing new in this ancient Greek myth or cluster of myths with Man as the tragic hero. Could we expect it to have been otherwise? If this theme is universal, it is so with a special hopelessness, for in it there is no time pictured when death did not exist or a future in which death would be abolished. Mankind is eternally balanced over the jaws of death, while the afterlife, the great Stygian swamp, remains forever the shadowy land of exile from the land of the living. It was the pagan vision at its very cruelest.

Yet, for all this, there is a unique element in that myth. Man, despite his fate, remains the hero as long as he resists. Death and humanity are locked in mortal combat, and *physically* death always wins. But heroism itself does not die, for out of this engagement a victory for the human *spirit* can be won. More than any other of these ancient myths, the paradox of the tragic hero has paved the way for a belief that, despite the chaos of creation and despite the maliciousness and stupidity of sin, the human spirit will never, and must never, give up its "impossible dream."

B. Myth and Evolution

How are we to relate these ancient myths to our own understanding of the evolution of life? Or why should we even attempt to do so? The fact is that in terms of its value systems, mankind lives by myth, so much so that evolution itself has become, at least from this perspective, the great all-encompassing myth for modern man. The problem remains, however, as to whether any one myth can convey the total picture, and it is here that the ancient myths can supplement the modern, just as the modern mode of understanding can help us solve the riddles posed by the old.

We have already seen how the ancient myths of the chaos in some ways come closest to the picture presented by evolutionary science. Yet they do so in terms and concepts that are incredibly grotesque. Theologically speaking, the Babylonian myths seem to be monstrosities (as they seemed to the biblical writers as well). Nevertheless, they express, perhaps more effectively than any of the stories that appeared later, the primitive disorder of the material from which the universe is made. For present purposes, they best reveal the universal presence of that force which is antithetical to all created order, and which remains an ever-present threat lurking within the depths of our physical, material existence. For all practical purposes, the myths or stories of primeval chaos are the revelation of physical evil.

In a similar way, but in terms that are, like the Greek civilization that produced them, humanistic and highly refined, the myths of the tragic hero depict the universal and paradoxical condition of a humanity aspiring to immortality but faced with certain death.

Out of this conflict arises suffering or psychological evil in its most relentless form, one that poses the conflict of the unattainable ideal against the ever present real in terms of relentless and protesting struggle. It is significant that modern philosophers, both the evolutionists who foresee mankind's victory over the mechanisms of evolutionary struggle, and the more pessimistic existentialists who see humanity's effort as eternally doomed, have reincorporated these myths into their outlook. Nietzsche's Zarathustra, the Persian hero who proclaims that "God is dead," becomes the prototype of the modern *Übermensch* or Superman who is destined to subdue the forces of evolution for the eternal benefit of humanity. Albert Camus' recall of Sisyphus, on the other hand, was meant to depict the futility of the struggle, one in which humanity, like the doomed hero of old, is forced to roll the weight of ambition uphill against the fatal slope of evolutionary law. But the price of life remains death. The Prometheus in each one of us is not dead, but the Fire of the Gods has turned from immortality to the power of mass destruction.

What can be said for the Adamic myth in the face of this renewed eloquence of the pagan myths? Surely it not only remains as one of the most poignant expressions of our universal folly, but even more it stresses that moral evil is the major obstacle frustrating God's creative plan. Through sin and the corruption consequent upon death, not only is creation dragged back toward the chaos from which it came, but there would also be an end of all human aspirations and divine hopes for God's image in humanity, unless—. But here is found the major difference from the other myths. In the biblical story, paradise has never been entirely lost, or if it can be said to have been lost, it can also be found or regained. It awaits us still, guarded by an angel until that day when mankind regains its primal innocence and is reconstituted in the image and likeness of God.

What factors lead to such a conclusion? First, there is the internal evidence of the story itself. It ends with just such a promise, a hint of ultimate victory in the prediction of the seed or offspring of the woman, who shall crush the head of the serpent. A Messianic addition to the text? Perhaps, but one that colored the interpretation of the story for all time.

However, there are additional, structural reasons for this claim. Despite the timeless character of all of the myths, or rather despite their deliberate location at the "beginning" of or before all time, each of the major myths of evil displays in its own way a

distinctive temporal character. While the biblical stories of creation
are mostly a setting for the drama of the human fall, and the Greek
hero myths almost avoid the question of origins entirely, the
myths of the primeval chaos restrict themselves more exlusively to
the form of a cosmogony or creation story. From this frame of
reference we can single out the chaos myths as being primarily
symbols of the past. Not unlike the spate of modern books on
sociobiology and other phases of evolution, their focus is on prehuman origins, and what they have to say for the present, much
less for the future, is even less encouraging.

The myths of the tragic hero are, preeminently, depictions of
the present. Like most Greek thought, they depict the past as the
archetype of the "eternal present," while the future exists only in
another world, one apart from time. Mankind's "eternal" frustration is thus "timeless" only because, paradoxically, it is presently
bound up with time. There can be no true evolution in such a
world, only repetition of the present. Past and future are only
illusions.

With the Adamic myth in particular, as with biblical thought
in general, we enter a new dimension. Only in light of the revelation of a future can the past and the present attain any real
significance. The Jews, it has been said, "invented history." Without a real future, time remains bound up with myth, and the past
remains only as a symbolic statement of the ideal (like Confucius's
Golden Age) or else as a prototype of things simply as they are.

The Bible is so different that this difference is the source of
much of our present confusion. Where myth, couched in terms of
the past, is used, as in Genesis, to usher in a new vision of the
future, the two become intertwined in a way that is apt to mislead.
For example, was there really ever a paradise? Or put another way,
it has been asked, "How long did paradise last?" To this question
some medieval rabbis are supposed to have responded, "About
twenty seconds!", which is to say, it never really existed, or that it
existed only in our minds. That is not, however, to rule out its
possible future existence, or at least some final state that it sym-
bolizes.

If the Jews can be in some way credited with inventing history, that is, discovering time as a truly significant factor in the
unfolding of God's creative plan, it must also be said that biblical
thought paved the way, in its own nonscientific manner, for the
concept of one-way or irreversible time in the modern scientific
sense of the term. True evolutionary time, in any philosophical,

biological, or even cosmic sense is inconceivable without any concept of an actual beginning and at least a hypothetical end. Even the Marxists have had to admit as much.

For some, of course, such an imposition of evolutionary thought patterns in interpreting Scripture represents an attempt to read the Bible backward. Yet, if this charge be true, then we would also have to claim that the Bible itself was, to some extent, written backward as well. The Book of Genesis, in its present state, dates from the time of the high point of the classical writing prophets. It may not be directly their work, but it does incorporate into its message not just the mythic forms and legends of antiquity but, even more important, the prophetic vision of an "end-time," a completion of human history when sin, suffering, and death, and even cosmic history, with all its ups and downs, its uncertainties as well as its recurring lapses, will have come to an end. It is in this total prophetic and eschatological perspective of Scripture, and not just in the vague but very important hint found in the promise of the seed that shall crush the head of the Serpent, that I feel that we are entirely justified in seeing paradise not as a lost garden of Babylonian mythology, much less a location of impossible geographical description, but as a shimmering symbol of a reality yet to be revealed and attained.

What, then, of the devil? Does he exist in his own right, or is he, as Dostoyevsky's Ivan suggests, a creation of man "in his own image and likeness?" Insofar as he is the personification of mankind's own perversity, the devil is the worst in man revealed to himself. Just as surely, he, or "it," is the superhuman force of disorder and dissolution that threatens to drag all creation to the brink of the chaotic nothingness from which it emerged. However we choose to think of this evil spirit, the really important facts that remain and that we must never lose sight of are not only the reality but also the extent of evil that dogs the creative act of God. If myth is truth that never happened, then the devil must be seen as part of that truth. If this truth has taken on the mirror image of ourselves, the parody of what God intended us to be, it has had to be at the same time the conscious symbol of whatever it is, whether in ourselves or in the universe, that stands between the ideal and its fulfillment. No more could be asked of such a symbol, but at the same time, in the face of the odds, nothing less.

Notes

1. Although I here adopt Ricoeur's terminology, I do so with some reservation in its application to the biblical story of the Fall. As Herbert N. Schneidau carefully points out in his chapter on "The Mythological Consciousness" in his book *Sacred Discontent* (Baton Rouge, La.: Louisiana State University Press, 1976), there is a paradoxical element in the Hebrew use of myth approaching almost what amounts to anti-myth. Thus while admitting Levi-Strauss's emphasis on the essential structure (rather than the stories as such) underlying myth as the key to its adaptability from one culture to another, Schneidau emphasizes that it is precisely this element that has been subverted in the Hebrew scriptures. In their desacralization of nature, the biblical writers made more of the story elements than the underlying structures which they contained, perhaps at some risk to the writers' central purpose. Nevertheless, Ricoeur's analysis of the basic functions of myth would seem to fit the biblical story of the Fall quite accurately.

2. More properly, "Eve" *(ḥawwāh)* may be derived from all life *(ḥāy)*. See *The Jerusalem Bible*, Genesis 3, note e. Alexander Jones, ed. (Garden City, N.Y.: Doubleday, 1966).

4

The Reality of Evil

Christ on the Cross, the greatest harm inflicted on the
greatest good: if one loves that, one loves the order of
the world.

—Simone Weil

Simone Weil, the late French philosopher and author, Jewish by
birth, Christian by conviction, and churchless by choice, was also,
at least in her own mind, one of the late pure Platonists. Yet her
shattering remark,[1] rife with the cry of protest, is most revealing. If the classical myths of evil fail to explain evil and only
succeed in restating the problem in all its human intensity, the only
alternatives remaining are either to deny or explain away evil or to
embrace it as the ultimate tragedy of the universe. The mystical
Christian Platonism of Weil paradoxically attempted both.

When we speak of *Platonism* we are dealing with both the last
of the great myths of evil and the first great bloom of the perennial
flowering of philosophical idealism. Idealism in this sense is not
merely a matter of holding high ideals, although philosophical
idealists are also generally committed to upholding humanity's
greatest aspirations. Rather, this idealism is one that would, beginning with a division of the world into conflicting forces of good
and evil, end up, as far as possible, rejecting the world of materiality, change, and suffering—in a word, repudiating the harsh
world of reality as we know it and substituting the realm of ideals
in its place.

Obviously, such idealism in the full-blown sense of the word seems to be an attractive alternative to grappling with the horrors of the world as we know it and accepting them as being somehow part of the world that was destined or ought to be. However, the myths of evil also imply that the world ought to be other than it is. Are we to believe, then, that philosophical idealism has succeeded where the myths have failed? Perhaps for many people it has. Yet, for many Christians as well as many others who have believed, like Simone Weil, that the power of evil has full sway over this world we experience, does not the answer of idealism end up becoming the basic problem itself? For rather than solving the problem of evil, would not idealism only throw us into deeper conflict with and alienation from the world in which we must live?

Christianity has been accused, perhaps not without cause, of being world denying, and of having taught generation upon generation of its faithful that we have here, on earth, "no lasting city." The implication of this charge is that Christians, almost by nature, are incapable of taking the world and its evils seriously or, almost paradoxically, of taking the world so seriously *as evil* as to lead to a total indifference to the world and its capacity for good. I shall not deny this charge, for there is ample evidence that it is, at least in part, all too true. Yet I shall deny that what is true in this accusation is exclusively or even specifically Christian; it is a great deal older and more widespread than that. The question of how much older and more universal deserves serious consideration, for until we recognize the basic lines of this thought in all its major forms, we shall not be able to fully recognize it in our own. This vein of philosophical idealism is, Ricoeur maintains, the final great myth regarding evil, and it may represent the philosophical refinement of the existential statement behind them all. If so, then we must come fully to grips with it and wrestle with it. Unless we do so, we shall, as a result of our tendency to deny the reality of evil, end up immobile beneath its weight.

A. Idealism and the World of Evil

Recall, for a moment, the Babylonian chaos myths, particularly the ones that see the origin of the world in a battle between two gods, one good, one bad. The material part of the universe, with all its physical parts, is seen as taking its origin from the slain body of the bad god; and while spiritual forces of evil in the form of devils continue to harass the human race, the main source of its woes is inherent in humanity's existence as physical, corporeal beings. Now it very well may be that philosophical idealism took its immediate origin, as Ricoeur suggests, as an explanation for the Greek tragic myth of mankind's futile struggle against death or that the tragic myths themselves were but popular stories designed to convey the meaning of what was already a widely held but still only a half-articulated philosophy or attitude toward life. But such a "chicken or egg" debate may be pointless for present purposes in view of the fact that such a view of life did not remain confined to Mesopotamia or Greece but seems to have spread even farther Eastward. The Aryan peoples, moving into India at least several thousand years before the time of Christ, appear to have incorporated this same line of thought into the native Indian nature religions to produce that religious-philosophical amalgam we call Hinduism, or more properly Vedic Religion. Later, but almost simultaneously, in the fifth and sixth centuries B.C., both Greek philosophical idealism and Buddhism began reworking this ancient vein of thought.

I call attention to this not as simply a curious historical footnote but rather to stress the fact that the most significant civilizations of the time, intellectually speaking, with the exceptions of Egypt, China, and, of course, Israel, were rapidly coming under the influence of this idealism or its dualistic roots. However, even the exceptions, like Judaism in its later Wisdom Literature, would feel its attraction. Greek civilization and its thought would later spread over the whole Mediterranean and Near Eastern world. Buddhism was to take over all Southeast Asia and to influence, with strong modifications, both Chinese and Japanese thought. Even Christianity could not be expected to be entirely immune to the lure of idealism or even dualism.

If I have begun to speak of dualism as a significant component of this philosophical and religious trend, it is because the kind of idealism I have in mind is that which ultimately finds its roots as well as its expression not just in an ethical dualism of good and evil but in a metaphysical dualism of spirit and matter. The most obvious and widespread symptom of such thinking is belief in reincarnation, where the soul is seen as a separate spiritual being that takes up residence in a succession of bodies, living one life after another, as was widely held in ancient Greece, or even in animal bodies, as is believed in popular Hinduism. Buddhism, as we shall see, attempted to break with this idea, but it seems to still permeate a great deal of the Buddhist world.

Less obvious, but perhaps even more widespread than belief in reincarnation, is the general idea of the soul as a kind of substance that is imprisoned in the body, to be released from its earthly existence by death. Despite the fact that this concept sometimes included a belief in the preexistence of that same soul before its life in the body, a view that was repudiated by Christian orthodoxy, it is quite clear that Western religions even today tend rather strongly to such a "Platonic" idea of the soul.

It should be noted that the basic biblical idea is something else; in fact, the Old Testament writings, at least in the original Hebrew, know no such word as *soul* or its equivalent! The *nepeš* (often mistranslated as "soul") designates simply the living being in its entirety—the *bāśar* or flesh that has been given life by the *rûah* or spirit/breath of God.[2] Consequently, although in the New Testament the Greek word *psyche* is often used, especially by St. Paul, it generally refers to the mental (as well as often the emotional and volitional) functions of the human body. This is not to deny outright the idea of an "immortal soul" in the common way of speaking, but again, it must be stressed, any real life after death is, at least in the sense that we can look forward to, the result of the granting of the "spirit" or the Holy Spirit, the *pneuma* (the Greek New Testament word corresponding to the Hebrew *rûah*).

If all this seems a bit complicated, it is nevertheless of vital importance, for I think that the contrast between these two ways of speaking about the human soul show us just how far Christian thought has been influenced by Greek concepts, so much so, in fact, that the New Testament has been generally misinterpreted by means of ideas drawn more or less directly from metaphysical dualism rather than remaining true to the integrated, holistic view of human life, even life after death, that the Scriptures represent. This basically nondualistic view found its more developed expression in the doctrine of resurrection, where any form of life after death must be seen to be, at least in some form, a *total* restoration to life and not just the nebulous existence of a disembodied soul. Skeptical "realism," which borders on materialism (as was the case of the Sadducees of Jesus' time), would of course reject this concept, but so too would philosophic and spiritualistic idealism. Paul's scoffing audience at the Athenian Areopagus most likely represented both extremes.[3]

Such divergent ideas about the nature of the human being have strong implications regarding the problems of evil, particularly physical evils and the meaning of death. Yet the influence of dualistic thinking does not stop merely at the consideration of these problems as they affect human life. It also greatly affects our thinking about the world as a whole. If physical reality is afflicted with evil or is in some way the source of all evil, while spiritual reality represents and embodies the highest good, then which of these realities is *really* real?

This may sound like a tautology or a begging of the question, but it is not entirely so. At least we must ask, if we assume that both the material and spiritual sides of existence are part of reality, which is the more important? We all know what we have been taught, and yet we all know what generally assumes more importance in our lives. However "spiritual" our hopes and aspirations, it seems that most of us live our lives almost totally immersed in the "mire" of physical, earthy existence.

Whether we find the question as posed in such terms to be congenial or repugnant, the fact that such terms are common in Western "spiritual" literature surely indicates how far down the road of dualism we have, in fact, traveled. We may not have gone as far as a Hinduism in which the word *maya*, which originally meant "change," has generally come to be understood to mean "illusion" or the illusionary side of reality. Yet more than two millennia's worth of Western thinkers, including even some contempory scientists, have repeated Plato's famous argument, one way or another, that things, especially physical things, are not what they seem to be. "Now you see it—now you don't!" Can this be reality? Or is it a case of such material things being, as Plato said, a mere *eikōn* or image of reality, a reality that is immaterial, belonging to the realm of pure ideas, reflections of an ideal or spiritual world? Could it be that what we take to be real, in our common sense view of things, is nothing but an illusion, a dream produced by an eternal thought, a will-o-the-wisp conjured up by an ultimate, all-embracing Mind?

There is a great attraction, and perhaps a good deal of truth, in such a view. We must "seek the things that are above" and strive to rise above what is merely sensual and prone to corruption. This, indeed, is "the perennial philosophy," which has given the human race its greatest impetus to the soaring achievements of art and culture. But what about the world "below?" Is it only to be used, abused, and finally be discarded? Is it only a second-rate "reality," as the great Hindu philosopher Shankara taught, one that is prone to capture the mind in the morass of illusion, preventing us from the realization that indeed "we are that"—that the true self, "Atman," is identical with the ultimate reality, "Brahman" or God? For if that is true, or at least if we have come to the conviction that it is, then we have passed beyond the realm of ethics, beyond the conflict between good and evil, into the pure level of undifferentiated being, where neither life nor death, sin nor suffering, nor even the illusion that we exist in our own right as independent personalities, can any longer touch us. To fail in this saving realization—not to achieve the great liberation provided by such "enlightenment" into the ultimate "Advaita" or "nondual" truth of existence—is to be condemned to repeat the endless cycle of rebirth and death, with all the suffering it entails, at least until such time as one has finally seen the light and finds release from the world of self-delusion.[4]

If classical Hindu thought and its Vedantist refinements represent the Indian solution to the problem of evil by minimizing the metaphysical reality and ethical significance of the present life, except insofar as it represents a barrier to our existence in a state beyond all materiality and change, Buddhism, at least in some of its purest forms, represents in an even more radical form, an all-out attempt to come to terms with the specific problem of suffering. "To live is to suffer," said Siddartha Gautama, the "Enlightened One," Buddhism's founder. But "suffering is caused by desire." Hence the solution is to eliminate all desire, at least all selfish desire. To accomplish this, the Buddha proposed a totally different approach. Forget self, even a supposed higher true self (thus the Buddhist doctrine of "anatta" or "no-self" as against the Hindu doctrine of the Atman). Forget all attempts to describe the indescribable Brahman and instead aim for the great void of Nirvana. In this alone will all desiring and suffering be overcome.

It may be argued interminably, and it has been, whether or not Gautama was actually a materialist who denied the reality of the soul and of God, or a spiritual idealist who proposed a radical psychological break with all metaphysical and self-concerned thinking. What is clear is that he did, in fact, find a solution to the problem of suffering and death that has proved convincing to countless millions, even billions, of people. Even when his teachings became strongly modified, especially in its "Mahayanist" or "Greater Vehicle" forms combined with the more down-to-earth "Taoist" world views of China and Japan, Buddhism in its many forms has provided a way of coping with life, suffering, and death that even Christianity might envy.

But should Christians envy this solution? Maybe the question should be "Have we not already come close to (too close to according to some) adopting the same solution ourselves?" According to one Western critic, Arthur C. Danto, Buddhism, failing to overcome much of its metaphysical roots in Indian dualism or the idealist escapes from this dualism, can never take suffering and evil with any ultimate seriousness. Despite its apparently direct psychological confrontation with the problem of suffering, Buddhism would release a person from pain by having him escape or bypass the whole "illusion" of personal existence in the body. According to strict Buddhist teaching, our imagined "self" is (in terms not much different from those proposed by the rationalist philosopher Hume) merely "a bundle of sensations." Moral evil, or its principal cause, according to Buddhism, is nothing but our own complicity in our own self-delusion in taking life seriously. Good, or the highest expression of doing good (Buddhist "love" or "compassion") consists in leading others to this self-realization of the nonexistence of the self! As Trungpa Rimpoche, the Tibetan ex-lama who now teaches Buddhism in the United States, has been quoted as saying, "Americans are suprisingly happy to learn [from him] that "they do not exist!"[5]

This is not to say that the mass of Christians or that much the total population of the Western World is in mortal danger of forgetting its all-consuming passion for self-fulfillment or quest for personal happiness; we might even welcome a bit of this Buddhist antidote to our mania of self-preoccupation. But is a metaphysical denial, even one only implied for healthy psychological reasons, any real solution to the problem of evil? Have we not already had enough, even in our own Western religious traditions, of the attitude that this life is not really what "counts" or that the millions upon millions who suffer in this world should really consider themselves "blessed" or "happy" for their reward is great in heaven?

I realize that in saying this I am coming perilously close to contradicting the words of Jesus in his "Sermon on the Mount." But what he offered as consolation to the poor and suffering does not constitute the ideal of justice for "the Kingdom of Heaven." Jesus was violent in his denunciation of those who caused such suffering and especially of those who invoked the will of God to justify it. On the other hand, while the way of the Christ would eliminate needless suffering, as Buddhism would do, its means of doing so differs even more radically from the Buddhist way than did Gautama's from that of classical Vedic Hinduism. Jesus would not escape suffering or evil through a path of enlightenment. Rather, he defeats the power of moral evil, the positive power of prideful human rebellion, by entering most directly into the process of human suffering that sin has produced, as well as all the other pains that belong to the struggle of emerging life. Perhaps deeper insights, especially in the psychological realm, can detect a common ground of agreement between what lies beneath both the Christian and Buddhist attempts to overcome evil, but somehow the Cross itself remains the great sign of contradition. Could there be any more significant contrast than in the deaths of the Christ and the Buddha? Jesus, who died in his prime on the most hideous instrument of torture that era could devise, seems to have suffered a blackout of even that "enlightenment" or sense of oneness with the Father that was the mainstay of his faith. Gautama, on the other hand, slipped quietly into his Nirvana at an advanced old age, complicated, it is said, by a slight case of indigestion.

This is not to say that we should wish a death like Christ's, particularly his suffering and abandonment, for all Christians. I myself would much prefer to die as did the Buddha, and as did many Christian saints—peacefully. Unlike the Buddhist, however, I would hope not for a Nirvana of emptiness, nothingness, or whatever (the nearly untranslatable term literally means "a snuffing out"), but rather, emptied of all self-pretense as effectively as any Buddhist might be, I would also hope to be "filled with the fullness of God."

It may very well be, as the Zen philosopher D. T. Suzuki constantly insisted, that the Buddhist "emptiness" of Nirvana is really an enigmatic way of speaking of the fullness of the ultimate, that "zero equals infinity and infinity equals zero"; but somehow such "enlightenment," while it might lift me above the vicissitudes of life, at the same time would weigh me down. It would make me indifferent not only to my own troubles or sorrows, but also, I fear, to the pains of others. If so, as the Buddhist might object, I would fail to have that "compassion" which Buddhism would demand of me. But how could I have "compassion" unless that passion or suffering of others is real and I really make it mine? Is suffering or compassion only a state of mind, and that only a mind that imagines it exists?

I don't think so. I do not believe that the one view of evil and suffering that Christianity can accept and still remain true to its revelation in the person of Christ is that suffering and evil are but an illusion or at most a changing phenomenon with no lasting significance. On the contrary, in accepting this world as the real world, Christianity is constrained to accept the tragedies and sufferings of this world, and even its moral failures, as part of a process in which this world, the only one that exists, achieves its fulfillment in God.

B. The Nature of Evil

If Christianity, as well as Judaism and Islam, has been influenced by or at least tempted to deal with evil along the lines of the various solutions offered by metaphysical dualism, it has nevertheless been forced, ultimately, to reject them. Any view that holds that the material, as well as the spiritual, side of reality is not only *real* but also basically *good,* can only at the very most adopt some limited psychological approach to the problem of suffering that resembles, for example, the Buddhist solution to the problem. But at the depths of the problem, despite any surface similarities in the manner by which we cope with evil, lies a vast metaphysical difference. Suffering is more than simply the result of self-deluded ego-consciousness. Despite its constant state of change, the universe is not simply *maya* or a realm of illusion or unreality. Death, not the misfortune of being born into life, remains the great barrier that seems forever to bar the way to the unlimited fulfillment of all good.

If all this is true and we are determined to reject all views of evil that would subvert our view of the world as a totally good expression of God's love, then the major problem still remains. What, in fact, is evil? No doubt, perversion of the human will (moral evil), chaotic disorder (physical evil), and suffering—at least unnecessary, useless suffering (psychological evil)—are all expressions and varieties of evil. Even the metaphysical dualist or outright idealist will admit as much. Still, if we hold that even these are but negative or disordered elements in what is otherwise basically good, can evil be said to be anything or entity in itself?

This may seem to be a totally futile and useless question. It may also prove to be ultimately unanswerable. Yet it is an important question, even if the answer eludes us, for we shall find that the way we ask the question as well as the way we attempt to answer it will determine, to a large extent, our basic attitude toward creation, life, and ourselves.

One basic approach to this question, that was considered by

Aristotle and has dominated Western thought since St. Augustine's time, is that evil is, in fact, *nothing*, that is, not a created entity or a *being* in the concrete sense of the word. Starting with the basic biblical assertion that all creation is good, as well as with the metaphysical premise that being, or existence in itself, is a perfection, Augustine concluded that evil is basically a lack or privation. It is a kind of vacuum, a nonexistence where there should be existence. It is a lack of order or an imbalance in what is otherwise good.

Such a notion may seem rather odd at first glance, or even inadequate upon further examination, but it has its advantages, so much so that the great medieval theologian St. Thomas Aquinas took over Augustine's idea with very little modification. After all, take physical evil. Is there anything wrong in itself, as I asked before, with alcohol, despite the rantings of some religious moralists on the subject? No. Even Scripture says that God gave man wine "to gladden his heart." What is wrong is the abuse of alcohol. Likewise, but on a more purely physical level, what is the evil in a flood or an earthquake? Is not the evil in the interruption of the more usual or predictable behavior of the earth? But are even these interruptions an absence of "order" or "balance" in nature? Earthquakes seem to be a necessary part of that ongoing process by which the crust of the earth was formed and continents took their shape. Floods may likewise seem to be a disruption of natural tranquillity, but without them the fertile soils of the flood basins would not be renewed, as the Egyptians have found out to their dismay since the building of the Aswan Dam. Clearly, from this point of view, many physical "evils" are, for the most part, evil only from a human perspective, and, as these last examples show, often a very time-bound perspective.

This same ambivalence affects our understanding of what is good or evil in our own life process. Biological evolution is built on the two foundations of genetic mutation and death. The tragic element in human psychological suffering comes, to a large extent, from our own unwillingness to accept these facts of life. Certainly disease and innocent suffering, even in animals, present special difficulties that we cannot minimize. Yet viewed through the broad spectrum of biological life, it is more a question of imbalance or temporary disorder—for example, too many individuals for the available amount of food, or a rampant multiplication of microbes in a weakened host population, rather than a question of individuals, microbes, or anything else being evil as such.

As for sin, while we may very well see something diabolically malicious in human perversity, still it is not the human will that is evil, but rather the disordering of the will. The essence of sin, as Augustine carefully analyzed, is the *disorder* that results when the will chooses some limited, relative good in preference to a higher or even the absolute good. Even pride, at the level of basic self-esteem, is not all bad, but rather it is the pride that is based on a lie that is bad. Yet, despite the uniquely human quality involved, what is a lie in most cases (even in the case of pride) but a defect, a deformed element, in what is otherwise the truth?

However, the question still remains as to whether or not this view of evil as being merely a defect in what is otherwise an organized harmony is adequate. Is there not something a little too optimistic about it? Like Socrates' claim that no one does anything except by being drawn toward the good (a view also adopted by Augustine and Aquinas) and that evil only occurs when we fail to take in the whole picture of what is *really* good for us, the "privation of good" explanation of the nature of evil seems just a little too simple. It does not seem to fully account for the enormity of the evils we see around us. What was the disordered good that, even in a perverted way, motivated the genocide perpetrated by Hitler and Stalin? Is it possible for even one man to so delude himself as to the true nature of what is good on such a massive scale as to never once entertain a serious doubt about it? Is there not something about evil that is a kind of law into itself to such an extent that even consciousness of good ("the law," as St. Paul describes it) gives a kind of mysterious new power and existence to that same evil? Does not the evil born of simple ignorance become, in the face of the full disclosure of the truth, not just mere disorder, but true perversity?

It is for reasons such as these that the story of the original Fall in the Bible must be understood in a much deeper sense than its apparent mythical simplicity first suggests. So too, St. Augustine's visualization of Adam's sin as a sudden turning away from a primeval perfection would seem to contradict his view of wrongdoing as a mistaken choice of a lesser good, for if our first parents were perfect in all respects, how could they have been trapped by a bold-faced lie? How can perfection be squared with prideful self-deception? Perhaps St. Irenaeus was closer to the truth when he naively pictured Adam and Eve as children (at least psychologically speaking) or as innocents in a paradisal wonderland, whose half-sleeping awareness was destined for a rude awakening as their eyes were opened to the realities of their existence.

Even in such a view, which lends itself easily to an evolutionary reinterpretation, the question remains—what, in itself, is evil? The early Alexandrine School of Christianity, perhaps influenced by Platonic notions (so we should be careful here), speculated on a "precosmic fall," not simply in terms of angelic beings falling from grace, but even in terms of a possible fall of God himself! By this they were implying that the act of creation represents a kind of precipitous slide of "pure being" in and by itself (which is God in his solitary existence) into a state of shared existence with a multiplicy of as yet unorganized and half-formed beings. God steps down from being simply and purely God (or "Godhead," as some would put it) to becoming Creator, with the consequence of becoming involved in all the evil as well as good that creation implies.

We can perhaps already see how such an interpretation is, for all its philosophical sophistication, close to that of the creation myths of chaos. It also seems to imply a distinction similar to the Hindu one between God as the Absolute (Brahman), impersonal and unmoved, and God as the Creator (Brahma), personal and active in the universe. This would allow, in terms of Hindu thinking, for a Creator who is responsible, in a direct way, for all evil as well as good in the universe, while leaving the eternal Godhead uninvolved. Whether the authors of Genesis intended a rebuttal of such an idea of creation as itself a kind of fall (and there is good reason to think so in light of the repeated insistence on the goodness of creation), there is even more reason to think that they would have had objections to any attempts to distinguish a Godhead from a creator God or to define evil as a mere privation of the good. The personification of the tempter as the serpent can be seen as a naive, perhaps crude, attempt to depict evil as a positive force to be reckoned with. True, this personification has its own negative symbolism (the sentencing of the serpent to become legless and henceforth to crawl in the dust), but on the whole the symbol of the serpent is that of a positive and objective embodiment of evil at its very source.

Of course, the problem with this "realism" is that, while it maximizes the fact of evil as a counterforce to God, it also maximizes the problem of ultimately blaming God for evil's existence! If we are to understand evil as a positive force, even if there is a great deal of insight to be gained from seeing it as metaphysically negative (a real being, but a legless or disordered one for all that), we have to reread the story of the fall in another light. But how?

If we may follow the earlier suggestion that the Genesis story of humanity's paradisal existence should be read backwards, as a revelation of the possible future rather than as prehistory, we might go a step farther. Why not apply this reverse approach not just to the possibilities of future good but also to the consequences of future sins, and even to our understanding of the source and power of evil itself?

If paradise is yet to be achieved, might it not also be that its opposite is also yet to be realized? If this could be true, then might not the cause of our woe, its full personification, have yet to take its final and full form? Indeed, this is more or less hinted at in the apocalyptic Book of Revelation with the "Anti-Christ," or the succession of those who wield the destructive powers of this world.

If this is possible, then I would also suspect (as did Teilhard de Chardin) that the original sin is not to be found so much at the dawn of the human race (unless we take it to simply be concupiscence, or all the tendencies toward disorder with which evolution has left us) as in the twilight or dusk of the human race before the final darkness falls. If there is something positive about evil, something malicious, even diabolic, it has not diminished since the first appearance of humankind but has increased. Compounded by generations of ignorance and stupidity, but even more by the dreams of empires both personal and universal, human pride feeds upon itself until in its madness it would have for itself "all the kingdoms of this world and their glory," or else, frustrated in its pretense to self-proclaimed divinity, reduce the cosmos to nuclear ash. Having unlocked nearly all the secrets of life (and death), we imagine ourselves the captains of our own ship, but we may find that we have instead run aground or worse. Most of all, we aspire not only to be simply "as gods, knowing good and evil" for what they are, but to be God, deciding for ourselves what is right and fit, without reference to the Source from which we came.

At this point I may seem entirely to have disposed of the existence of Satan as a personal, fallen, angelic being. It is not my intention to do so. I would only relocate him in time. Like its vision of paradise, humanity's vision of itself is to "be as angels," unencumbered by the limits of bodily existence, impervious to weaknesses of passions and ignorance, exempt from disease and death. Very possibly some day we shall achieve this, but not without a price, for what may be turned to good may just as surely turn out for ill. Man's creation of the devil in his own image and likeness has just begun.

What, then, is the nature of evil? Who can say? Surely it is negative, nonbeing, disorder, pure nothingness, where being, order, and harmony should exist. Just as surely it is positive, for it is equally something, anything or anybody that stands in opposition to the self-donation of God in love. Disorder, nonbeing, and nothingness are abstractions. Disordered beings, evil persons, deformed societies are not. They are real, they exist, and we shall probably see more of them and worse in time to come.

Did God then create evil? In one sense, yes, he is responsible. He is the source of all good or bad. Disorder and nonbeing can be thought of as standing outside of or as opposed to God and his creation insofar as "being in itself" is God and "ordered being" shares his existence. There is, however, such a thing as disordered being, and God has allowed it to exist as well. One of our main problems has been to read the process backward and to assume that the disorder that we have engendered and encountered in ourselves in its worst, even diabolic form, was also God's idea instead of our own.

C. How Bad Is Evil?

The question I am posing may seem like a silly one, almost like asking, in another way, "How good is bad?" There is definitely a serious question to be faced here, for in any true estimation of the reality of evil, beyond its actual existence and metaphysical nature, lurks the question, "but in the end, is it really all that bad?"

This question can occur in several forms and be approached several ways. For one, does not the division of evil into kinds (physical, psychological, moral) also imply that there might be a certain hierarchy or grading of evil? For example, a modern French Catholic writer has claimed that "there is only one real tragedy in life, and that is not to have become a saint." This position, a popular Christian sentiment, implies that physical and psychological evils (suffering) are not to be compared with the reward of having escaped or overcome the moral evil of sin. St. Paul said as much, and even Jesus himself when he warned us "Do not fear those who kill the body . . . fear him who, after he has killed, has the power to cast into hell . . ." (Luke 12:4–5).

Likewise, was not Gautama's doctrine of negating all selfish desire to eliminate suffering also something more than simply a way of reducing psychological evil to mere physiological pain? The whole Eastern tradition, both in the Hindu as well as the Buddhist form, seems to agree that the ultimate evil is ignorance. The loss of, or the failure to discover, the nature of the true self, however it be conceived, remains both the source and culmination of all evil. Indeed, such a disaster is, in Eastern thinking, the equivalent of a total separation from ultimate reality or God.

So too Socrates, the sage of ancient Greece, calmly underwent his self-inflicted death, confident that the life of his soul would not be diminished, but rather enhanced, by his devotion to the truth for which he had been sentenced.

In the minds of these men, commonly held to be among the world's greatest thinkers, moral evil (however it may be envisioned) is worse than physical evil, and the sufferings of the body are minor in comparison to the sufferings of the unfaithful spirit, and temporary torment is far preferable to eternal loss.

In much the same way, but for more immediate and even "worldly" reasons, the whole science or study of ethics and the art of politics are founded on a similiar set of assumptions: a hierarchy of values and a recognition that some evils have to be tolerated for the sake of greater good. When it comes to evil experienced as purely physical pain, although sometimes the cure seems worse than the disease, do we not put up with the pain (the dentist's drill, the surgeon's scalpel) rather than suffer the longer-term consequence of neglect?

Such a line of thought suggests another, perhaps false, solution to the problem of evil. If the reality of evil is not to be denied, perhaps then the ultimacy of evil can be. If physical pain can be considered to be less serious than psychological suffering, which in turn is less evil than moral corruption, is it not possible that this ultimate depravity, which we call sin, is also canceled out? Would not even moral evil lose permanent significance in the light of some overall purpose and victory of goodness in the universe?

Certainly the temptation to see this as the final way out of the problem of evil is very strong. Some have suggested that the gradual emergence of belief in an immortal soul was evolved simply to make it possible to see all evils canceled out through hope for a heavenly reward. In fact, we can see that the Hebrew prophets struggled mightily with the dilemmas of evil and divine justice in the absence of any clear idea of an afterlife. Prosperity, long life, a good name, and the honor conferred by generations to come were each given prominence at one time or another as the reward of a just life. Yet none of these proved adequate. So no doubt there is probably a strong element of truth in this accusation. The belief in an afterlife made possible through a resurrection of the just was the culmination of a long process of struggle with the riddle of divine justice in the face of evil. However, along with this belief there also emerged a corollary belief in a resurrection of the wicked to further, delayed punishment in retribution for a sinful life. Nor was this punishment seen only as corrective; for some it was deemed to be eternally punitive. Thus, for all but the "Universalists" (those who believe that everyone will be saved, despite what they have done) the usual doctrines of an afterlife predict eternal damnation for the wicked.

One of the more persistent criticisms of orthodox Christian teaching in this matter is that despite the threat of such an ultimate tragedy as eternal damnation, certain theologians such as Augustine, Luther, and Calvin have nevertheless seen such damnation as a kind of triumph of God's goodness and power. Thus, in effect, the critics say, there would be no real evil in the universe because all evil would be considered relative to the absolute and the ultimate—the triumph of the Kingdom of God. That this is no minor or outdated objection is evident from objections leveled against the thinking of such modern Christians as Karl Rahner and Teilhard de Chardin. Along with criticism of Teilhard's alleged minimalization of evil is paired the condemnation of Teilhard's view of hell as part of the "Pleroma" or fullness of God's creation (he likened it to the dump of a well-planned city!). More subtle criticism may be reserved for Rahner's concern for the possibility of "anonymous Christians" who are saved without explicit belief. Does not this concern for the salvation of unbelievers also amount to admitting the possibility of damnation as well? In either case the implication of the critics is that to accept even the possibility of eternal damnation is to somehow trivialize the ultimate tragedy it would represent.

To face this objection squarely, it must be asked if such protests against the doctrine of eternal punishment do not contradict themselves. Orthodox Christianity, as well as all biblical religion, sees God's kingdom as ultimately triumphing, but one should hesitate to claim that all its principal theologians (at least the more saintly ones) rejoice in the failure of those who do not make it. Origen's famous espousal of a universalistic belief (for him even the devil would be saved in the end) may have got him into serious trouble with the bishops, but at least it proved that his intentions were good. Can we not then suppose that most orthodox writers, whatever their views on the victory of God's goodness and his saints, at least secretly mourned the tragedy of those who threw away their chance?

In addition to the limitation that the doctrine places upon belief in the otherwise total triumph of God, we must also consider its opposite implication, the partial victory of evil. Even in this victory there is something of a natural good, for whatever else one may think of a doctrine of eternal punishment, it remains the last bastion of defense of belief in free will, at least in the context of immortality. Just as there could be no meaningful salvation without the wish to be saved, damnation is the last and not entirely feeble protest of the creature who would insist on its own will against that of God, no matter what the cost. One can only suspect that the real reason for the widespread rejection of a belief in hell is not a reaction to the distortions of medieval painters or preachers, or even simply a tender-hearted view of God. At the root stands, more likely, a modern disinclination to accept any ultimate human responsibility for tragedy in the universe—indeed, to accept the possibility of any lasting tragedy at all. For rather than minimizing the tragic potentiality of human freedom, belief in at least the possibility of eternal loss protects it, even at the cost of diminishing the final success of God's plan. If anything, those who damn themselves to isolation from divine and human love are "tragic successes." They are, in C. S. Lewis's words ". . . in one sense, successful, rebels to the end; [for them] the doors of hell are locked on the *inside*."

What more can be said about the reality and tragedy of evil in the universe? Perhaps Weil in her Jewish-Christian Platonism said it all in a form calculated to outrage us or at least to refute whoever among us claims to be an optimist.

> God has created a world which is not the best possible, but which contains the whole range of good and evil. We are at the point where it is bad as possible. For beyond is the stage where evil becomes innocent.[6]

Can this be true? Can it be, that while formerly the world had been passing through eons of evolution, now, with the emergence of the human race, there has been only a moral devolution? If so, must we then accuse of God having deliberately created the worst possible world or simply one in which the fullest range of possibilities for good or for ill exist? If it is the latter, then it must be, in fact it can only be, that God so values the higher good of human freedom that he allows things to come to such a pass, even if the next stage were to be one where evil has become so pervasive that it would be a kind of perverted innocence, a kind of diabolic ignorance of even the vestiges of good or evil. Few of us (thank God!) have had to live through what Simone Weil did, or have experienced her extreme hypersensitivity to evil, and we have not deliberately gone out of our way to share, to the extent that she did, the sufferings of the unfortunate, but I think that we all can sense the outrage she felt. Despite her avowed Platonism, no one can accuse all idealists (especially all Christian ones) of minimizing the problem of evil.

At the same time, I question her statement that things are as bad as possible. She wrote over three decades ago. She died before Nagaski or Hiroshima. Did she have any inkling of the extent of brutality at Auschwitz or Dachau or other extermination camps where one-fourth of her own race would be eliminated? Perhaps she did sense what was happening and it was these things that prompted her to write as she did. But have things become any better since then, or have we even begun to slow that headlong plunge into a ghastly innocence in which we no longer even want to know, much less judge the extent of, the difference between good and evil?

In effect, Weil's vision of evil is that of an Eden in reverse. Just as we should perhaps see paradise as a possibility to be realized in the transcendent future, and just as the full dimensions of evil are yet to be measured, perhaps, too, the terrible possibility of the total dehumanization of the human race still awaits us in the complete loss of all moral sensitivity. If this should happen, we shall have reached the end. Evolution will have exhausted all its possibilities in a stillbirth—the total wreckage of God's hope for this favored child of his creation. Is this possible? Christian belief holds that it could not be so, that the victory over evil and sin is, in principle, already ours, that Christ has already prevailed. But the casualty lists have not yet been revealed. Unfortunately, they are not even yet complete.

Notes

1. *First and Last Notebooks*, Translated by Richard Rees in the edition first published in English by Oxford University Press (London, New York, Toronto: 1970) from the French *Cahiers* (Paris: Plon, 1970) and *La Connaissance surnaturelle* (Paris: Gallimard, 1950) and

as quoted by George A. Panichas, *The Simone Weil Reader* (New York: David McKay Co, Inc., 1977), p. 427.

2. The transliteration of these Hebrew words follows the system utilized by *The Jerome Biblical Commentary* and a number of other modern translations seeking a more exact rendition of the Hebrew. For purposes of rough approximation, however, the above words can also be transliterated as *ruach, nephesh,* and *bashar.*

3. The reader should be cautioned that the use of such terms as *realism* and *idealism* is rather relative. The same is perhaps even more true for the opposites *dualism* and *monism.* Not only are the latter terms applicable to ethical, metaphysical, and other categories of meaning, but very often they interrelate in a paradoxical fashion. Metaphysical idealism, in its stress of the superior or primary function of the spiritual, often simultaneously expresses itself in a dualistic antithesis of spirit and matter. However, it is perhaps just as apt to ultimately reach a point where the spiritual aspect becomes so emphasized as to subsume all reality as mere (or more or less) illusory aspects of a single all-embracing (hence *monistic*) principle. Monistic pantheism, generally associated with Hindu mystical philosophy, is probably most typical of this trend, with its stress on all, particularly the human *atman* or soul, being one with the divine *brahman.*

Western or more typically "nature" pantheism, on the other hand, tends to stress the particularity of each individual being as nevertheless interrelated in a divine "all." If for the latter "*All* is God," for the former "*God* [or his equivalent in nontheistic systems] is all." Despite Paul's appeal to the somewhat pantheistic words suggestive of Epimenides of Gnossos ("it is in him that we live, and move, and have our being," cf. Acts 17:28), he seems to have lost his audience, containing, as we are told, both Epicureans as well as Stoics, upon his mention of the Resurrection of Christ. Apparently whatever pantheistic leanings his audience may have had, the dualistic tendencies that accompanied it, whether the stress be more on the material, as with the Epicureans, or on the spiritual, as Stoicism may have been evolving (as evidenced by the direction of later Christian stoics), Paul's biblical realism was too much.

4. Shankara or Samkara (or more accurately still, Śaṁkara), who lived somewhere around the eighth or ninth century of our era, still remains a very controversial figure. His system of "non-dualism" *(Advaita)* is manifestly an attempt to modify the pure doctrine of metaphysical idealism that was current in the Vedantist philosophy of his time, with the intent of allowing for a modified form of realism regarding the phenomenal world. For this attempt, among other things, he was denounced as being a "crypto-buddhist" of sorts, while others, even such modern innovators in Indian philosophy as Sri Auribindo Ghose (1872–1950), continue to reject Samkara's philosophy as unadulterated idealism. For more on this, see R. Puligandla, *Fundamentals of Indian Philosophy.* (Nashville, New York: Abington Press, 1975).

5. This remark, reported in *Time* magazine some years ago, illustrates well the danger of distortion that popularizations (as well as critiques) of ancient philosophies are all too apt to undergo when taken out of their original cultural milieu. Indian, as well as Buddhist philosophy (although in somewhat different terms) is certainly prepared to admit the phenomenal reality of the individual person (the *jiva* of Hindu thought). Christianity too is replete with warnings against the "false self." More reflections on these matters are contained in Raimundo Panikkar's *Myth, Faith and Hermeneutics: Toward Cross-Cultural Religious Understanding* (New York: Paulist Press, 1980).

6. Quoted by George A. Panichas (op. cit., p. 390) from Simone Weil's *Gravity and Grace,* translated by Arthur Wills (New York: G. P. Putnam's Sons, 1952).

5

The Evil Within

> I cannot understand why the world is arranged as it is.
> Men are themselves to blame, I suppose; they were given
> paradise, they wanted freedom and they stole fire from
> heaven, though they knew they would become un-
> happy, so there is no need to pity them.
> —Feodor Dostoyevsky
> *The Brothers Karamazov*

Ivan Karamazov, who has become our principal protagonist in this discussion of evil, has a point; for the most part, mankind has only itself to blame. Among the problems of evil, moral evil or sin is, with certain reservations, the easiest to understand. St. Augustine, despite his insistence on the absolute all-powerfulness and all-knowingness of God, insists that mankind is *free* and *responsible*. In fact the only real evil, in Augustine's mind, is sin; everything else is secondary.

Is it really that simple, even if we ignore the predestination implied in the concept of an all-knowing and all-disposing God? Part of our uneasiness with such an apparently simple solution, which holds that human freedom accounts for all evil (leaving the devil aside), is that it gives merely an abstract answer to the problem of a specific kind of evil. It is not in itself an adequate explanation of the specific problem of your or my or anyone's concrete sinfulness. As Ivan Karamazov says, rather paradoxically, "Men are themselves to blame . . . though they knew they would become unhappy. . . ." But did they know, really?

Perhaps this is why Augustine had to lay such great stress on the original sin. Adam's fall is the sin of all humans, infecting us to our very core, making it virtually impossible that any human being ever after be without sin. Every other evil that befalls us is, in Augustine's view, a punishment designed by God's justice as either a retribution for sins already committed, or a warning lest we sin again. Seen in this way, there is nothing that happens to us that we do not deserve! We are all guilty. None of us is innocent, even the most blameless little child.

This solution of Augustine's, despite its apparent grotesqueness, has also a certain simple grandeur, particularly in light of his doctrine of God's saving grace. However interpreted, Augustine's concept of original sin (based on his own personal interpretation of St. Paul) has had immense influence on Western theology, whether it be along the lines of Luther's concept of the total corruption of human nature, Calvin's correlative idea of God's totally predestinating will, or the Roman Catholic doctrine of the "gracelessness" of mankind in both its "natural" and fallen states. Yet there also seems to be a certain heartlessness and inexplicability in these views that appear to contradict the presumed mercy and goodness of God. Despite the qualified use of the concept of guilt (more often restated as the "stain" or basic condition of being born in the "state" of original sin), it amounts to a kind of initial curse, presumption of guilt without a trial, a punishment without personal responsibility. Is there not a better way of accounting for the human condition, a way that both explains the human propensity for sinning and also preserves the intuition of the basic innocence of every child born into this world?

I believe that there is, and that it can be found in the suggestion made earlier that what we have called original sin could be reinterpreted in terms of an "ultimate sin," in much the same way as the suggestion that the paradise of Eden may represent the possibility of the future rather than the memory of the past. As unorthodox as these suggestions may at first seem, they should be given a hearing. Such a reinterpretation would not be simply for the sake of providing the way out of the embarrassment occasioned by an ancient doctrine that has proved a source of scandal to modern sensitivities. Of much more importance, it would help us to deepen our understanding of our own situation, one in which the human race seems to be bound up more hopelessly in its present sinfulness than can ever be explained by a mere appeal to the past.

A. *"Original" or "Ultimate" Sin?*

At first, an inverted notion of original sin—in this case, more that of an ultimate sin—may seem as strange as that unusual scientist-mystic Teilhard de Chardin himself, who to my knowledge was the first to suggest it. Yet everything fits.

Current thought regarding the biological origins of the human species would indicate that the idea of the existence of a single, isolated "first" human couple is problematic if not highly questionable. The majority opinion still holds to the concept of a single race or type of human as ancestral to our own.[1] Nevertheless, the lack of an identifiable first pair makes the idea of a transmission of an original sin in terms of a kind of genetically related or inherited guilt rather improbable. Aside from this difficulty (of the biological as well as the theological orders), can we really conceive of such an emerging human type as being morally or psychologically capable of such a sin (whatever it was) that would forever after plunge the human race into a state of automatic alienation from God? Certainly Irenaeus's depiction of our first parents as naive and blundering innocents rings more true.

No doubt, as even Teilhard admitted, the subsequent course of human development seems, at least as far back as we can go, to be marred by some "primeval catastrophe," a penchant for wickedness and perversity that is more than mere naivité. Could not this basic tendency be better explained as a war between conflicting instincts, or between instincts inherited from our biological past and a present situation wherein they are no longer appropriate? May it not be that our basic drives are no longer even instinctually governed but have been set adrift as the result of the emergence of the higher faculty of reason, like an aircraft that has had its "autopilot" replaced by a still-to-be-trained human substitute? Whatever the origin of this conflict, such a view would be surprisingly close to the medieval idea of original sin as being manifested primiarly in concupiscence, or the driving passions of the flesh.

Even granted such a basic propensity for evil and other forms of self-defeating behavior in human nature, can we conceive of sin in terms of deliberate transgression except where there is a basic awareness of ethical limits or moral demands? It seems hardly likely. This was partly St. Paul's point when he said that it took the Law to make mankind fully conscious of sin. A person can do wrong or act stupidly, to the detriment of his own best interests as well as those of others, without being fully conscious of what he is doing. But sin, properly speaking, is something more. It implies at least a minimal awareness of evil that in some way involves a malicious opposition to the will of God. Unless the first humans were an unaccountable exception to all that we can observe in both primitive cultures and human childhood, it seems difficult to imagine a first human or a primal group of proto-humans who were anything more than barely self-conscious enough (never mind God-conscious enough) to do anything more than engage in passion-driven tantrums.

On the contrary, when we look for real malice, we must also look for real reflective awareness. Traditionally, we have seen pride, pure pride, classed as the worst sort of sin because it is the fruit of a self-centered awareness in opposition to the claims of a higher awareness centered on God. Sins of passion, stemming from violence, lust, or avarice, may be more common, but they are also less malicious and more forgivable precisely because they are very often the result of being driven by forces beyond our full control. By any such analysis, if the so-called original sin is consummately a sin of pride, then we must look for the full manifestation of such sin in the growing self-awareness of the human race and in the perfected ability of humanity to act in total rebellion against God and in total inhumaneness toward itself. Prehistory seems an unlikely stage for such capability; have we not just recently reached that point, or nearly so?

It must be admitted that this inversion of the idea of original sin into an ultimate sin appears to fly in the face of long-standing Christian interpretation. Yet it is rather curious that those who have made so much of "biblical religion" have seemed to overconcentrate on the Adamic myth of the Fall in trying to explain humanity's sinfulness, while the people who gave us these Scriptures have been very reticent about jumping to any such conclusions. As Paul Ricoeur has remarked, with the major exception of St. Paul's Letter to the Romans (and two brief allusions in the Book of Wisdom) almost no further reference is made to the sin of Adam by either the Tanach (or "Old Testament" Scriptures) of the Jews or the Christian New Testament. Jesus himself seems to have referred to the Genesis story of the creation of the human race only once beyond his allusion to the devil as "the father of lies," and that is in reference to the monogamous pattern of marriage. His other references to sin as depicted in Genesis were rather to the stories of Cain and Abel, Noah, and Sodom and Gomorrah. If we were to look for the locus of the major sin of the human race as

Jesus depicted it, we would have to look to the future, to the time of the great apostasy that will be the prelude to the *eschaton* or final coming of The Son of Man and the subsequent final judgment of the human race.

Perhaps too we have misunderstood Paul's purpose in resurrecting the Genesis myth. The major point in his argument does not seem to be how "all have sinned *in* Adam" (the phrase in Romans 5:12 that defies translation—does it mean "because of Adam," or "like Adam?"—even Augustine was stymied by it) but more that mankind has a new progenitor, a new spiritual head, in Christ. Perhaps Paul was attempting to utilize what J. T. W. Robinson called the Hebraic concept of "corporate personality" (Abraham standing for all Jews, Joseph for all exiles, etc.). In any case, Paul appears to have been more intent on explaining that just as all people have become living souls (that is, living beings)[2] in sharing the human existence of Adam (who for obvious symbolic as well as genetic reasons stands for us all), so, even more, all human beings are enabled to become spiritual beings, immortal sharers in God's life, through the sacrifice of Christ. That such a transition involves a cancellation of the debt of our Adamic sinfulness is obvious. On the other hand, it is less clear that Paul actually meant that Adam's or any ancestor's sin produces a guilt inherited automatically by being born human. In fact, this last idea seems to have been more St. Augustine's interpretation of St. Paul than Paul's own idea. Even Augustine himself, who was more concerned with eleborating a theology of grace than producing a doctrine of congenital sinfulness, seems to have been hard-pressed to explain how this could be. At one time Augustine even tried to blame sex for our sinfulness, rather than simply our humanity! There can be little doubt that St. Paul's primary intention was to insist on the gratuitousness of God's favor toward us, and that this grace was earned for us by Christ. That sin itself, rather than a tendency toward sinfulness, can be inherited is another matter—a conclusion deduced from reading Paul's analogy upside down.

What we did undoubtedly inherit from Adam, at least in St. Paul's mind, was our mortality, our susceptibility to death. It is very interesting to see what Eastern Christian theology has done with this concept. At least one line of the Oriental Church tradition has chosen to see our mortality (or death taken as a collective condition) as the very root and deepest condition of our sinfulness. Perhaps influenced more by the Greek tragic myths than by St. Paul directly, this theology sees death less as a punishment for sin than as the central motivating cause of our sinfulness. We sin because we are afraid to die. We are avaricious (piling up treasures on earth), we are lustful (seeking to indiscriminately misuse our powers to propagate life), we are violent (resisting our death with the death of others), all because we ourselves are afraid to die. But die we must. No man or woman can escape it. Nor did Jesus. In that is the tragedy, but from his willing submission came the victory, for in rising he overcame death.

We shall have more to ponder concerning this Eastern Christian view of original sin and its relation to death, but it is quite obvious at this point that such a view requires a readjustment of our understanding of St. Paul's controversial chapter in Romans. At face value, Paul seems to have imagined that death itself, as a biological fact, entered the world only because of Adam's sin. Did he mean this to apply to the death of animals as well? If so, then how could humans before the Fall use all the animals, at least for food? (Perhaps we have read St. Paul, as well as Genesis, in a much too literal fashion!) However in 1 Corinthians 15, St. Paul, although he says that both death and sin come to us in Adam, also clearly says that "sin is the sting of death!" Again, in Romans 6 he says "the wage paid by sin is death." Which is it? What is first? The two seem to be intrinsically allied, bound up in a vicious circle. When we attempt to cheat death by sinning, we only reap more death.

In terms of biological evolution, it only makes sense to see physical death as a natural phenomenon, long antedating the appearance of the human type. Yet psychologically, and especially in moral terms, it is sin that has given death its real power—the power to destroy humanity's soul, its life of divinely given freedom, its genuine chance to become "like gods." Death and sin, then, taken together, are both original and ultimate, for death and the futile attempt to escape it have been with us from the very beginning; and sin, as the expression of and protest against our fate, will surely increase as the universe draws nearer to its own death. The fact of death has become the agony of dying, and the curse of the first sin has become the compounded perversity of us all.

How has this actually come about? How is it that the human-race, born into the slavery of death, could aspire to life, and yet, for all its noble hopes, bring upon itself only more death, and this a death not only of body but of spirit as well? To answer this we must face a further paradox, perhaps one even more puzzling than the relationship between death and sin. Sin and death are, in so many ways, correlative, at least in their relation to freedom; and yet, in their failure to find it, find themselves ever more closely linked. Can it be then that it is really freedom, not death, that is the great enemy? Or is it that only in the awareness of freedom can we at last fully experience the bondage of sin?

B. Freedom and Sin

Just as the logic of original sin as formulated by Augustine breaks down in what appears to be a series of irreconcilable contradictions, so too his defense of human freedom seems to lead to just the opposite conclusion. For just as Calvin was to draw his doctrine of double predestination (God's willing of some people's damnation as well as the salvation of the rest) from Augustine's view of divine grace alone rescuing humanity from the universal guilt of original sin, so Luther believed that he was following in Augustine's footsteps when he denied that humans, suffering as they do from a total corruption of their God-given nature, have any real capacity to exercise free will. Yet Augustine himself stoutly maintained that we do in fact possess free will. It is this free will that is responsible for sin; and, after we have sinned, it is this free will that makes it possible for us to accept God's grace as a remedy, or to reject it. But there remains the question of how we can be seen to be free enough to do even that when the very acceptance of grace requires a special help from God, the outcome of which God knows from all eternity! Subsequent argument over the matter of God's grace and human free will seems to have led nowhere, with one Counter-Reformation pope even calling a halt to the great Thomist-Suarezian debate on the question. Clearly we have gone in circles and have gotten nowhere, except perhaps to have defined our terms a little more precisely. What then is amiss?

Assuming the reality both of God's grace and of human freedom, no matter how much they seem to clash, let us suppose that Augustine got off on the wrong foot on this matter of God's presumed all-powerful foreknowledge of events. Let us even forget, at least for the time being, this whole matter of mankind's having already sinned in Adam. Let us simply begin with what we think we experience as freedom.

Suppose we take freedom to be the ability, or even the desire, to do other than what we feel constrained or forced to do. To put it in a more theological way, would not freedom mean that at least some of the things that we do are not a direct result of God's having willed them? This means, even if one reintroduces the idea that God already knows how things will turn out, that nevertheless God only permits some things to happen as they do, but does not directly cause them to so happen. Free creatures, then, ultimately derive their origin from God and in that sense their freedom can be seen as "caused" by God, but the exercise of their freedom, the result of their free decisions, is something they themselves carry out in their own right. My decisions are my own free-will acts, not somebody else's—not even God's.

Yet we know that what we often take to be freedom is not all that simple. Just as the idea of God as the ultimate cause of our existence and our freedom keeps intruding on the concept of pure freedom, so too a host of other causes, whether genetic, environmental, social, or otherwise, constantly calls our freedom into doubt. Is freedom then truly a given, something that just appears out of the blue as part and parcel of being human, or is it something that is slowly acquired or won?

Note what Dostoyevsky's Ivan says (perhaps with more insight than he realizes): "They *wanted* freedom and they stole fire from heaven." Were the first humans, whoever they were, really free? Even if we regard a certain basic freedom as part of what it means to be human, would it not be more logical to suppose that freedom was, at the earliest stages of humanity, more of a tendency than an actuality? Would not "stealing fire from heaven" or wanting to "become like gods . . . knowing (deciding for oneself) both good and evil" be really more an impulse toward freedom than freedom already obtained?

True, one may argue that to grope for freedom is in itself a beginning of freedom, a kind of decision, or at least an acquiescence to a kind of vital impulse. In that case, depending on how you look at it, it was either a free act or a driven act, or, more likely, a combination of the two. Regardless of how much actual freedom there might have been, the first sin seems to be bound up with a quest for *more* freedom. The result of that sin only further complicates the matter, for in asserting a certain autonomy from God, the first sinners also experienced a new kind of slavery. Thus it is more than just a question of sinful disobedience; there is rather a certain ambivalence, even a self-defeating paradox, contained in this first real exercise of human freedom. To "know" in this way, that is, to decide for oneself what the standards of good and evil shall be, involves at the same time the loss of the freedom that comes with innocence. If "ignorance is bliss" it is because, at least on one level—that of childish innocence, not to know is to experience the freedom from the responsibiblity of decision. But who would choose to remain a child forever? Freedom on this level involves almost no self-determination, the very essence of any fully human freedom. Such primitive freedom is illusory, being born of ignorance more than of anything else.

Yet, for all this, can we say that the freedom we seek is much more free? Is there not something truly sinister about it? There is a kind of "drivenness" about it, reminding us of Sartre's phrase about our being "condemned to freedom." It is as if evolution, even when conceived as a process set in motion by God, will not rest until it has produced a creature that has stumbled, to its own regret, upon its own independence. Having found it, this strange creature we call Man has mixed feelings, both celebrating his freedom as proof of his humanity and rueing the burden of responsibility brought in its train.

If this existential insight into the dual or mixed good/bad nature of freedom is correct, then where does it lead us?

To begin with (and this is not too different from what Augustine and many others have said), it means that freedom, even at the cost of much deviation, is a value which the creator of the universe apparently considers to be of great importance. Like Henri Bergson's view of evolution, the direction of the creative process is toward freedom, or the emergence of a multitude of free beings. Biblically speaking, we were created to be in God's image and likeness, and we presume that to be God is to be absolutely free.

Second, freedom, for created beings, is necessarily limited. Our freedom, unlike God's, is neither total nor absolute. It is limited by the same creative drives and impulses that bring this same freedom into existence. It also must contend with the claims advanced by the freedom of others.

Third (and this follows directly from the second point), being limited, this same freedom is defective. It has evil aspects; one of them, perhaps the most significant, is that even partial freedom contains a certain rivalry with or duplication of the freedom of God, without ever being able to equal God's freedom.

Finally, and perhaps the most crucial point, is the paradox that the only sinless use of human freedom seems to be in giving it up! At first glance this statement seems outrageous, both logically and humanly speaking. It appears flatly to contradict not only what we, especially in the Western world, hold most dear, but to undermine our profoundest intuitions about the nature of human dignity. Did God, as Eric Fromm insists, really not want us to become "as gods"? True, but it is quite another thing to become as gods on our own terms, defying God's plan and going off on our own to refashion things in our own image and likeness. Yet, does not any such restriction of our freedom, any such conforming of our will to God's will, truly make us "a little less than gods" (or "the angels"—depending on how you translate the biblical phrase)? Thus it seems that we must be content to be second, or even third-rate gods—but is this not enough? Apparently it is not, at least not for many individuals when faced with an actual contest between the human will and the divine will. It is one thing to accept gracefully the honor of being like gods in our freedom, although not exactly God's equal. It is quite another thing to accept the responsibility of patterning our individual actions along the lines set by God.

This last point is why only a specific, concrete approach to individual evils can solve, so to speak, the problem of sin. The existence of freedom as a "specific abstract" (to use Ahern's phrase) quality does, in fact, explain the possibility of equally abstract moral evils. It does not, however, answer the question of why this or that particular sin. The answer to that is to be found only in the particular situations in which we as individuals are confronted with specific choices. Either my decision brings me into greater conformity with God's plan and thus a share in his freedom, or it does not. If it does not, then my divergent use of freedom becomes a nonfreedom, a capitulation to the blind and driven forces of nature, and to the unfreedoms by which they are compelled.

C. Sin and the "Excess" of Evil

Although freedom is a positive value, it brings in its wake both good and ill. We must, then, see sin as a distinct possibility in God's universe. "What is able to fall does fall at times," said St. Thomas Aquinas. Apparently God so values the existence of free creatures, even if they only poorly resemble himself, that he is willing to pay the price of our possible, even probable, failure. But the question is: are *we* willing to pay the price? Apparently we are—but not without some misgivings. It is especially in this re-

spect, when we come up against the horrible excesses of evil, all the
terrible things that could have been otherwise, the "could have
beens" that never were, that second thoughts arise about the whole
price that has been paid.

Toward the very end of Ivan Karamazov's impassioned debate
he admits that there might be, after all, some "higher harmony" to
be achieved out of or even despite all the sin and sufferings of the
human race. He himself, however, must protest or even attempt to
disaffiliate himself from such a horrendous process, one that demands the sacrifice of so many innocent victims for the sake of
some elusive freedom or its by-products. Ivan does not doubt the
possibility of such higher good. Rather, he doubts that any such
good is worth the price being paid. He would just as soon turn in
his ticket and refuse to participate in such a dreadful lottery.

Of course, what we witness in such a protest is not merely a
denunciation of all the atrocities perpetrated against innocent victims. Even more, it implies a protest against the terrible misuse of
human freedom and even the freedom of God to start such a
process. It is not that freedom occasions some incidental abuse. It
is rather that the chronic misuse of freedom is so widespread, so
ingrained in the human condition, that no amount of good seems
sufficient to balance it. It would be a plausible, even just, arrange-
ment if each sinner were punished for his crime, but it seems as if
instead it is the innocent victims of sin who suffer. In this, even
innocence itself is corrupted and the whole human race becomes an
embodiment of evil.

Thus there is a certain "communal" aspect to sin; it is conta-
gious, afflicting the sinner and victim alike. Like a single virus that
finds a vulnerable host organism, it multiplies and transmits itself
in a new, virulent intensity to all around. Evil becomes epidemic.

There is no need to enumerate all the forms of this phenomenon, ranging from the betrayal of individuals to mass genocide.
Let us simply recall how this excess or multiplication of evil has
not only scandalized the skeptics but even puzzled the prophets of
old. "The fathers ate sour grapes and their children's teeth were set
on edge"—so goes the old Hebrew proverb that Ezekiel wished to
see repudiated. Can it be? Certainly God's justice would seem to
require that the sinner alone be punished (which Ezekiel an-
nounced would be the case); but, unfortunately, it rarely seems to
work out that way. Not only do the wicked often prosper (at least
in worldly terms) but they seem to do so mostly at the expense of
the innocents to whom it must seem that indeed crime *does* pay!

In this way evil, especially communal or shared evil, is self-perpetuating. Take, for example, the evil of slavery which, paradoxically, so many of its original perpetrators in our era did not seem to think to be a sin at all. For the Arab slave traders, and the American Christians who sailed the "slavers" or otherwise engaged in the trade, it was just good business. For the Americans who bought and used slaves, it was the advance of civilization. Even Catholic religious orders who owned them could point to one pope who defended the whole practice if "souls" could thereby be "saved!" The first victims of all this rationalization were, of course, the slaves themselves and, as immediate beneficiaries of their misery, their children. But what of the slave owners themselves and their descendants, who found themselves locked into a social system based on human exploitation? Even after a bloody war to end slavery, is not our society still rife with the mutual distrust and ingrained injustices that slavery sowed?

Examples like this have been multiplied all over the world. The situations in Northern Ireland, Palestine or Israel, and South Africa are only some current instances in the so-called Free World, while, in the rest of the world, no pretext need even be sought. By merely adding examples, however, we might miss the most significant aspect of communal evil—its "snowballing" effect. The process is not so simple as it looks, for there are other factors at work that go beyond mere human malice and the direct responses it invokes.

Like Thomas Aquinas, who observed that "what can fall will fall at times," Teilhard de Chardin also spoke of the inevitability of sin. Taking Christ's words in Matthew out of context, Teilhard often repeated the warning, "It must be that scandal will occur, but woe to the man through whom it occurs." Teilhard pointed to this saying as indicating what he believed to be "the statistical *necessity*" of evil, especially sin. Many claim to be scandalized by such an assertion, arguing that such a view reduces sin to a natural phenomenon, just another by-product of evolution. I think these critics miss the point, which may also account for what seems to be a peculiar application of Matthew's verse. Although it is statistically inevitable that there will always be sin in the world, humans are theoretically capable of avoiding it. We are in control at least of ourselves, and our personal reaction to evil is ultimately our responsibility. Sin there will undoubtedly be, but it does not have to be our sin.

Even this may be an oversimplification, but not in the direction that the critic decries. If anything, the case for the statistical necessity of evil is stronger still, despite the strong affirmation of personal responsibility. Constant repetition and accumulation of evil does more than confirm statistics. It is truly self-replicating in the infectious manner described earlier, but not simply in an arithmetic progression. Moral contagion, not only in terms of the number of its victims, but even more in terms of the conversion of victims into carriers of the same disease, proceeds in what is more like a geometric progression. Sin is not only communal, but cumulative!

Another way of looking at this "snowballing" effect of moral evil might be seen in what is sometimes called "feedback." In terms of cybernetics we know that when information is programmed for use in a computer, the interpretation of that information is often prejudiced by the "yield," or data that the computer was preprogramed to produce. People who have been refused credit cards because they have never owed anybody anything have some inkling of what all too easily happens! In a similar way we can see that it is not just a matter of sin affecting the sinner (like debt affecting the debtor) or affecting the victim (the holder of a bad debt), but a matter of the whole moral atmosphere becoming poisoned, complete innocence being interpreted as some kind of guilt! Evil can no longer be recognized as evil, or good as good. In such a morally ambiguous situation, even a good person becomes like one who is "sighted" among the blind, only to find out that the world itself is in complete darkness. Sight is then useless. In such a situation, how would one even know if one possessed sight?

Thus, the statistical necessity of sin turns out to be more than a mere contrasting of the percentages of failure with those of success. Rather it becomes like one of New York's now famous electric power blackouts, where the breakdown of one small segment of the power grid brings on an overload of neighboring generators to the point where one generator after another fails in rapidly increasing succession until the whole region is plunged into darkness. Rather than the "brownout," or reduced-power situation that the engineers anticipated, a total failure occurs. In much the same way, moral evil, when sufficiently multiplied, tends to fulfil that philosophical dictum of Engels that sufficient *quantitative* change eventually effects a *qualitative* one. Enough individual sins, sooner or later, create a society that is sick to its very core. Personal sin, multiplied to this extent, becomes what theologian Piet Schoonenburg has aptly termed "the sin of the world."

Such an "excess" of moral evil would not be, in some people's judgment, a total loss since, in their estimation, there resulted a corresponding "excess" of good, even if in a concentrated form. Augustine, while lamenting the fact that the mass of humanity was surely damned, seems to have believed that even the existence of a "chosen few" who had achieved heavenly glory would be a justification of God and a triumph over evil. That a loss in quantity may be balanced by a gain in quality seems logical enough, until we remember that we are dealing with human persons and, as we are taught, immortal souls!

The story of Abraham, bargaining with God over the sparing of Sodom and Gomorrah and getting God to agree to relent if even "ten just men" could be found there, illustrates my point. Ten could not be found, so the two towns were destroyed. So today Jewish legend holds that if the whole world has not already been destroyed, it is because there are at least ten such "just men." If so, it would only speak of God's patience and the power of prayer, not necessarily of a final victory of the good.

After the living nightmare of Hitler's Holocaust, of the Communist purges, and of the atomic incineration of Nagaski and Hiroshima, as well as of the torture cells and internment camps that still defile the face of the earth, the word *excess* seems like a cold, clinical abstraction. It is not simply that over twenty million lives were lost within the decade of World War II, or that millions more have disappeared in such far-flung countries as Turkey, Nigeria, Cambodia, and other places almost too numerous to count. These facts are too horrible to be blithely termed mere excesses. Nor can we begin to measure the suffering of tens of millions more who survived, many of whom may judge the dead to have been luckier than they.

The reason that the word *excess* seems far too mild is that we are dealing with a kind of malice and collective guilt that is all the worse for never having been totally admitted. To admit an excess is to acknowledge a deficit that might be canceled, but like the good people just down the road from Auschwitz or Dachau, we have refused to recognize the stench in our nostrils or acknowledge the evidence before our eyes until it was too late. For what is the "greater good" that came from these atrocities? Repentance? Ask the average German today. Revived faith in God? Ask the average Israeli today. Reconciliation with enemies? Ask the displaced Palestinian Arab. A lesson for humanity? Ask the South African (black or white) about that.

The fact that the effects of these crimes are allowed to continue today in many places in the world, even in the so-called
freedom-loving nations, and not only the superpowers, but even
the second-rate powers and third-world nations (when they can)
are jealously hoarding and building up stockpiles of conventional
and even nuclear weapons in order to guard their sovereign territories and to preserve inalienable rights (as if there would be any
territories or people left to enjoy them) seems to point to a condition that defies any description as mere excess, although absolute
madness might come close. How can such a state of mind come
about?

Psychological studies (such as those of Jean Piaget or Law-
rence Kohlberg) have shown that a child's sense of justice or of
moral decision-making proceeds through different stages, beginning with motivations of mere punishment-avoidance and reward-
seeking, through a rudimentary sense of fairness, and going on
through a more developed sense of socially shared standards of
human decency and justice. Yet none of these is a mature moral
sense of rightness, for none of them point to a sense of
"oughtness" in terms of goodness or rightness for its own sake. In
fact, these studies indicate that very few adults can even comprehend such a higher criterion. Would this not seem to indicate
that the excess of suffering in the modern world is due to a basic
failure to even begin to grasp the *moral* root of evil?

Augustine, of course, would have said that such an awareness
is impossible without an "illumination" from the source of all
goodness and justice—God.

It may be that St. Augustine can be faulted for having seen
everything in such a dualistic-supernaturalistic perspective that he
could calmly envision the triumph of God's goodness in the face of
mass damnation. But at least he had more than an inkling of where
the origins of true goodness and the ability to perceive rightness
lay.

If people, even high-principled idealists, persist in thinking
that true goodness is instinctive with humanity, it is hardly surprising that populations under the sway of political rhetoric consistently underestimate our capacity for self-destruction. If the
concept of a "revealing" God is problematic for many of the intel-
ligentia of the modern world, for even more of them the idea of an
original sin remains a theological joke. If Sir (and Saint) Thomas
More's exercise in pure rationality was realistically entitled
"Utopia," the reason he so named it seems to have escaped the
deeper capacities of the modern wit.

In this rationalistic escapism we are not unlike Dostoyevsky's Ivan Karamazov in quite another way. As an intellectual man of the world, and as a person of highest humanistic sympathies, the ultimate evil for him is to be seen in the death of the innocent. Even though he excoriates the bestiality of people who would inflict such tortures, he sees such senseless deaths as a symbol of something still more evil. Yet he is unable to recognize wherein it lies.

Dostoyevsky, it should be remembered, had himself been a social revolutionary; in fact, he had even been exiled to Siberia on the charge of subversive activities against the Tsarist regime. Ivan Karamazov represents, to a lesser degree, that type of person described more completely in another Dostoyevsky novel, *The Possessed*. In it he depicts, with self-critical insight, the mentality of a great many politically involved men of humanistic ideals. Their ineffectual regret over the violence carried out by their more activistic comrades reveals the arbitrariness of their sense of justice, and the persistence of their deluded idealism proves the shallowness of their understanding of evil. Yet it is from just people as these—Engels, Marx, Lenin, and Stalin (to halt this chronology of one line of social reformers at its apogee of violence)—that the movement of international Communism was born. The excesses of evil that these people saw in human society they correctly ascribed to the devil of human selfishness. They simplistically believed that this demon could be exorcized by a restructuring of human institutions, especially the relationship of labor to capital. Yet the very fact that their vision of evil was in materialistic terms (in which physical suffering and the death rate are the highest evils) ended up in their paradoxically inflicting much more death and suffering, psychological as well as physical, than that which they sought to remedy. Thus "All justice comes out of the barrel of a gun," as another great social revolutionary, Mao Tse-tung, once said.

It may be, as Alexander Solzhenitsyn has claimed, that from all this a new moral fiber has emerged, one that puts to shame the spinelessness of the Western capitalistic world. If so, the West has only its own materialistic humanism to blame. Perhaps Solzhenitsyn, like a new Augustine, is calling us to a revived appreciation of the true nature of the good and its intolerance of whatever we mistake for worthwhile goals in the world. But is the lesson worth the price? Are moral pride and self-righteousness any better than slackness and corruption? Have not both East and West, each in its own way, confirmed the same ugly truth about ourselves? Have we not proved, beyond a doubt, that one excess breeds another?

Ultimately, the moral evil within our hearts breeds and festers unchecked, not simply through the excess of man's inhumanity to man, but because of its deepest roots in our original estrangement from God.

For the Christian, of course, things are not hopeless. The estrangement between humanity and God is not irreparable, for there has taken place that incomparable Atonement or at-one-ness through the sacrifice of Christ on the Cross. If there continues to be an excess of sin, suffering, and death in this world, there is also the excess of God's love shown to us. Yet we may not relax our efforts or take too much comfort in believing that all is well. The evolution of the human spirit is a door that swings on the hinges of human freedom, but it swings both ways!

If this chapter on moral evil seems to have belabored the concept of original sin far beyond the insights discussed in chapter 3, or if it has also seemed to unduly prolong the discussion of the amount of evil present in the world (which ended chapter 4) the reasons for doing so are most critical.

For a biblically based Christian theodicy, the whole conflict has tended to draw its battle lines around these issues. For even if all moral evil and a great deal of the physical and psychological evil in the universe could be traced to an original sin, there is nevertheless a tremendous amount of suffering and death that seems to be nobody's fault except God's—a conclusion that most believers find to be totally unacceptable. It is at this point, therefore, that most theodicies break down, leaving us with the alternative visions either of a heartlessly cruel God or else one who is incompetent. It is also at this point that the reader is asked to shift to a whole new mode of thinking about God's creative activity, that is, to evolution and particularly its relationship to human freedom. For it is at this point that we shall have to reach far beyond such suggestions or adjustments as reversing our time perspectives about original sin or paradise; those were only preliminaries designed to smooth the way. What is called for now is a whole new vision (a new myth, if you will) that can make sense out of *all* the facts—many of them just as unpleasant to the modern mind as any threat of damnation was to the medieval.

If such an effort can succeed, as I believe it will, not only shall we be able to make a lot more sense out of the universe but we shall also, I believe, make a great more sense out of our ideas of God.

Notes

1. This opinion, scientifically termed *"monophylism,"* is held by the majority of paleontologists as against a polyphylism that would look for human origins among diverse species. The more common term *monogenism*, often used in place of the above, strictly speaking denotes a single couple, both members truly human, as the ancestors of all subsequent humans. The papal encyclical of 1950, "Humani Generis," while rejecting polyphylism as incompatible with Christian doctrine, only cautioned about the difficulties of reconciling polygenism, that is, the idea of a number of couples of the same species, as co-progenitors of the human race, with traditional teaching. For a more recent discussion of this matter, see Karl Rahner's article "Monogenism" in *The Encyclopedia of Theology*, edited by Karl Rahner (New York: Seabury Press, 1975).

2. See notes *l* and *m* for Corinthians 1:15 in *The Jerusalem Bible*, edited by Alexander Jones (Garden City, N.Y.: Doubleday, 1966), "The New Testament," p. 309.

6

Evil and World Process

Each one of us is a statistical impossibility around which
hover a million other lives that were never destined to be
born—but who, nevertheless, are being unmanifest, a
lurking potential in the dark storehouse of the void.
—Loren Eiseley
The Unexpected Universe

The problem of physical evil is most complex. It oscilates between
the warp of random chance and the woof of the seemingly invariable laws of nature. It includes not only the conditions that are part
of the essential constitution of the natural world, but also those
accidents and calamities which, to the human eye, the world could
do very well without. No doubt part of the problem is to distinguish between those happenings which inevitably take place as a
result of the lack of total perfection in the great "chain of being"
and the psychological reaction of suffering that these things occa-
sion in humans and perhaps in animals as well. Setting this last
consideration aside for the present, let us focus on those things
which the world might run more smoothly without.

Even here there is a wide range of opinion. Could, for example, the continents have been formed without the continuing
aftermath of earthquakes? Could any agricultural activity flourish
without the existence of other areas, like frozen wastelands and
deserts, that seem utterly useless for agriculture? Could there be
any food chain without the existence of animals of prey or even

parasitic organisms? (Are not we ourselves beasts of prey and para-sites in respect to the ecological scheme of things?)

In addition to this order of give-and-take in nature, which seems to work out to the benefit of some if not all, there is the nearly constant occurrence of other problems afflicting plant and animal life as well as mankind; phenomena that appear to serve no good purpose—unless the "culling" of vast populations can be seen as somehow a stage preliminary to renewal. Even in such cases must we not question whether it is somehow "better" to die from some sudden disaster than simply have a population die off slowly through lack of food?

Finally, we also have to face the problem of genetic defects, which affect all forms of life. While, as we shall see, the chance of mutations is integral to the process of evolution, is it necessary that there be physical, and in humans mental, defects that wreak so much havoc with the otherwise orderly development of life?

Obviously, much depends on how we view the whole process and how we define physical evil in relation to it. Certainly we cannot help but look at it from the viewpoint of the human experi-ence of pain and suffering, yet, even if we discount this an-thropocentric point of view, it appears that there are true physical evils aside from whatever pain is caused. A three-legged calf, even if it should never become aware of its deformity, is defective nonetheless. To borrow from the classical philosophers and the scholastic theologians, at least some kinds of evil can be seen as a defect of being or order in what is otherwise good. In much the same way, while death itself must be necessary, it is nevertheless an evil (perhaps, for mankind, the greatest evil) for the individual creature whose existence we take to be a good in itself.

If all these evils are in some way natural, even necessary in the long run, how can they be said to be "evil?" Are they considered to be evil only because of a flaw in human perception? Or even if real, is physical evil merely something relative, containing no final, ab-solute significance in itself? (It is strange how such modern ques-tions suggest the ancient Vedic reduction of evil and the world that contains it to the category of *maya*—of mere change amounting to illusion.) With the greater portion of humanity, we refuse to see it that way. We tend to consider even relative evil as something actual in the world, something existing outside of our own percep-tion and evaluation of it. Yet it is clear that there is a riddle here, one that for more than just our own satisfaction must be solved. Both the riddle and the answer lie in the creative process itself.

A. Chance and Choice

Albert Einstein is credited with the statement: "I refuse to believe that God plays dice with the cosmos." Thus this world-renowned theoretical physicist, whom very few considered to be an avowedly religious person, was personally convinced that the universe invariably followed set laws of physical behavior. This apparent denial of the place of chance occurrence in the development of the universe is surprising, especially when his own formulation of the general and particular theories of relativity almost completely upset the hitherto-accepted Newtonian ideas of a clockworklike universe.

In contrast, the priest-paleontologist Pierre Teilhard de Chardin, whose avowed purpose in life was to promote a general harmony between scientific and religious thought, proclaimed that "God plays creatively with chance." How are we to account for this rather surprising divergence of views concerning the role of chance in evolution?

Obviously the explanation can *not* be traced to differing theological stances. If it could, one might expect just the reverse situation, with the committed Christian downplaying the chance factor and the pure scientist doing just the opposite. More likely the difference can be traced to the mathematical basis of theoretical physics as opposed to the more experimental approach of the life sciences. Even here, however, there is something of an irony, for it was another great modern physicist, Werner Heisenberg, who first introduced what amounts to a major reassessment of the place of chance in the basic structure of the universe.

One application of the Indeterminacy Principle holds that, beginning with the smallest particles of matter (a fact often experimentally verified in these smallest bits of energy), behavior is to a large extent unpredictable.[1] Rather than seeing the laws of nature as inflexible rules to which all things must conform (whatever be the correct formulation of these rules), Indeterminacy sees these laws merely as statistical predictions of how most, but not all, particles will react to given conditions. It is only when the individual particles are lumped together that behavior seems to take on a predictable uniformity. Even more important is the fact that when they are combined into more complex atomic and molecular structures their elemental "freedom" becomes hemmed in by more invariable patterns of performance.

Certainly there is a paradox in this, particularly when we

compare this modern view of chance to classical notions of cause. The medieval scholastic idea of *chance* was simply of a word used to describe the lack of sure information about the immediate cause of any effect. Since God, however, was seen as the ultimate "cause" of everything, ultimately there was no such thing as chance! The Indeterminacy Principle, on the other hand, seeing everything as ultimately based on chance, is claimed by some to all but eliminate the whole notion of cause! By such standards, despite the nearly complete dismantling of the old Newtonian ideas of a universe ruled by a clockworklike mechanism of cause and effect, Einstein's universe of Relativity still seems to be ruled by a God who has disposed of everything according to a fixed plan! Surely there must be room for another possibility—of a God who can allow things to be caused by chance.

Admittedly, then, the notion of chance is a very slippery one, having different overtones for different people. Yet on the whole, as the biologist Jacques Monod says, we tend to think of chance in terms of a certain "randomness" or the "quality of an event that results from the intersection of two totally independent chains of events."[2] Such, for example, would be an occurrence like that of person A who just happens to be walking by a building when person B who just happens to be working on the roof at that very moment accidentally drops his hammer. Assuming that B has no murderous intent against A, we conclude that if A just happens to be struck in the head and killed, this is an accident, an entirely chance occurrence, even if the old adage about not walking near or especially under ladders, or the common precaution of wearing a hard hat around construction sites, indicates the probability of such accidents under certain conditions. The element of chance is surely present here, but just as surely the element of cause as well.

Of course, if we were to assume that B was waiting for A and actually aimed the hammer at him, we then could assume that B was causing a homocide. Yet even here, chance, in the form of various other circumstances, could intervene to frustrate the murderer's design. Thus, while every event logically would seem to have a cause (or a whole series of causes), some of these causes are not only difficult to discern, but likewise they defy any sure predictability, especially when it comes to forecasting any simultaneous interaction of causes to produce an invariable result.

While definitions and examples could be multiplied endlessly, and words like *chance, indeterminacy, accidentalness,* or *randomness* more or less interchanged, it should be evident that such factors are part of the chain of causality. The idea that chance somehow eliminates any otherwise intelligible element of cause would seem to be an outworn part of a strategy to argue against the existence of God as the First Cause. As such, this tactic seems to reproduce the same error that is involved in many people's problem with evil—the assumption that any First Cause must necessarily be directing the occurrence of any secondary causes. For both kinds of mentalities, God would seem to be a kind of homocidal workman who could not only aim his hammer blows unerringly, but who would also control the movements of all pedestrians! Such a picture of God or the world is unreal.

On the contrary, this element of basic indeterminacy or chance, taken precisely as a cause, is of capital importance. Once we survey its effect on the evolution of things, we shall see that not only has indeterminacy *determined* the course of events but, even at this very fundamental level, without chance there would be no evolution at all, at least in the accepted scientific sense of the term.

To better understand this fact, we must become more specific. Evolution, in the sense of biological transformism, can be understood as the development of one biological type from another. This phenomenon can be understood narrowly in terms of offspring not resembling their parents in every respect, thus allowing for gradual variations within a species leading to the formation of distinct races or types. Or, understood more broadly (as the present-day general theory of evolution would have it), this biological transformism would include the emergence of wholly distinct new species which, although they share common ancestors, can no longer successfully interbreed. In either interpretation, evolution depends initially on the occurrence of genetic mutations. After a century of argument, it has been generally agreed that, while the effects of such mutations tend to follow more or less set laws (beginning with those formulated by Mendel), the actual occurrence of such mutations in terms of the alterations in the DNA coding of the chromosomes is extremely unpredictable. We not only do not know the exact cause of the mutations, although solar radiation and "mistranslations" of the genes are commonly thought to be major factors; moreover, the predictability of a single mutation happening in a certain specified way is about as random a matter as forecasting the impact point of a hammer falling from a housetop. All that can be known are statistical averages.

Thus Monod estimates that the rate of even easily detected mutations (the ones that can be seen in microscopic examination of genetic material) averages on the rate of 10^{-4} to 10^{-5}, which translates into an incidence of 100 to 1,000 billion mutations (as multiplied by $X^{\#}$ of genes per individual) occuring in an overall population of three billion humans within a single generation. At this rate, as Monod exclaims, ". . . the amazing and indeed paradoxical thing, hard to explain, is not evolution but rather the stability of the 'forms' that make up the biosphere."[3] Part of the reason for the stability, however, is that rarely if ever will a single mutant gene cause a significant change in a general biological type. More often only a certain combination of mutations will effect a significant change, a process that has been compared to a couple of masons rummaging through a pile of rubble to find a suitable number of reusable bricks; most of the material they come across will prove to be entirely unsuitable.

Even here the odds are not very favorable for any mutation turning out to be a beneficial change. As George Gaylord Simpson repeatedly points out, the great majority of genetic changes result in organisms that are less able to survive than their well-adapted predecessors.[4] It is only the changing environment, acting as a "sieve," that favors any variant gene or gene combination out of the raw material that mutation provides. Statistically, mutant forms of life are much more likely to be biological failures, or at least to be severely handicapped, if they survive at all.[5] Still, considering all the factors favoring survival in the stable forms of life as against the "loaded" dice of random mutation, the incidence of harmful genetic defects is imposing. Over 1,500 single-gene hereditary defects are possible in the world's population, with conditions like cystic fibrosis afflicting Caucasians at a rate of one out of every three thousand (with one out of thirty as carriers!) and Down's syndrome (mongolism) afflicting one out of two thousand live births (and one out of fifty children born to women over 40!). One out of every four hundred males is born with an extra X chromosome, a condition often resulting in mental retardation. Eighty percent of achondroplastic dwarfism apparently results from fresh genetic mutation with no previous family history of the condition.[6] Such figures are hardly reassuring for those who would credit God with disposing all things for human benefit!

While genetic mutation remains the greatest "chance" element in evolution, it is not the only such factor. According to Simpson, fluctuations in genetic frequencies (or what is called "sampling errors" in a given gene pool) as well as the inflow of genes from other populations within the same species are two other highly variable and equally unpredictable factors. These chance elements, coming from "outside" in terms of the influence of selective or differential interbreeding of individuals and races, only further increase the chance of genetic mutations in the offspring of parent stock that is already susceptible to the possibility of mutation from "within."

If all these factors form the element of chance in evolution, there also remains what might be called the element of choice. For most purposes, this element might be better termed necessity or determination, to stress its quality of certainty or inevitability. Even here we are only dealing with relativities, with what amounts only to a certain predictability in the face of unlimited randomness. Evolutionary biology has generally thought of natural selection as the limiting or determining factor, the anti-chance element that balances or even to some extent cancels out the nearly complete randomness of mutation and other chance factors. In old-fashioned Darwinian terms, this natural selection was thought to operate on the basis of a "survival of the fittest." The climate, the competition for available food, or even just the comparative strength of the mutants was thought to determine which organisms would live and reproduce, and which would lose out in this brutal competition and die. Thus the wild prodigality of chance mutation would be relentlessly "screened" and trimmed by an almost automatic process that would inevitably harden biological efflorescence into a highly predictable series of types or species.

It is not that such ideas were wrong, but the whole process of natural selection has turned out to be considerably more flexible than was once thought. For one thing, it is not so much a question of the survival of the fittest as conceived in an individualistic way (the strongest ape, the fleetest horse, etc.) as it is a question of which type of organism proves most successful in terms of "differential reproduction." It is not that characteristics such as strength, speed, or cunning in selected individuals are negligible factors (if we breed race horses or hunting dogs, we had better believe it!), but that the decisive factor in the battle for survival is now thought to be the ability of a whole population successfully to reproduce itself as a distinct species in comparative reproductive isolation. Species that can maintain reproductive superiority without diluting their genetic pool by interbreeding with other types will very often end up winning out over a line of supposedly superior physical types that do not reproduce so readily or successfully. Thus researchers and theorists in the new field of sociobiology are close to claiming that it is the genes alone that are the controlling and motivating force of evolution. Neither the individual organism nor even the whole group or species are seen to exist for their own sake; they are merely host populations used by the DNA sequences which, according to sociobiolgist spokesman George Pieczenik, "exist to protect themselves and their own information" (*Time*, Aug. 1, 1977, p. 55). The individual organism, or even the whole species, really doesn't count!

The point I am trying to emphasize here is that if this current trend in biological theory is correct, then we must see that even the supposedly anti-chance or determining factor of natural selection as it is now understood seems to be largely a matter of chance! If teleology or the attribution of some kind of purpose in the process of evolution has always been a touchy subject, one that has tended to credit Nature with some kind of creative foresight not unlike that which theologians have attributed to God, the tenets of sociobiology would seem to be forcing us toward the uncomfortable conclusion that it is particles of protein that alone "plan" the course of evolution. Whether or not the sociobiologists are correct, the result of this reexamination of the so-called determination or necessity that governs natural selection or differential reproduction is unsettling. On the level of the biological process alone, understood in isolation from whatever other forces may be at work in the universe, the choice or determination is apparently a matter of random chance. No one, not even the sociobiologists, credit DNA with having a conscious mind of its own. Determination of a sort there may be, even a kind of choice in a brutish world of basic indeterminacy, but pushed this far, such words tend to loose all meaning.

Further evidence of this basic randomness in the midst of what supposedly limits the results of chance mutation is even more striking when one comes to paleontology (the study of ancient forms of life). Simpson tells us that "throughout the whole history of life most species have become extinct, without issue. The statistically usual outcome of evolution is not, then, the progressive appearance of higher forms but simply obliteration."[7] The reasons for this are several. For one, most mutations, as we have seen, are nonadaptive, that is, they lead toward extinction rather than improvement. More decisive yet, those mutations which do prove adaptive and of some advantage in the struggle for survival usually do so only on a strictly limited and limiting basis. Most adaptations are highly opportunistic, fitted to a particular climate or a lucky abundance of a certain food supply. If the climate should change, or the food supply be wiped out by some other sudden catastrophe, the happy accident will soon turn out to be a curse.

The case of the famous Irish elk is a striking example. For reasons unknown, in the times following the last ice age, this large species of deer evolved enormous antlers, males sporting racks well over six to eight feet in spread, presumably to fend off rival males. Suddenly the species died out. Did the growth of forests make their moving around nearly impossible? Did the nutritional drain of growing a new set of these gigantic appendages each year (or even their sheer weight) prove to be too much of a strain? We can only speculate on such a profligacy in nature. Fortunately for us, it was the brain that expanded in the ancestors of the human species. In the long run it is is not the opportunistic specializations that favor success, but the specialization of not becoming too specialized. There seems to be a lesson here that extends beyond biological evolution.

In this discussion of chance and choice in the role of evolution, it should be quite evident by now that this randomness is, for the most part, what is behind not only the "progress" of evolution but also its failures. Statistically, the failures far outnumber the successes when we judge them as individual ventures or experiments of nature. That we should call these failures evils is, of course, a human judgment, which must be balanced by the realization that evolution as a whole has been a success. And that success we judge, like the Creator in the Book of Genesis, to be "good"— indeed, "very good."

Such judgments aside, the overwhelming evidence is that life has evolved only at the expense of most of the forms of life other than those which presently exist. It could well go on that way, with most of the present forms of life doomed to someday disappear. Not that the overall process has been automatic. It has involved many random events, any one of which could have set the whole course of evolution in a completely different direction, or even have nipped the whole thing in the bud!

Theodosius Dobzhansky, the famous and highly respected geneticist, insisted (despite the contrary opinions of many other scientists, most of them physicists and astronomers venturing outside their respective fields) that while there are undoubtedly many other planets in the universe that might support life of some sort, there is very little probability that such life would duplicate the same course of evolution as that which occurred on this planet. As Simpson points out, it is not just the randomness of genetic mutation that supports such a conclusion, but even more the randomness of all the factors involved in natural selection that would affect the results. It is not just ourselves as individuals, as Loren Eiseley has said, who are "statistical impossibilities." The whole human species, or even life as we know it on this earth, comes very close to having been such an impossibility!

Being ourselves the children of chance, it is not surprising that there also lurks, both within the void of the universe and within each one of us, a "dark storehouse" from which unknown potentialities may manifest themselves. There are not only all the genetic mutations that may occur in ourselves; there are also the rapidly evolving viruses and bacterial parasites that hover, seemingly ready at a moment's notice to change themselves into new forms that defy with impunity the weapons of modern medicine. We carry within ourselves a perverse potential for our own cells to go berzerk and to multiply in wildly cancerous forms, whether triggered by viruses or other outside agents, or simply by the caprice of genetic factors within us. If chance, whether from within or without our own organisms, can wreak such havoc, it may be just as much a question of chance that we can survive. Jacques Monod believes that there is good evidence that even the antibodies that form the front-line defense of our own immunity system are themselves only able to arm their host against invading cell growth by means of a fortuitous or random matching process.[8] In this case chance recombinations and mutations would be the only means by which the right combinations are found—not unlike a wrestler attempting different holds on an opponent, or a gambler betting on different numbers. We always hope that the statistics will remain on our side, but unfortunately even a winning streak must eventually end. The odds are stacked in favor of the house. Not only have the vast majority of species sooner or later died, but each individual, be it a member of a successful species or not, must die. Chance leaves no choice in the end.

B. Evolution and Death

If it can be said that evolution is built upon the contending variables of genetic mutation and natural selection, it can be just as truly said that it is also built upon the invariant of death. A strange paradox, perhaps one that would not exist in a "better" world, but one that necessarily exists in our own.

Life feeds upon death. New life as we know it requires the

death of what has already lived. The successful evolution of new types of life depends, to a large extent, upon the disappearance of former types. Conditions that favored the age of the dinosaurs would not have favored the appearance of the primates from which we have taken our remote ancestry. Whenever some earlier and more primitive types still survive, it is almost inevitable that newer, higher forms of life prey upon them. This is what largely constitutes the pattern of the food chain today. Microscopic bacteria prepare the soil for plants, animals in turn consume plant life, other animals consume them, and humans consume them all. Of course many exceptions exist, some of them anticipating the end of each higher organism, when the bacteria turn on plant, animal, and human alike and consume them. In either case, the major point remains; no form of life survives except at the expense of other life, always feeding upon the nutrients of life that belong, have belonged, or could have belonged to another creature.

There remains another fact that is just as basic. In an even more intensive fashion, sexual reproduction, although responsible for new life, is the harbinger of death. The only living creatures that are, in a certain natural sense, immortal are those which reproduce asexually, that is to say, those which prolong their existence not by an exchange of genes with others of their kind, but which simply divide or split in half. Even this mode of reproduction involves a kind of "death" for, while the primitive protoplasm may live on (at least until such a time as it is consumed by something else), still, it ceases to exist as an individual. It is not amoeba A plus amoeba B, but amoeba A becoming amoeba B and C.

Although simple protoplasmic life loses only its numerical identity in the act of reproduction, this is not the case in life that reproduces sexually. While the genes involved in sexual reproduction can be said to "live on," albeit in new combinations, the individuals of which they are a part are themselves doomed. Thus, on the biological level, sexual reproduction alone guarantees true individuality, an individuality that is more than just a numerical difference from its source. Yet just as sexual reproduction results in the statistical impossibility that is our own organism's uniqueness, so too does sexual reproduction make it impossible that our offspring ever be exactly like us. Biologically speaking, only cloning could produce that result in higher animals, yet even then the parent remains subject to death. True individuality implies mortality. The price of being totally unique is death.

What, then, can be so wrong with death? Is it not just part of the overall scheme of things? How can something so necessary and natural really be considered as an evil in the real sense of the word—a disorder of sorts, or even something that should not be? Is it not just our sense of individual self-awareness that protests— quite unreasonably at that? Perhaps. But I think it goes deeper than that.

We protest death in the name of our own uniqueness but so, in some sense, does the animal world, at least the higher animals. While it may be improper to speak of an animal fearing death (because man alone, as Dobzhansky said, can contemplate the fact of his impending death), still animals share a common drive toward life and generally manifest a certain instinctual avoidance of death-dealing situations. Allowing for certain "altruistic" behavior, such as defending their own kind, especially their own offspring, to the point of death, animals nevertheless will generally struggle to keep themselves alive, at least to the point that there can be said to be any hope of survival left. Without such an instinct neither the individuals nor the species would have long survived. No doubt our own fear of death also has its roots in this subconscious drive to live.

There is, however, something more. Individuality and the spontaneity it implies also seems to be a value or "good" of evolutionary significance. If we speak of higher forms of life, it is not simply because they have a long evolutionary pedigree that culminates in a perfected type of species in their line. The common housefly, as Simpson points out, is the culmination of its line of evolution, partly for the same reasons (perhaps because of its adaptibility to nearly all types of environments) as humans represent the culmination of primate development. Yet we do not think of houseflies as higher forms of life. This is because they lack the spontaneity and hence the individuality of the truly higher forms, particularly as found in the mammals. So too, while honeybees may have developed very intricate and well-ordered societies (which some people would like to see emulated by our own), no one mourns the loss of an individual bee, including the other bees, all of whom live, with the exception of the queen, for only about six to eight weeks. All bees, at least of their own class, are equally alike and equally expendable (especially the drones) for the sake of the whole colony. In contrast, the loss of a beloved dog, or even of a particular wild animal with which one has become familiar, is something else. These higher animals approach true individuality. Anyone who has tried to replace a faithful dog companion of many years' standing will never believe that one dog is just like another even if, through careful breeding, the new dog looks just like its predecessor. While it may be true that pets, especially dogs, reflect to a large degree not only the training given to them but also the personal habits of their masters, no one who really knows dogs believes for an instant that they are all pretty much alike.

One may be accused of too much anthropomorphism in a discussion like this. Naturally we value in animals those traits which reflect aspects of ourselves. Simpson once commented that elephants might perhaps question our supposing of ourselves to be the highest of all animals, considering that they weigh a lot more, live just as long or longer, and have, undoubtedly, longer noses. That they might but in fact are unable to ask such questions is exactly the point. Nor is the ability to ponder as we do simply a result of large brains (again the elephant and most certainly the whale should win the prize in this category) or even the size of the brain in proportion to the body—not only the porpoise but even the common house mouse outclass us in this! There is something else.

The reason that humans can be said to rank highest on the evolutionary scale is to be found in their powers to reason and reflect. One may, of course, object to our setting the scale on the basis of these powers, but in order to object one must rely on these same powers. There is no way around this. Nor is there any way around the fact that humans alone can consciously think of death precisely as an evil. Animals indeed can fear or shun death, but only humans can "know" death in anticipatory awareness, not only knowing death as a phenomenon around us, but "knowing that we know" and dreading the revelation of that which we can not escape. Just as our individuality is not merely a question of a unique set of genes or a numerical distinctness, but of human reflective awareness, death too is something that we do not just avoid by blind instinct or even by a simple awareness that death is the end of life. Death is the end of *me!*—the period at the end of a sentence that can never be repeated.

Is death, then just a peculiarly human hang-up? No, there is something more to it than that. We do not consider death an evil just because we do not like death, particularly our own death. Evolution, although it is built upon death, is the story of *life*. No species, no individual, exists *in order to* die, even though the death of individuals, and even sometimes of whole species, is necessary to make way for further life. The goal of evolution, if it may be said to have a goal or purpose, is life. In the peculiar sense of the word assigned to it by Teilhard de Chardin, there is a true "orthogenesis" (or goal-directed process) within evolution as implied in the very catchword *survival of the fittest*. What is survival or life but a kind of purpose in itself? If being or existence in this sense seems to be the whole point of evolution, then the nonbeing of death is an anti-value, the counterpoint of life that evolution flees even while using it. Death is the physical expression of nothingness. No amount of life, by itself, can make death or what leads to nonbeing or nonexistence into something good in itself.

Viewed from these perspectives of death as natural, as necessarily part of the whole process of evolution, yet, at the same time, as metaphysically the antithesis of the emergence of the life for which evolution exists, we seem to be caught in an irresolvable paradox. God appears not only as The Author of Life but also (despite the statement in Ecclesiastes) as the author of death as well. Yet we believe that God irrevocably stands for life and the enhancement of life. God has committed himself in the struggle against death, yet even here there is a further paradox, for the one whom Christians believe manifested God's will to live ("I have come to bring you life and life more abundantly") himself knew that he must undergo, indeed sacrifice himself in, death. Why? Where is the answer to this riddle? Or is there one?

C. *The Final Enemy*

Death may well be the ultimate negation of individual life in this world. For the believer, it may also be the threshold to greater life. For believer and unbeliever alike, however, it remains the inevitable cessation of the life we have known. Perhaps, for those for whom life has ceased to be tolerable and for whom continued living is too wearisome, too painwracked, or too psychologically torturous to be endured any longer, death comes a a liberation. Death then assumes the guise of a Janus, a two-faced god, whose visage scowls upon most of life and yet, when life itself can no longer be sustained, turns a merciful smile toward the victim of life.

Death, like all physical evil, but perhaps even more than any experience of pain, displays a certain ambivalence. Like pain it remains a condition of life. Just as the sensation of pain warns us and protects us from what is harmful to life, so too death must provide for new life and to a large extent even sustain it. Yet, taken in itself, death still remains the great barrier, the inevitable enigma, that consumes not only the banquet it sets but the guests as well. How then can we deal with such a host if we are not at liberty to refuse the invitation?

One thing is clear—if death must be faced, we would choose to face it on our own terms. If the ancient warrior often chose to die in battle rather than languish as a prisoner, even at the risk of being left abandoned or unburied in an alien land, it was because he believed the loss of control over his life or afterlife was preferable to the loss of control over the very act of dying. The moment of our death is, as theologian Karl Rahner insists, the summation of our life, thus it should be the recapitulation of how we have lived. So if a man lacks the ultimate power to avoid death, at least he would aspire to choose the mode of his dying.

All this suggests that the worst aspect of death is its unpredictability. It is significant that the movement for euthanasia and living wills has grown in proportion to the modern ability to prolong physical survival. If the unpredictability of chance or random mutation has been seen as an enemy in the first protoplasmic beginnings of our lives, it is not surprising that many would protest its having the final say in our demise. To die at the end of a long, happy, even prosperous life, full of years and blessed in the memory of descendants and friends, is a bittersweet tragedy, an end that is not without its grace. But to be striken with a lingering terminal illness in one's youth, or to be consigned to a prolonged senility or useless confinement, these are the kind of living deaths against which death itself seems a welcome friend. Innocents cut down before knowing what life is about seem lucky in comparison.[9]

I am now speaking, of course, of human suffering, of psychological evil, which must be distinguished from the biological phenomena of pain and death. To separate our reactions to these experiences from the hard physical facts themselves remains psychologically impossible. However we may choose to attempt to thwart its effects, chance continues to play its capricious game with life (our lives!) through all its phases: conception, birth, growth, prime and decline, and even in death. Like the shadowy character in Tennessee Williams's *Suddenly Last Summer*, we gaze spellbound and horrified. Our world is like the beach at the Galapagos where we, like the newly hatched sea turtles, rush headlong toward the sea of life, only to be slashed to pieces by the hovering, diving birds of prey. In this death- and life-filled scene we too can see the story of evolution and perhaps even the face of God!

To grasp this vision in all its brutishness and simply to cast it off with a casual shrug is too little, or too much. If humans must die, they are intent on at least dying with a sense of purpose or dignity. It may seem strange that we are so concerned to make the greatest common denominator in life, which is death, in some ways the very climax of our existence. Why is it that for us there may be only one greater indignity than having lived in vain, and that is to have died in vain? To have both lived and died as a victim of chance is for humans the epitome of senselessness, and for a rational animal, for one who seeks purpose above all, such meaninglessness seems the height of all evil.

But is it? Observing the seeming irrational choice of death in the face of the otherwise overwhelmingly universal desire to live, Freud at one time postulated the existence of a death instinct. He believed, at least for awhile, that some force rooted beneath our conscious self was quite capable of driving us to death as surely as lemmings sometimes unaccountably drive themselves into the sea. Is such a thing possible for humans? Altruistic motives can propel a person to willingly accept death. Is this, however, for the sake of dying or is it not for a vision, the hope of a better life for oneself or for others? Even in the case of suicide, especially since it is almost universally agreed that it is psychologically impossible to really envision our own death (we can only imagine ourselves as live bystanders at our own funerals), it would seem that what we really imagine is not death but somehow another, better life.

If this is true, then what we instinctively fear is not death so much as nonbeing. So much do we fear this that we seem incapable, for the most part, of even imagining it. Yet, it is said, herein lies the "key" to all philosophical reflection—why do we exist? What is existence? Why is there something rather than nothing? Useless questions perhaps, in the eyes of many, yet to avoid them, to brush them off as idle speculation, is to run the risk of never having fully, humanly, lived. What is more, the fear of facing them may block any realistic appraisal of the power of evil in our lives.

Ernest Becker, in two brilliant books published shortly after his own untimely death, attempted to link the "Escape from Evil" with "The Denial of Death." Despite its being awarded a Pulitzer Prize, Becker's *Denial* was termed "wrong-headed" by at least one critic and was very unsettling to many humanistically inclined reviewers. Following in the footsteps of Freud's disciple, Otto

Rank, Becker made the bold claim that all human culture and civilization, all religion, all personal ambition, whether crassly expressed in the piling up of wealth and power, or more subtly and lastingly in artistic creation and intellectual achievement, are motivated by the refusal to accept death as inevitable. All these things, just as surely as doting on one's offspring or building a marble mausoleum for ourselves, or even giving an anonymous bequest, are attempts to purchase immortality.

That these things can be a force for good is obvious. Equally obvious is that these pursuits can become expressions of evil. Unlimited wealth and political power, selfish family concern for prestige, even religious causes, have all been "good" excuses for tyranny, economic slavery, and murderous crusades. Not only do these things promise a type of life after death, but they also bestow a certain illusion of deathlessness, flaunting defiance of the danger of dying itself. As Becker recalled Winston Churchill exclaiming, "Nothing in life is so exhilarating as to be shot at without result!"

If the young Churchill emerged from his first brush with death with a sense of immortality, what are we to say of the kamikaze pilots of World War II or the waves of Chinese infantry in Korea, some of them unarmed, who rushed enemy emplacements to form a human bridge, whether dead or alive, for their comrades to clamber over? It is said that they were high on opium. Perhaps; but they need not have been. They were already high on a sense of their own immortal destiny. There is nothing new in all of this. Man has repeatedly sacrificed himself and his fellow man in his eternal war with death. If the twentieth century seems to be a landmark era in this revelation of the power of death to pervert human life with its propagandized ideologies of "Thousand Year Reichs," and utopian socialism, it has been, according to Becker, only a "refresher course" in the annals of human folly. The flight from death has always been and, unfortunately, will always be the greatest motivation for evil in the world. Unable to defeat death, humanity will first deny it, then flaunt it, and finally try to make death serve man's purposes beyond the grave.

Christianity is, according to Becker (himself an unbeliever), the only religion that has attempted to fully confront the power of evil, which can be overcome only through the acceptance of death. It would do so by the power of the Cross, by which death is turned against itself. Perhaps non-Christians, especially those who reject Christianity as too "death-centered," have realized this better than Christians have. Perhaps Christianity, in this very central sense as well as others, has, as G. K. Chesterton once said, "never been tried." If it was tried in its beginning, it soon became, as Bonhoeffer suggested, like all the other "religions"—an escape hatch from reality, the "opium of the people" that the Marxists claim it to be.

The lure of such an escape is strong. As the poet Montaigne once wrote: "It is not so much death we fear, but dying." Death, for all its capriciousness, is nevertheless inevitable; dying—the willing acceptance of death—is not. We shall all some day be dead, but not everyone will fully experience dying, consciously and voluntarily commending our spirit back to the Source of all life. The hallmark of all false religion has been the promise of immortality, the release from death, without having to face the process of dying. Such has been the great Escape from Evil, which has only bred more evil in turn. Each of us in our uniqueness, as the "statistical impossibility" that somehow we came to be, fears return to that dark void of nothingness from which we came. That void, however, has another face, the face of God. Indeed, death is the final enemy, but it is in dying that we live.

Notes

1. Another aspect of the same principle, of less immediate concern here, but nevertheless of importance to the question at hand, is that the act of measurement or observation itself contributes to the indeterminacy of particle behavior. Ironically, while the uncertainty introduced by this latter factor may call into question the accuracy of the first application of the principle, the extension of this same principle into the realm of the social sciences only further confirms the complementariness of these two insights. Similarly, Louis J. Halle, while asserting that the Indeterminacy Principle applies directly only to particle physics, believes it has its counterpart in the evolution of life by natural selection. See Louis C. Halle, *Out of Chaos* (Boston: Houghton Miffin, 1977), p. 625.

2. Jacques Monod, *Chance and Necessity* (N.Y.: Knopf, 1971), pp. 121f.

3. Monod, ibid, p. 121.

4. George Gaylord Simpson, *This View of Life* (New York: Harcourt Brace and World, 1964), p. 207.

5. Ibid., p. 18.

6. I have gleaned these statistics from an old (8th edition) of *The Merck Manual* (Rahway, N.J.: Merck & Co., 1950). While anmiocentesis and other modern techniques may have reduced the incidence of live births afflicted with such defects, these older statistics best reflect the play of chance in an unmodified genetic pool.

7. Simpson, p. 21.

8. Monod, p. 125.

9. One observation of this sort provokes another; this concerning the irony (considering the usual line up of "pros" versus "cons" on such issues) displayed when one juxtaposes the issues of euthanasia and abortion. If one assumes the right to die when one chooses and

provides a "living will" to insure that this choice is not left up entirely to others, it would seem only logical to extend that same right to others regarding their own lives. In the case of self-willed euthanasia a decision is made concerning what is only a potential situation, while in the case of an abortion, all potential for decision-making on the part of what is almost certainly to be a human subject is foreclosed. One may, of course, argue that the fetus is, of yet, only an object, not unlike a comatose person with no chance of recovering consciousness (thus no longer possessing a potential for a meaningful human life). But it is precisely in view of this latter circumstance (i.e., irreversible coma) that the parallel, at least on one major count, fails.

7

The Price of Freedom

If all must suffer to pay for the general harmony, what do children have to do with it . . .? It's beyond all comprehension why they should suffer, and why should they pay for the harmony? . . . I understand solidarity in sin among men. I understand solidarity in retribution too; but there can be no such solidarity with children.
—Feodor Dostoyevsky
The Brothers Karamazov

Do all explanations of suffering fail when it comes to the case of innocent children? All the proffered explanations down through the ages, even the "ultimate" theological justifications, seem to make no real sense. Even if innocent children who suffer are somehow turned into equally innocent children of God and citizens of heaven, that in no way explains why they should suffer to accomplish this. No doubt, in agonizing over this riddle it is we who actually suffer more. Innocent suffering, be it of little children or even of animals, seems to make little or no sense in the scheme of things attributed to a supposedly good God.

By *suffering*, in this context I mean primarily psychological evil as distinct from, although connected with, the moral and physical evils that give rise to it. We might begin with the moral evil of sin, which perhaps causes some physical loss or even death to a victim, but even more, in that same process we almost surely inflict psychological suffering on the victim (and, perhaps more justly, on ourselves too). On the other hand, physical upheavals like earthquakes hit and thousands die, causing untold human misery and perhaps an untold amount of moral evil—looting, degradation of human life, even loss of faith in God.

Truly, moral evil (sin), physical evil (death, sickness, violence) and psychological evil (suffering, emotional breakdown, loss of freedom, etc.) seem to form a vicious circle. At whatever point one kind of evil enters, the other kinds invariably follow in its wake. It may be argued that moral good nearly always accompanies such upheavals—heroism, repentance, conversion, and the like—but is it possible to say that such elements balance the evils or that, even more, good has emerged victorious, allowing us to say that things are "better" for the evil having happened? As we know, it is impossible to reckon this with any certainty. Again, even if we believe that these things must turn out so, we may, like Ivan, still be forced to protest. Is some imagined eternal harmony worth the price, even though it be only the death of one innocent person or infant who can suffer pain, separation, or the loss of existence?

The real crux of the problem is to be found precisely in the situation just described. There seems to be some link between physical and moral evil, and this link is shown unmistakably in the experience of suffering. Yet the questions persist—why this link and how necessary is it? We can see, quite clearly, that freedom necessarily opens the way not only to the possibility of, but even more to the probability of, moral evil. We also know that physical evils, or the occurence of pain and death, which we take to be evils, are a necessary part of the evolutionary process, so much so that we are hard put to explain how they are really evil unless it be in terms of the suffering they entail. Thus we can, like Ivan Karamazov, admit a certain human "solidarity" in sin and retribution, and we can, in a similar way, discern a kind of "solidarity" with the rest of nature in our experience of pain and death. We may, for our own comfort, even project some strong reasons why the two should complement each other, with physical evil serving both as a punishment for moral evil and as a spur toward moral excellence. Yet it is here, in this claim that one serves the other, or that they are necessary to each other, that the problem posed by suffering, particularly innocent suffering, receives its most critical test, and the claims of theodicy their stiffest resistence. It is when the condition of innocence is coupled with suffering that the theological consistency of the link between moral and physical evil seems to fail. It is here, in the lack of any clear grasp of how and why there is necessarily a kind of "solidarity" in suffering, that all pretenses to some kind of an eternal harmony become, as it were, a cosmic joke, and the claim of a "good God" a blasphemy in reverse.

Any way around or through such an impasse will have to involve the discovery of some more vital, even organic connection between moral and physical evil, one that avoids the pitfalls of all past attempts. While it is clear that there is very much a moral issue that is involved (the whole question of God's justice), it is equally clear that the solution can no longer be sought in a presumption of some universal guilt. For despite the manifold connections between moral and physical evil, it is just as obvious that suffering exists in countless occasions without any possible imputation of sin as a justifying cause. Instead, our path must take us through a better understanding of suffering itself and its role in creation. It is only when we have probed its place in the evolution of the cosmos and its relationship to human freedom that we will be able to understand its solidarity with all that happens. Only then can we even begin to judge whether or not there is some "eternal harmony," and, whether such harmony is worth the price.

A. Suffering: Human Affliction or Universal Lot?

It is a paradox that the principal obstacle to our understanding of the place of suffering in life has been primarily its identification with our own experience of psychological evil. Experienced by humans mostly in conjunction with reflective awareness of both physical pain and the consequences of moral evil, suffering is often reduced to the status of an epiphenomenon (a kind of sideshow or evolutionary spin-off) and regarded as a peculiar by-product of the human capacity for anxiety and regret. No doubt there is much truth in this, perhaps even the promise of salvation from suffering. Thus if, as Buddhism teaches, one can eliminate ego-centered desires, not only the pains of life and the fear of death but also the sources of moral deviation can be rendered harmless as well. Somewhat in the same way, Christians are taught; "Neither death nor life . . . neither the present nor the future . . . neither height nor depth nor any other creature, will be able to separate us from the love of God. . ." (Romans 8:38–39).

Are we then to conclude that suffering, the psychological experience of evil, is of little consequence, except to alter our perception of the hard facts of existence in the world? I do not think so. In fact, I believe that such a reductionist approach, rather than eliminating suffering, could have just the opposite effect. If we remove suffering in this way (if indeed we can), we shall have eliminated neither pain nor sin, but only our sensitivity to their existence. On the other hand, if we admit suffering, contend with it, we shall have come to grips with the universal struggle of life.

However, such a claim—no matter how self-evident it may seem—involves a great deal more than just our awareness of the laws of life. In some way, suffering is the key that alone can unlock the problem of evil in much the same way as the problem of innocent suffering remains the lock that seems to bar the door to understanding or acceptance. If there can seem to be no comprehensible solidarity in suffering that would allow for the death of the innocent, it is because we have failed to grasp the true nature and scope of suffering. It is something more than our psychological reaction to evil or even our awareness of a universal condition. It is, in itself, that condition, human awareness or not!

To make such a claim is to venture, I fear, into unpopular territory. Such a view smacks of universal pessimism. Life, after all, is for living! If pain and death there must be, or even sin, well then, let them be. But no need to dwell on these inevitabilities or aberrations. If they must be admitted to consciousness, then they must also be dismissed from it as quickly as possible, lest we suffer or doubt life itself.

Suppose, nevertheless, that we open our consciousness to this inverted view of life. What shall we find? For one, rather than seeing suffering as an unfortunate by-product of human awareness of that which it would rather not acknowledge, suffering takes on a new shape. Not that it becomes good in itself, for it remains the sign of incompleteness, imperfection, and of being struggling toward fulfillment. Suffering, which is passive by definition (the Latin word *passio* itself means suffering), would nevertheless take on, at least in many cases, a new active meaning. Not that suffering should ever be sought for its own sake. It remains something that is passive in the sense that it is to be endured, even avoided when not strictly necessary. Most suffering is inflicted by disorder and failure, by deterioration, by anxiety and alienation. This suffering must not be merely endured; it must be fought and, as much as possible, overcome. However, there is also the suffering that is entailed by struggle toward further growth. Such suffering, like the work of a farmer who turns, pulverizes, and rakes the soil clean of foreign growth, must be undertaken as part of a task that is actively pursued and sustained.

Suffering, understood from this perspective, is an intregal part of all created reality. It is, in a way, the moral dimension of physical evil, if physical evil be taken to be the incompleteness and frustration of fundamental existence and morality is understood as the quest for fuller being and life. So too, suffering is the physical dimension of moral evil, if by *physical* we mean concrete existence and in *moral evil* we include the failure, at least when caused by ourselves, of nature to achieve its full potential for good.

How is such an expanded vision of suffering possible? What are its presuppositions?

First of all, we must reject all dualistic or other related idealistic views of the universe, views that would separate the world of ethical life and moral decision-making from any logical or even metaphysical connection with the world of physical being. The consequence of such a bifurcated view of reality, when applied to the problem of evil and suffering, is all too evident. It results in a kind of schizophrenic world view in which statements, such as this one from H. J. McCloskey's discussion in "God and Evil," are all too readily taken to represent the logic of the standard theistic position:

> if free will alone is used to justify moral evil, then even if no moral good occurred, moral evil would still be said to be justified; but physical evil would have no justification. . . . Physical evil is not essential to free will.[1]

Do we live in such a world—one in which human freedom could stand in such isolation, and is so much an absolute good in itself—that any amount of misuse of free will could not detract from its solitary splendor? Or can we suppose that any connection between physical evil (which for McCloskey includes psychological evil or suffering) and moral freedom, whether it be for good or ill, is purely accidental, or at best the caprice of some sadistic whim of God? Would not such a view lead quite logically not only to the rejection of any such God but equally to the denial of any intelligible order in the universe?

Rather than reject out of hand such a God, whom we cannot see, is it not more logical to first question our understanding of the universe, which can be seen? Does the universe in fact present such a disjointed picture of the relationship between human freedom and the physical order of things? Do we not need, first of all, instead of a new faith in God despite the things we think we see, a new way of seeing, a fresh way of interpreting all the evidence that lies before our eyes?

Thus the second step in remedying this state of affairs must concentrate not so much on some kind of theological apologetics, or even a moral reevaluation of traditional theodicy, as on a new understanding of basic physics and biology, somewhat like Teilhard's "ultra-" or "hyper-physics," which instead of separating the physical from the metaphysical world, would unite them. What we need is a world view that integrates the physical, biological, and psychological levels of existence, not by reducing any of them to one or another, but by incorporating all of them within a single spectrum of being, in which their modes of existence are seen as interrelated, and their values in terms of that existence begin to make new sense. Only in such a way will physical, psychological, and moral goodness as well as evil be understood in terms that are comprehensive in respect to each other and comprehensible to the modern mind. Only then would the full dimensions of the relationship between suffering and freedom be revealed.

Seen in this fashion, the world is one in which matter and spirit not only coexist, intertwined on all levels of existence, but one in which the material and the spiritual form two aspects of one and the same reality, two manifestations of a single, all-pervasive "stuff."[2] On the level of creation, matter, or what we take to be the purely material side of reality, is but the fragmented, particularized, unorganized diversity of created existence. Spirit, or the spiritual side of this same reality is, on the other hand, manifested in the organized, unified, and, most of all, conscious level of existence.

The evidence for such a view is all around us, at least for those who are open to it. No atom, no subatomic particle, is without its spiritual potentiality in the rudimentary sense that it is capable of entering into a higher, more complex, more organized unity with others of its kind. But as we know equally well, no organism living upon this earth, least of all ourselves, is so entirely spiritual as to be free from the material side of being. On the contrary, we find that the higher an organism stands on the scale of psychic capability in this world the more complex on the physical level it is. Each is an interwoven system of highly organized and integrated molecules and cells and organs, all of them composed of the most basic material elements of the universe. We, as much as, or even more than, the lowest protoplasmic life, depend on a delicate balance of physical and biological interactions and processes that make even the most complicated atomic reactions look like basic mathematics in comparison to higher calculus.

In terms of this incredibly complicated interdependence of the physical and psychic elements in nature, it is unreasonable to restrict what we call "suffering" to the purely human segment of creation. No doubt humans suffer in a unique way, especially as a consequence of moral evil. But there can be no question that animals also suffer. While it is quite evident that their suffering arises primarily from physical causes, such as starvation, cold, heat, and death as it comes in its many violent ways in the wild, still it is no mere anthropomorphism to ascribe to animals, at least the higher ones, the capability of suffering the psychological experiences of loss, separation, or even a kind of neurosis induced by confinement in captivity. Nor can there be any doubt that domesticated animals, in particular our companion pets such as dogs, often exhibit the same psychological or emotional traits as their human masters. Nature, it appears, is a single, interconnected whole. Any view of evolution that would affirm a merely physical interdependence of species without allowing for a certain amount of psychic relatedness would be a strange and disjointed hypothesis indeed.

In this total evolutionary context, one in which spirit and matter interpenetrate, suffering is more than merely a psychological accident or by-product of moral or physical evil; it is the basic condition of the universe, while physical pain and moral evil are the subspecies of this universal fact. Suffering is that core reality which ties moral and physical evil into a shared destiny, linking them together not just as a mental or verbal construct (in which physical defect is in some way likened to moral evil) but even more as actually constituting that underlying reality of which both physical and moral evil are particular manifestations. "All creation groans and is in agony . . . eagerly awaiting the revelation of the sons of God" (Romans 8:18–23). These words of St. Paul are no mere analogy! They reveal a vision of the universe where all forms of evil—physical, psychological, and moral—form the background for one great expression of a cosmic longing for perfection, a world where incompleteness and defect on all levels of created being share a common travail until all things are consummated in one great ecstasy of union with God.

B. Freedom and Chance

If we accept, with the help of a Teilhardian "hyperphysics," this Pauline vision of all of creation caught up in a universal condition of suffering until its redemption is achieved, then we may also find ourselves in a better position to understand the link between physical evil and human freedom. Suffering, in this context, would no longer be seen simply as the human awareness of physical pain or as the psychological effect of human failure, but as the price exacted from all creation in its struggle toward consciousness and freedom. Born in the creative play of chance, true freedom is won only through suffering. Pain, ever present within the struggles of the material side of existence, is deepened in the human consciousness, which suffers not only from the whims of unorganized matter but also from misuse of human freedom.

Freedom, particularly human freedom, is not an easy concept to define. There are many varieties of freedom: physical freedom (lack of physical confinement or constraint), political freedom (with its right to participate in government as well as its responsibilities toward others), ideal freedom (the opportunity to act according to one's highest values), creative freedom (the ability to bring about new ideas and expressions), or even the freedom to do what one pleases. But most of all there is the kind of freedom that we have so far taken for granted, simply the freedom to choose, or what is generally called "free will." Of all the varieties of freedom, this concept is the most difficult to pin down, for self-evident as its existence seems to us in our immediate consciousness, it turns out to be less obvious when subjected to close analysis.

It will not be necessary to go into the historical controversies that have raged over this question, ranging from the intellectual determinism implicit in Socrates, through the theological predestinarianism drawn from Augustine, to the modern behaviorist school of psychology as championed by B. F. Skinner and his followers. What suffices for present purposes is that we see human freedom or, more precisely, free will, as that power of self-determination which exists within us, no matter in how limited a way, in the face of whatever else determines our lives. Thus no matter how constrained our freedom is, we resolutely defend its existence, even if the proof is only in our refusal to deny it in the face of all the evidence to the contrary (the same kind of proof the critics of free will inadvertently supply when they choose to deny its existence!).

If there seems to be a kind of stubborn resistance to any theories of complete determinism, it is not merely because little in human life and culture makes sense without the presumption of freedom and a corresponding responsibility. Very little in the whole pattern of evolution as well makes sense without it. Perhaps evolution can only be understood, as Bergson insisted, as the evolution of freedom. Thus, if we are constrained or "determined" to believe in at least a minimal freedom (at least enough to choose to imagine we are free!), it may only go to prove the truth of the paradox voiced by Sartre, that "we are condemned to be free."

Rather than retreat in confusion from this paradox, could we not exploit it? If we find ourselves continually forced to defend our own freedom, does this not tell us something about its nature? Could it be that freedom, even in the strictest sense of free will, is more a potentiality than an actuality, that our imagined freedoms are more an illusion, or perhaps a goal, than the reality we take them to be? (In this, B. F. Skinner's *Beyond Freedom and Dignity* may be much closer to Eric Fromm's *Escape from Freedom* than Skinner's critics might wish to admit!) Whether one argues that other freedoms have either grown or diminished, it may be that true freedom, at least on the level of completely undetermined human choice, has yet to exist.

This partial concession to deterministic behaviorism would destroy belief in the existence of free will only if one adheres to the dualisms of the past. Rather than seeing ourselves as either determined or free, can it not be that we are *both*—impelled by the forces of the past and self-directed toward the future? Although such a view runs the risk of an oversimplification of a very complex matter, still, does not the play of determinism and chance (or better, the determinisms of chance) in the basic origins of the evolutionary process point to a new and higher, more self-conscious level of the same process on the level of human life? As beings who are rooted in the materiality of creation as well as manifesting its psychic potentialities to a high degree, we either tend to place too much emphasis on one sphere or the other, adopting either a strict materialism or an equally strict idealism, or else ending up taking a disjointed view of both, which like Descartes' view of the soul as the Ghost in the Machine ends up creating more problems than it solves. Thus while either of the extreme positions leave us at a loss to explain the paradoxes of human existence, a merely superficial juxtaposition of materialism with a corresponding spiritual idealism abandons us to a morass of outright contradictions. Not only do the counterclaims of determinism and freewill remain irreconcilable, but in addition any coherent relationship between suffering and sin, except by way of punishment, would disappear. Innocent human suffering (and in such a world only humans could suffer) would have to be explained either as an accident of blind nature or as the whim of a cruel God.

No doubt there are accidents in nature, but "whims" are dis-

tinctly human. More partially aware of possibilities than fully conscious of our responsibilities, we make innumerable choices during
our lifetimes. But, as Gabriel Marcel has pointed out, choosing is
not the same as willing. We choose again and again, impelled by
our predelictions, our inborn, inbred, even indoctrinated "determinacies." Rarely, if ever, are these choices made with anything
resembling full reflection. Not unlike the case of love at first sight,
we are driven, attracted, even compelled against our better judgment. But only subsequently are we faced with true decision-
making, a fully conscious willing that depends on reflective
awareness. It is at this point, usually long after we made the
choices that have determined the circumstances in which we find
ourselves, that truly free willing becomes possible. No doubt, even
when this point has been reached, there remain hidden motives,
unrecognized determinisms, and unconscious drives that continue
to affect us. The Freudian revolution has made us supremely wary
of them. Yet it was the avowed purpose of Freud's psychoanalytic
therapy to free persons from such determinacies so that fully conscious and truly free decisions could be made.

But to free ourselves from such determinacies is not to eradi-
cate them. Freedom consists not in the wiping out of the past, but
in its utilization, and in the transformation of the chance influences
of the past into the material for new, conscious, self-
determination. We cannot alter our own genetic make-up or
change the circumstances of our birth, rearing, or education. These
are fixed in the past. Nor can we control, for the most part, even
the chance occurrences of our present lives; we can at most only
trade one set of uncertainties for another. The only thing we can
have complete control over, and this in theory more than fact, is
our intentions for the future, and as we know all too well, often
these have very little effect.

For some, all this is a cause for despair if not an outright
denial of free will. But again, need it always be a question of either
determinism or free will? Is it not rather a matter of both? Rather
than all determinisms being enemies of freedom, which so often
seems to be the case, can they not be seen, at least in certain
aspects, as a basic constituent of freedom, if not the very material
from which all created freedom is made?

To begin with the most basic levels of the physical-biological
universe, the so-called determinisms are themselves under the
sway of chance. If we accept as so-called laws of nature statistical
averages that express the normal outcome of the play of large

numbers of particles displaying basically random behavior, what is to prevent us from seeing chance itself as a kind of determinism in its own right? Likewise, without the play of chance (as in random genetic mutation) biological change would be impossible. Yet without the relative stability imposed by determinisms that control the result (as in the formation and preservation of distinct species), chance alone would produce only chaos. If there is a paradox in this, it is again only a matter of perspective. Not unlike the old riddle about the chicken or the egg, the relationship between determinism and chance is one of organic interdependence. We can imagine one without the other, or even isolate them as objects of analytical inspection, but in the reality of evolutionary growth they are inseparable.

Taken a step further, this same interplay of chance and determinism forms both the background of and the material for the acting out of human life. Without the variety rooted in chance occurrence, what could be object of free human choice? Isolated in a world of predetermined, robotlike actions and reactions, what would there be left to choose? Conversely, if the exercise of free will were not itself a kind of "determinism," a regulating force imposed on nature and modifying our own behavior and attitudes, would human freedom have any meaning at all? Would it not be reduced to an exercise in wishful thinking conducted in a vacuum of nonresponse?

If this last point strikes one as a sophism or seems like some kind of verbal conceit, I would suggest that the real relationship between freedom and chance lies deeper still. If this overall view of the universe as the product of the interplay of chance and necessity be admitted, should it surprise us if our own inner universe is not much different? If we admit, as an evolutionary interpretation of the universe would demand, that we ourselves are a product of this same creative process, must we not then look at the universe as not only the field of opportunity for our exercise of free will but also the organic source of our power to choose or will?

No doubt such a suggestion is threatening to many who may have been schooled in more classical or humanistic philosophy, and even to the scientifically oriented it may appear as a simplistic reduction of a very complex human issue. Likewise, any assertion that the human intellect or will could have evolved from lower stages of biological life may also appear to be particularly subversive of traditional religious views, which insist on the uniqueness of mankind as creatures made "in the image and likeness of God."

Even Teilhard de Chardin hesitated, for religious (or "religiously diplomatic") reasons, openly to draw such conclusions. However, once they are understood, the implications are not so destructive of traditional human values as they might seem.

On the other hand, if the possibilities offered from an evolutionary perspective are ignored, the consequences would be very grave, especially for philosophy and theology as disciplines claiming relevance to our interpretation of all reality, and even more for any humanism or religious belief that looks to these fields for intellectual assistance. More specifically, such a refusal, I think, would be completely destructive of possible success in any further attempts to arrive at a fully comprehensive as well as fully comprehensible theodicy. After many centuries of deadlock, the fear of reductionism or theological heresy must be put aside long enough to explore new possibilities. No doubt, any first attempts in such complex questions will appear reductionistic and highly unorthodox. In this, like many other matters in life, "a tree is known by its fruit." No fair judgment can be made unless the fruit is allowed to appear.

This much said, the next step should be simply to take the basic insights of such an evolutionary approach and allow them to be carried to their logical conclusions. The most basic of these insights is a phenomenological one, that is, based on our observation of the general pattern of the facts of evolution. It would hold that the degree of consciousness present in an organism is in proportion to the complexity of that organism. It is this basic pattern, generally seen to be on the increase in the universe (see again the Darwin Centennial definition of evolution above), that Teilhard went on to formulate as the Law of Complexity-Consciousness,— a phenomenon he described as a general drift toward "convergence" or "unification" in nature.

Furthermore, considered strictly on the phenomenological level, the uniqueness of the human type is not in the fact that humans can know things, for so do animals, but that "man knows that he knows." This is to say that he has the power of reflective thought. How explain this phenomenon? Teilhard suggests that there is nothing in the uniqueness of the human thinking process that cannot be quite readily explained by the extraordinary complexity of the human brain, particularly in the overwhelming dominance of the neocortex or "gray matter" when compared even to other primates. As to why or just how this came about, Teilhard, as both prudent churchman and prudent scientist, chose to remain silent (or noncommittal), but that it came about as part of the course of evolution there can be no doubt. Nevertheless, he insisted that it was no mere quantitative difference that resulted—that is, not just more brain matter leading to more intelligence—but a real qualitative "leap" resulting in a whole new kind of intelligence—reflective thought.

However, suppose we take this phenomenological description of human uniqueness and couple it to Teilhard's "hyperphysical" theory which, as we have seen, postulates the existence of spirit and matter not as separate entities in the created order, but as distinct yet dynamically interdependent manifestations of a single *Weltstoff* (perhaps better described today in terms of distinctly manifested but conjoined energies). Understood in terms of this dynamism, the phenomenon of life, particularly the gradual appearance of life that is more and more sensitive or "conscious," but even more, the appearance of a consciousness that "leaps" into the realm of reflective awareness, becomes plausible. But there is more, particularly when this explanation of the origin of human intelligence is extended into the realm of human freedom.

According to Teilhard, human reflective thought is animal awareness or consciousness "squared" (a shorthand expression for "knowing that we know"). If we go back to our observations on human free will, particularly Gabriel Marcel's analysis of the difference between mere choosing and truly willing, we can in a definite sense observe a similar "qualitative leap," indeed, one that is based on the same advance as that of reflective thought over basic unreflective awareness. Is not what Marcel describes as mere choice capable of being described as a more or less random selection determined by the basic awareness of stimuli? On the other hand, to truly will something, and to do so freely, would mean that the immediate sense impressions, and perhaps even more, the instinctual drives and other psychological compulsions within ourselves will have to be reflected upon in such a way that we would "know what we are doing," as the phrase puts it.

All this is obvious, or should be, yet what so often seems less obvious is the connection that this whole process of choice and willing has with chance. Most basically, evolution depends on chance as a major element in its working mechanism; without chance mutations there is no evolution. Second, if chance also is a major element (as the behaviorists insist) in the reason why we choose one option over another (as it is also a major reason why we have any options to choose from in the first place), then we must also conclude that without chance there is no choice. Finally, the human act of willing in the highest sense of the word depends on reflective awareness in order to be able to exist, and that same reflective power of the brain is in turn a product of organic evolution (involving its own complement of chance). We must therefore conclude that without the element of chance in the universe, the exercise of free will as we know it would also be impossible; in a word, without chance, no human free will. If a little linquistic shorthand of my own is permissible, it might be said that free will is "chance squared," or chance raised to as many powers as one can detect quantitative leaps from its role in physics, to biology, to psychology.

Certainly, thus formulated, the charge of reductionism has to be taken seriously, but almost every area of human knowledge involves some degree of "reduction" from the complexity of the facts to an approximate formulation of the truth. In this same field of thought the Eudaimonism of Socrates, which held that no one chooses except in terms of what he or she thinks is best for him or herself, is certainly also such a reduction, a kind of intellectual determinism that explains most behavior, but not all of it. Aristotle voiced reservations about the principle, but no one has ever come up with much else adequate to replace it—except perhaps diabolic possession or its psychoanalytic equivalents! Thus even this account of the element of chance working in the operating of choice depends largely on Socrates' old principle.

As for the charge of unorthodoxy in terms of the highest valuation of human nature given by the Judeo-Christian tradition, while the 1950 Papal Encyclical "Humani Generis" admitted the possibility of a physical origin of mankind from lower forms of life, it drew the line at the suggestion that the human "soul" might have similarly evolved. According to the encyclical, man was (and still is, in each case of human conception) created directly (or "immediately") and "specially" by God.[3]

Since then, Karl Rahner has pointed out (possibly following another suggestion of Teilhard's) that in terms of the Aristotelian categories of causality, direct and special creation need not apply in the sense of efficient or instrumental cause. It is hardly necessary to imagine God as specially engaged in a separate creative act every time a child is conceived. Instead, says Rahner, direct creation in this context would be best understood in terms of "exemplary" or "formal" cause—that is, in terms of God drawing or influencing the course of evolution in such a way that it would result eventually in the appearance of the human type exhibiting the "image and likeness" of God, expecially in its intellectual-volitional capacities. Finally, what is special about man's creation seen as part of the evolutionary process is most of all the operation of the divine "final" causality, which is to say that each individual has a transcendental capacity or potentiality for sharing God's life forever.

Understood in this way (and no serious objections seem to have been raised to this approach since Rahner's exposition in the early 1960s), the door seems to have been left open to this more evolutionary view of mankind's origin and, along with it, to the immense advantages that this approach affords theodicy.

In the course of this rather technical but altogether necessary discussion concerning the relationship of freedom to chance, the whole point has been not that evolution is in some way compatible with traditional theodicy. Rather it has been that none of the traditional theodicies made any sense, especially regarding the problem of the suffering of innocents, because they did not in effect really allow for evolution to take its place in the organic, much less the theological, scheme of things. Traditional theodicies, beginning with Augustine, for the most part tended to stress human free will as the reason, one way or another, that most evil occurs, but in doing so the theodicies also tended to reproduce (indeed, if not sometimes cause) the proclivity of the Church to, as Whitehead observed, "teach all the right things—for the wrong reasons!"

Human freedom is indeed the reason evil exists. On this point we can be in complete agreement with Augustine, Leibnitz, Bergson, or whoever else would champion mankind's sense of self-responsibility. But we must pay the price. Human freedom, like all forms of awareness and like life itself, depends not only on the existence of a world where accidents happen, but also on chance itself as a precondition for the emergence of anything beyond a dumb and sterile existence enmeshed in a world of sameness and predictability.

Yet merely human freedom as we know it is not the whole answer. In a very real way God has "subjected" the whole world of nature to chance, but not for its own sake. Rather it is for the sake of infinitely higher stakes. God has taken a chance on chance, or so it seems, so that not only ourselves but all of nature might "enjoy the same freedom and glory as the children of God."

C. *Freedom and Futility*

If, in the above allusion to St. Paul's theology of suffering as found in the eighth chapter of the Epistle to the Romans, the word *chance* has been substituted for the *vanity, futility,* or even *dec-*

adence as found in the various translations, the substitution was quite deliberate. In the Pauline perspective, which must always be understood with the primary emphasis on the place of Christ rather than on a doctrine of original sin, creation suffers as a result of the sentence imposed upon it because of humanity's fall. Taken less literally, the situation may be seen the other way around, with a fallen humanity suffering along with the rest of creation as a result of the very nature of things. Either way, the import of Paul's message is the same—Christ's victory will be total and final, and the universal condition of corruption and suffering will be reversed. Put in other terms, this belief expresses our conviction that true freedom will win out over the blind determinisms and fatal accidents of chance.

This is, of course, the answer of faith. But this is not to really answer the whole question that lurks beneath. For underneath any assurance of ultimate victory lies the doubt of whether or not such a victory would be worth the price. This is the hidden question that becomes manifest in the rebellious protest of Dostoyevsky's Ivan Karamazov; dare we speak of some kind of general harmony that can be won despite the suffering of even one innocent child, much less the suffering of millions of innocent humans or even billions of subhuman creatures? Does not our claim of a solidarity in suffering (unlike Ivan's refusal to admit such) only further complicate the problem? For even if we were to judge one such tragedy as being admissible as a part of some divine plan, then what are we to say of a plan that somehow includes untold amounts of misery? Wherein lies the "victory?"

The answer to this question depends, of course, to a great extent on how we understand this victory of divine goodness. If we persist in thinking of it in terms of an eternal harmony that admits of no discord, no false notes, then we are faced with an impossible task. The progress of the universe, for all its magnificent splendor, is not a perfect symphony. It is not a finished masterpiece. Even granted some kind of divine plan, it resembles more the fitful and halting rehearsal of an orchestra still in the process of trying to understand the idiosyncrasies of its members along with the expectations of a new conductor. To extend the analogy even farther, it may sometimes seem that parts of the score, particularly the conclusion, remain unwritten. Yet this "rehearsal" will turn out, as far as we know, to be the final performance!

Clearly, then, the answer to the second question, that concerning the price of victory, is just as much a matter of faith as any assurance of victory in the first place, for they both depend on some kind of vision of what victory can possibly mean. Faith may very well be, as Paul Tillich insisted, "ultimate concern," but even that must have some object, some faith that something or other is going to turn out in such and such a way, or else concern degenerates into mere anxiety.

For the religious man, of course, faith in a good God supplies its own answer—that the victory will be whatever God decides it should be and it will have been worth the price paid. But for the nonbeliever it cannot be that simple, unless he does not mind the accusation of sentimentality. Thus, for some, any such appeal, whether religious or otherwise, to a final, yet unrealized, state of things is an evasion, a kind of whistling in the dark to ward off the terrors of the universal void. For such as these, any talk of victory is the chatter of fools, any imagining of harmony an illusion produced in a world of silence. Such faith, whether it be religious or merely humanistic in its inspiration, is seen as the ultimate escape hatch from the world as it really is. To such skeptics nothing really can be said. Such words as *harmony* or *victory* are, in the final analysis, relative terms. *Victory* implies defeat; one man's triumph inevitably is someone else's failure. *Harmony,* for all its objective foundations in the contrasting frequencies of sound, still must be heard to be recognized, and some will persist in perceiving only one side of the contrast if they will consent to listen at all.

Thus there is an active aspect to faith as well, active in the sense that it may be just as or even more important to believe that a thing *can* happen than to believe that it will happen whether we believe it will or not. No one attempts what is believed to be impossible, whether it is a matter of landing on the moon or curing cancer. From the evolutionary standpoint, faith has been just as essential to the progress of the human race as intelligence or free will. Without this faith, this lure and promise of self-transcendence, whether it be either religious or worldly, any further evolution of the human race comes to a standstill.

It is then only in terms of some kind of faith that we can conclude that freedom is worth the price that must be paid. Yet such faith need not be blind. All the indications, the invitations to faith, point in one direction. Suffering in all its aspects, its physical and moral dimensions as well as its directly psychological repercussions, reveals a cosmic struggle on all levels. There can be no doubt that this struggle has taken a terrible toll, whether measured in terms of individual lives that have been sacrificed or even whole species. *Decimation* is far too conservative a word to describe the statistics of failure in the course of the evolutionary process. And yet the process itself has survived, and that in itself should tell us something.

In just what sense evolution can be equated with progress is for many still a matter for debate. Can the emergence of even one new species, one showing greater spontaneity and intelligence, be said to justify the disappearance of a hundred others that are less gifted, as the partisans of progressive evolution would argue? Or can we shift from that question to whether or not the survival of one solitary superior individual (which means obviously only a very limited survival!) could justify the sacrifice of numerous others? Or reverse either of these questions: is the sacrifice of a single superior individual or group justified by the survival of many less gifted individuals or groups or species?

It should be just as obvious, however, from the very nature of such questions (quite apart from how they are answered), that evolution, however defined and evaluated, involves struggle, struggle that in turn implies suffering, physical pain, and death. In the case of the human species, it also means moral failure, or sin. All these are a price that is unfortunately often paid, at least in part, by those who, whether they had much to gain or not, certainly did not deserve to lose—the innocents of this world. Yet, in a way, can we not also speak of the innocent species as well? True, we cannot place moral categories on amoral objects, but is that really the problem or part of it, when we talk of innocent human victims as well? They did nothing to deserve their fate. Yet they too had to suffer. If this is the price of freedom, it seems the more appalling when we realize how many who paid the price did so with no realization of what was being purchased. To accept this indeed takes faith.

Yet the pattern is clear. Freedom has emerged, and with it, sin, while life has always meant death, and any degree of sensitivity has brought suffering with it. None of these has been possible without the other, nor have any of these fated pairs existed over the eons of time without a direct relationship to the rest. It is all of one vast piece. There is a solidarity in sin, as well as in retribution for it, and there is a solidarity in freedom as well. But there is also a solidarity in suffering, which makes it one with life and death, sin, and freedom.

One may dream of a better world, even of a best possible

world. No one has forbidden us to do so, least of all God. We might even envision a world where no innocent ever suffers, only the guilty. We might even imagine a world where death itself has disappeared. We might even wish for a world where no moral failings occur. Religion, most definitely, biblical religion, does encourage such hopes, in fact even encourages us to do our best to make them come about, even guaranteeing that some day they will be fulfilled. On no account, however, are these wishes and visions ever to be confused with the world as it presently exists. Here another world is still supreme, one in which the price of freedom must be paid daily by all who would enjoy it and even by many others who never will.

No "mere biologist" (as Teilhard termed himself in his appendix to *The Phenomenon of Man*) could have said it, perhaps only one who, like himself, had fathomed the central, paradoxical mystery of the Christian faith. For once mankind's origins are clearly seen as linked to the whole history of our universe, it becomes all the more true that "the human epic resembles nothing so much as a way of the Cross."[4]

Notes

1. This statement of McCloskey, first published in the course of an article entitled "God and Evil" in *Philosophical Quarterly* (10, no. 39 (April 1960), 97–114) can be found reprinted in Peter Angeles's collection of articles appearing as *Critiques of God* (Buffalo, N.Y.: Prometheus Press, 1976) on pages 214–15. While McCloskey correctly underlines the fatal flaw in the classical theistic arguments, one seems to get the impression that he fully accepts the conclusion of a total lack of relationship between physical evil and free will as a premise for his antitheistic argument. It is this lack of correlation between physical evil and free will in the order of nature that I think must be rejected totally, even apart from any theological considerations.

2. Teilhard's repeated recourse to the German term *Weltstoff* (certainly a painful concession for a Frenchman) only underlines the quandry in which he found himself when trying to express the relationship between spirit and matter. It also, to a large extent, explains his extreme reluctance to describe his speculations on the ultimate nature of reality as a "metaphysics" in any usual sense of the word and his use of the terms "ultra-physics" or "hyper-physics" (more often the latter) in addressing the subject. For Teilhard, the only legitimate use of the word "spirit" in the sense of that which is completely removed from the material aspect of creation would be for the divine being in itself. This point, paramount for a correct understanding of Teilhard's thought, has been often overlooked by both admirers and critics of his system in their readings of his oft-used hyphenization of "spirit-matter" (or its reverse) and has resulted in misunderstandings of his thought as being both "panpsychic" in an exclusive sense or, on the other hand, as in the case of a colossal error in an early printing of a translation of *Le Phénomene humain*, the statement that all energy is ultimately "physical" in nature.

On the contrary, for Teilhard, all energy is "psychic" because its direction of development, as manifested across the spectrum of evolution, is toward higher consciousness. Cf. *The Phenomenon of Man*, as translated by Bernard Wall (New York: Harper & Row, 1961), p. 64; also Christopher F. Mooney, *Teilhard de Chardin and the Mystery of Christ* [New York: Harper & Row, 1964] p. 223, n. 8. It is evident however, from evidence in his later "Journal" notes (unpublished), that Teilhard remained quite dissatisfied with his earlier attempts to formulate a theory of "energetics" to explicate his "ultra-physics."

3. Closely connected to the question of monogenism discussed earlier, this insistence of the papal encyclical on the uniqueness of God's special creative action in the appearance of the human species seems to have been directly connected to Roman apprehensions over Teilhard's ideas, despite his having been denied publication. Père Sebastian Tromp, S. J., the papal theologian commonly thought to have been the principal composer of Pius XII's encyclicals, also seems to have been much alarmed by the ideas of another Jesuit contemporary of Teilhard, Henri de Lubac, especially the latter's ideas concerning the nature of and function of divine grace in bringing human beings to their full capacity or final destiny. The work of Karl Rahner, particularly in the area of theological anthropology in what is termed as a "transcendentalist" mode, appears to owe a great deal to the pioneering work of Teilhard and de Lubac as well as to their friend and mentor, Père Maréchal. Indeed, Rahner's suggestion (below) as to the precise mode of special divine causality in the creation of the human race, is very similar to those made in Teilhard's 1920 "Note on the Modes of Divine Action in the Universe."

Cf. Teilhard de Chardin, *Christianity and Evolution,* translated by René Hague (London: Collins and Sons, 1971) pp. 27–35 as well as his 1931 "The Spirit of the Earth" as translated by J. M. Cohen in the collection of Teilhard's essays entitled *Human Energy* (London: Collins and Sons, 1969). Rahner's decisive essay on the subject, translated by W. T. O'Hara, was first published in English with the title *Hominization: The Evolutionary Origin of Man as a Theological Problem* by Herder & Herder in 1966.

4. Teilhard de Chardin, *The Phenomenon of Man;* cf. p. 313.

8

The God Who Suffers

The existence of evil is not the only obstacle to our faith
in God, for it is equally a proof of the existence of God,
and the proof that this world is not the only or ultimate
one.

—Nikolai Berdyaev
Freedom in the Spirit

When all is said and done, at the heart of the problem of evil there
remains a mystery. Broken down into its various aspects, physical
evil, psychological evil, and moral evil (with the related question of
human freedom), this problem presents distinct questions which,
although they may yield to some extent to a common evolutionary
solution, nevertheless recoalesce ultimately around that mystery
which is God.

God and evil are contraries; of this we have no doubt. And "if
the problem of evil is altogether insoluable, there is an end of
theism." With this judgment of James Ward *(The Realm of Ends)*
we can also concur. But can we agree with his corollary "if God
exists, there is nothing absolutely evil"? I, for one, cannot, and I
doubt that many others can, but I shall not belabor this point. Still,
where does this impasse leave us, or what option does it provide us
with, except in the end to reexamine our concept of God?

To do so, however, means that we have to be willing to move
out of the realm of mere problems and brace ourselves to confront
mystery in all its fullness. For some, such a challenge is entirely
unacceptable, for is not the admission of mystery the confession of
ignorance? For others it is unthinkable, for to confront mystery is

to question the unquestionable, a near-blasphemous enterprise to which the creature can claim no right.

Yet is it not possible that we have misread the divine intention? Rather than seeing problems as grim signposts warning us lest we trespass unwittingly into a forbidden mystery, may we not see them as invitations guiding us in the direction of a mystery that must be shared and lived by all, including God?

A. *"The Lord of the Absurd"*

"The world stands on absurdities, and perhaps nothing would have come to pass without them." This final rejoinder of Dostoyevsky's Ivan Karamazov, a theme taken up by the atheistic Sartre and the agnostic Camus, may just as well, as Berdyaev indicates, turn out to be the turning point to faith.

It is not altogether so amazing as it may first seem that the Catholic theologian Raymond Nogar, who had achieved some notariety for his comprehensive book *The Wisdom of Evolution*, produced just before the end of his life a little work that appeared to present an entirely opposite view. Was *The Lord of the Absurd* a complete repudiation of all that he had held before, a total collapse of the world view that had led him to extol the glories of a divinely creative evolution? Perhaps it was, but I do not think so. What took place was a reversal of perspective, one in which the world of evolution was seen in a very different light. No longer, at least to Nogar's eyes, did evolution, for all its apparent directedness (the teleology that most scientists are loath to admit) seem to be something inevitable, or as Teilhard believed, "infallible" in its final outcome. Rather must it not be admitted (again something that the scientists seem unwilling to do, at least completely) that the "evolution of life, and the emergence of man, is a natural process in which chance, failure, waste, disorder and death will ultimately prevail?" This is a hard conclusion, and it is one that drove Nogar, when speaking from what he finally concluded was the completely natural verdict on evolution, toward another, faith-filled counterbelief, one in which God "did not hesitate to shake the cosmic frame to its foundations and turn it topsy-turvy at the slightest inspiration of Divine madness."

Nogar's about-face is, for present purposes, highly instructive. What he was saying seemed to be simply the inverse of Aquinas's celebrated cosmological demonstrations of God's existence. All of them depend on a presupposition that the universe does make sense. And all of them, following the lines of Aristotle's analysis of the various types of causality, argue toward the coherence of the universe as being explainable only in the light of a divine Prime Mover and Orderer of nature. But what if the universe does not make sense in the first place? What if, in the light of an overwhelming recurrence of evil, particularly senseless suffering, evolution is headed toward a dead end? This is the problem posed by the apparent absurdity of the universe and of a God who would make it so.

One answer to this is, of course, the leap of faith to a God who can make sense from nonsense and order from chaos. Such an existentialistic act of faith remains an equally valid alternative to disbelief, despite accusations of bad faith, for one man's risk may be another man's act of cowardice. Alienation from an absurd universe can follow as easily from an atheistic viewpoint as from a belief in which there is a God to set things straight. But I suspect that this kind of faith in a God who *alone* makes sense is no more satisfactory for the mass of believers than a nonsensical universe is for scientists. So where can we turn?

For the believer in the God of traditional Christian, Jewish, and Muslim theism, this question raises grave problems. All attempts to extricate this all-powerful and all-loving God from the dilemma posed by an "absurd" universe could easily lead the believer perilously close to the world-denying theologies of the East. However, the strong historical and revelational foundations of biblical religion, particularly the central incarnational doctrine of Christianity, will not allow this. God is truly involved, not only in the good, but also in the evil, of a real universe. This world may not be the ultimate world, but it is the actual world nonetheless. Despite the reservations expressed in the book of Wisdom,[1] the Scriptures as a whole are quite explicit in their directness. "He [God] made it, and it belongs to Him." Not only the good, but also the evil, is ultimately attributable to God, shocking as this conclusion may seem. Not only life, but death, not just prosperity but adversity as well, flow from the hands of a God who both sanctifies and "hardens hearts."

Even making allowances for the peculiarities of Hebraic thought, which tends to bypass secondary causes and ascribe to God directly even the moral failings of his creatures, we must conclude with Pascal that the God of Revelation has little in common with the God of the philosophers. Pascal's carefully con-

sidered conclusion was not lightly made. Periodically throughout
the history of Christian (as well as Jewish and Islamic) theology,
serious thinkers had repeatedly pointed out that certain aspects of
biblical belief were irreconcilable with classical philosophy on a
number of issues, not the least of which concern the nature of God
and his relationship to creation.

Not only was the world, as understood by classical Greek
philosophers, coeternal with its divine origin (thus ruling out, it
would seem, any act of creation in, or along with time) but this
origin was itself an "unmoved mover," a "pure act" or complete
actuality in contrast to a changing and imperfect world of unrealized potentialities and recurring defects. Western theology was
able to modify this classical view of the world by insisting on its
creation in time and later has even adapted it to an evolutionary
understanding. The attempt, however, to reconcile the classical
philosophical ideas of God with the biblical revelation, while leading to great theological advances, has left us heirs to considerable
tension if not outright conflict. The remote and uninvolved supreme Truth and Beauty or First Cause of philosophy, although
admirable, contrasts sharply with the supremely majestic but eminently personal God of Revelation who, for all his love and mercy,
appears to be surprisingly changeable, even angry and vindictive.

Such a contrast proved to be something of an embarrassment,
not only to the early Christian theologians but even to the Jewish
philosophers who, like Philo of Alexandria, were desperately attempting to defend Judaism, even before the time of Christ,
against the incursions of a more sophisticated classical culture.
Proponents of this culture tended to view biblical religion, despite
the attraction of its high ethical standards, as somewhat primitive,
if not outright barbaric, in its understanding of God. The more
loving and accepting Father presented in the Gospels may have
mollified the situation somewhat, but only temporarily, for with
the claim that this same God had become man, the rift showed
signs of becoming even wider. The Johannine writings, particularly the First Epistle of John, indicate to us a situation in which
the philosophically minded among the early Christians were being
severely tempted to jettison the basic incarnational message of the
apostolic preaching for an elaborate and philosophically acceptable
reinterpretation of Christianity and the biblical image of God. This
Gnosticism or "higher knowledge" was an attempt to have it both
ways, and despite its failure to gain a foothold in the Church, it
was soon to resurface in that Marcionism which totally rejected the

Old Testament God in favor of a totally new image of deity that could presumably be discovered fully in the Christ.

That such a solution must have been an attractive one, considering mounting Jewish-Christian tensions at that time, seems undeniable. Yet official Christianity resisted. Instead of taking what would seem the easy way out, orthodox Christianity insisted on the basic unity of the two testaments and the God they reveal. At the same time its theologians embarked on a difficult and perilous effort to interpret this biblical God in terms that were understandable and as fully acceptable to both doctrinal demands and philosophical reasoning as cultured ingenuity and spirited debate could devise.

Why this exhaustive and, as some like Pascal feel, exhausted effort? Was it merely for apologetic reasons? That is, was it simply to present the biblical message in terms that might be readily understandable and acceptable to the non-Jewish and, particularly, the more highly cultured segments of the world? If so, this Hellenization of the Christian message might appear to many as the primary intellectual sin of official Christianity and the root of all future distortions of the Gospel message. On the contrary, what the Church was then engaged upon was not simply an effort to "translate" biblical revelation into philosophical formulations— most ordinary Christians were probably not much concerned with the philosophical insights into God, any more than the Athenians were in the time of Socrates! What we see here was a genuine effort to deepen Christianity's insight into the true nature of the biblical God, and to wrestle with the tensions that were inherent in the biblical belief. For these tensions were not just due to conflict with ideas drawn from the pagan philosphers, but were already present in those paradoxes found within the biblical message itself.

What paradoxes? The biblical and Christian message is shot through with them from beginning to end: God, loving and/or just, eternal yet involved in time, impassible (unmoved) yet involved (thus moved), and both One and Three; Jesus Christ, God yet man, who claims that whoever sees him sees the Father, yet the Father is greater than he; and, finally, good and evil—which is really which? In the face of these endless contradictions, theology and faith seem inane.

As a solution some, claiming to follow Tertullian, would advocate retreat into a kind of fideism, an appeal to "believe because it is absurd," when confronted with an even more absurd world. Many others, however, would question whether the effort to make sense out of chaos or the whole project of theology, of "faith seeking understanding," need be given up as futile. May the difficulty not lie in an inadequate philosophical framework? The obvious solution, as Teilhard once said, is that when one's philosophy no longer fits the facts, one must change one's philosophy. This is exactly what has been required of philosophy when our understanding of the universe shifted from static to evolutionary terms. A similar shift in theology is in order if we seriously believe that the God revealed in Scripture is the same God revealed in the universe that surrounds us.

For example, nature reveals itself to be in a state of constant, seemingly chaotic, flux, in a evolutionary process out of which novelty and ever-greater variety occur. Should we, then, be surprised that a theology that based its concept of God on the categories of eternal sameness and transcendent repose not only conflicts with our changed views of nature but does not even fit the biblical image of a God constantly involved in the vicissitudes of human history? Something is amiss when a view of God as "our fellow sufferer" (as A. N. Whitehead put it) is rejected as anti-Christian simply because it does not tally with the orthodox formulations of Christian belief, even when these same formulations seem to contradict some of the most obvious statements of the Scriptures.

True, the Scriptures themselves more than hint of a God who is eternal, all-wise, and all-powerful. They even speak of a God who is "without shadow of change or alteration" (James 1:17). Yet they also reveal a God who acts, who creates, who in his faithfulness (his unchanging fidelity to his promises) apparently changes his mind when the situation calls for it!

If there seems to be something absurd in all of this, perhaps it is more in our persisting in the illusion that we can adequately define God, or even in our uncritical acceptance of the idea that the Bible can contain the whole of reality, despite the limitations of human language. No matter how divinely inspired these Scriptures may be, we constantly run the danger of misreading them or of failing to understand them, particularly isolated passages taken out of context. Even if these dangers are avoided, can we reasonably expect the limited powers of human logic, even when bolstered by the tools of "higher" scientific critical analysis, to lead us to unerring comprehension of the ways, much less the nature, of God? If there has been any single message from the mystics throughout the ages, it has been that any true knowledge of God escapes adequate human expression, that even the path to such knowledge is inevitably one of "unknowing"—a collapse of all human reliance on logic, doctrinal formulation, and even of the tranquil assurances of the state of belief!

This being said as forewarning, I shall nevertheless suggest that we have generally failed to fully use the more obvious resources at hand to cope with the mystery of God and his self-revelation as they relate to the problem of evil and suffering in the world. If the world and justice of God in relation to this world seem absurd, it may be because we have failed to read the evidence that is clearly set before us.

"Absurdity," it has been said, "is sin without God." Is it not also suffering without God? If the concept of sin is nonsensical when God is removed from the picture, even though the consciousness of sin might inexplicably remain, what of the fact of suffering? If, as Dostoyevsky tells us, "without God, anything is possible" (at least within the limitations of conscience), how can we conceive of a universe in which pain and suffering make any sense except in relation to a goal that justifies the struggle or gives it some eternal meaning?

At the same time, how can we conceive of sin, pain, or suffering as evil unless they affect the outcome of the process, and, in doing so, unless they affect in some way even God himself? To ask this, of course, raises the final problem. If we admit that God can be so affected, can we still say with any surety that God remains God?

The resistance of the traditional theologies to the idea of a suffering God is grounded in strong logic. A God affected by sin is a God who suffers, and a God who suffers is no longer a God in complete control. Indeed, he would be a God who can be diminished, even eliminated as an effective force in the universe. Who could be compelled to worship such a God? Suppose, there remained the possibility of a divine victory over evil. Would there not also be a possibility of a divine defeat, one in which the Lord of (i.e., over) the Absurd, would turn out to be, instead, the absurd Lord, one who is ultimately crushed by the senseless suffering and unredeemed sin of the universe?

The possibilities here are too staggering to contemplate. It is here that radical Christianity and the tradition of rational theism, long used to support Christian theology, part company for good. Perhaps the final break can be averted by a temporary separation, but the prospects do not look encouraging. Philosophically speaking, Christian theology seems to have exhausted itself on this final problem of theodicy. Yet without some kind of a solution, can Christian faith (indeed, any biblically based faith) remain anything but absurd?

B. The God Who Died

The basic answer of Christian faith to this dilemma, the Cross, has indeed been "a stumbling block to the Jews and an absurdity to the Gentiles" (1 Corinthians 1:23). For the gentiles of St. Paul's time, particularly the philosophically sophisticated who held to an impassive and abstract theism of a supreme beauty or truth, the Christian answer was indeed absurd. As Jürgen Moltmann has pointed out, the classical philosophical approach to God is based entirely on the analogy between the perfection of the visible universe (despite all its faults as a lower order of being) and the inferred perfection of its invisible source. For those today who hold to such a Deistic view of God as the Great Architect of the universe, the Christian answer still remains incredible. It is equally incredible for the Jew, i.e., the strict monotheist believing in the all-powerful and personal God of revelation who is the triumphant ruler and judge, imposing his will and guiding the course of human affairs for his own honor and glory. Such a God stands above human history and tragedy, and although compassionate and merciful, remains superior to all human entanglement.

For these, as well as for the Christian whose theology might lean toward either an abstract deism or an absolutist monotheism, the explorations of a radical Christian theology into the implications of Friedrich Nietzsche's proclamation that "God is dead" was deemed blasphemous. Bumper stickers and church announcement boards blossomed throughout the land with counterslogans such as "My God is alive and well . . . too bad about yours!" A good part of this reaction was sparked by widespread confusion over the varying interpretations of Nietzsche's phrase (a recently published philosophy text quotes ten variations ranging from outright atheism to a psychological "death" of God-consciousness in modern man).[2] No wonder that the passing of what seemed to be a peculiarly American theological fad has been greeted with great relief by mainline and fundamentalist churches as well as serious theologians!

In the aftermath of this brouhaha, it might be profitable to consider what Teilhard de Chardin somewhat whimsically jotted in his own notebook years before the slogan became a theological catchword. As Teilhard saw it, "God is not dead, he has just changed!" Before we hastily write off such an opinion as being a mere quip without serious merit, we should consider the possibility that Teilhard was not just referring to our changed image of the world, which necessitated a changed image of God. Could it be that the message of Christianity itself is one of a God who has radically changed his relationship to the world? After all, how should we consider such Pauline texts that tell us that God "did not spare his own Son, but gave him up to benefit us all" (Romans 8:32), making "the sinless one into sin" (2 Corinthians 5:21), becoming "humbler yet, even to accepting death, death on a cross" (Philippians 2:8)?

Perhaps the only benefit of the "Death of God" movement in theology has been its challenge to explore anew the implication of such passages for our understanding of God in his relationship to the world. Can we, for example, continue to think of God as entirely impassive or unmoved when even such a world-renowned European theologian as Moltmann concludes that God has indeed suffered inasmuch as the Father has undergone grief at the death of his own Son? Does not the attribution of such a "psychological" passion to the Father imply that not only must the image of the impassive God of Greek philosophy be exchanged for a more biblical view of a loving (and sometimes angry and jealous) God, but also that God himself has become in some way "changed" in the Incarnation, Passion, death and Resurrection of Christ?

Any such "change" in God, if it has actually taken place, should demand, of course, a corresponding change in our understanding, not only of God's relationship to the world, but also in our understanding of the nature of God as such.

Such a change in understanding has, in fact, already taken place. Underlying the "foolishness" of the message of the Cross is the even greater "scandal" of the Incarnation and, underpinning both of these affronts to the highest human ideas about God, there are the great problems posed by the doctrine of the Trinity.

Christians wrestled with the intricacies of trinitarian speculation, at least in the beginning, not to challenge existing ideas about God but simply as part of the attempt to make comprehensible their belief in Jesus Christ as both God and man. The groundwork that made possible the formulation in Greek philosophical terms of Jesus as God (by nature or "substance") incarnate in a truly human nature as a single person (or "hypostasis"), also enabled the

Church (through an analogous use of the same terms) to define God as a single divine nature manifested in three distinct persons. But once such an understanding became established, such phrases as "the passion of my God" (Ignatius of Antioch in his *Epistle to the Romans*) somehow lost their force inasmuch as one could now revert to the classical philosophical concept of God, deeming it impossible that God (at least as God) could suffer, much less die. At the same time, by affirming that Christ suffered death in his human nature, one could state through a kind of linguistic sleight of hand (the *communicatio idiomatum*) that "God died" in the person of Christ. But do such theological niceties really do justice to what actually took place, even granting their usefulness in avoiding crude misunderstandings?

True, in the light of such distinctions, the strict monotheist of the Hebrew tradition can be spared the scandal of being told that God in some way has ceased to be God. Likewise the philosopher can be reassured by continuing to see God as remote from all the vicissitudes of too close an involvement with the changing universe. So reduced, does not this old Christian balancing act run the greater danger of removing God from any real relationship to the world that Christians believe he sent his Son to save? The logical result of this tendency to save God's traditional image then rebounds with one of two results: either Jesus of Nazareth is seen to be a mere man (albeit an extraordinarily holy one) who suffered death in much the same way as the other prophets before him, while God looked impassively on the scene from heaven, or else Christ is seen as a God who play-acts his way through a semblance of human life and death, but who is really never affected by it. Early Christianity rightly condemned these watered-down and oversimplified views of Jesus Christ as heresies, whether under the guise of Docetism, Arianism, or Nestorianism (to take them in their historical order of appearance). Although the labels have long since disappeared, the tendencies have not, and regardless whether one begins with a bias toward eliminating the divinity of Christ (the natural position of the unbeliever) or his humanity (the recurrent tendency among believers), the result is much the same. Both the folly of the Cross and the scandal of a God who suffers death are weakened to the point where the message of redemption from the evils and the sufferings of the world is lost.

It was precisely to avoid such deformations in the understanding of Christ that the Christian Church came to its definition of God as a Trinity. (Although strongly affirmed in the New Testament, it is quite evident that the idea of God as somehow triune in nature is not particularly Christian in origin—both the Hindu Advaitist concept of God as absolute Being-Truth-Bliss and St. Augustine's "psychological" exposition of the Trinity demonstrate the natural tendency to see God in this way.) As such, although it was to develop much more profound insights about God on its own, the doctrine of the Trinity remains somewhat in a satellite relationship to the central Christian task of proclaiming Jesus as the Christ, the Messiah-Redeemer who is God Incarnate.

Historically speaking, however, it is noteworthy that the biggest battles regarding the Church's doctrine about Christ, (aside from the Arian heresy, which would have diminished Christ's divinity) were more often than not waged to protect the integrity of his humanity. It seems that *theological anthropology* (to use a more modern term), at least as it applied to the person of Jesus Christ, was most often the focus of concern rather than theology, the doctrine of God, as such. Why?

The reason, it appears, is that the classical understanding of God as supreme Truth/Beauty, unmoved mover, and the like was now so firmly entrenched in the Christian consciousness, along with a rethinking of the biblical God's transcendent majesty along much the same lines, that the primary problem became the reconciliation of the humanity of Jesus with his firmly accepted divinity. There seemed to be only two possible routes that would avoid head-on collision with the concept of a totally unchanging God. The first was to deny some part of Jesus' humanity (his bodily existence, on the one hand, or his human soul on the other, or perhaps just his human will)—anything that would either eliminate his real humanity (and with it the humiliation that it implied for God) or leave a gap in his humanity that would allow a place for God (so that the person of Jesus really would be God and his "humanity" always a kind of appendage). The secondary strategy was simply to deny that there was any real, personal ("hypostatic") union between the two natures; that, in effect, there was merely a man (Jesus of Nazareth) who was in close, even the highest, union of mind and will or "grace" with God, but, of course, who was not the person of God himself. Again, of course, the Church managed to officially avoid such distortions in its doctrinal statements about what or who Jesus was, yet it resoundingly failed to convincingly explain how this could be. Hence these ancient heresies are still alive and flourishing. There is no need to draw out the details of their modern counterparts, but simply to stress the fact that the reason they still exist is not to be found in the great christological problem of explaining the hypostatic union of divine and human natures in Christ, but rather in our assumption that we fully comprehend what is meant by the divine nature in the first place!

Hence it seems that modern attempts to redefine the human nature of Christ in a way that better harmonizes with our concepts of divinity are, to say the least, somewhat backward. All indications from Scripture point to the opposite approach, that aside from earlier, partial revelations and even human speculations about God, we can only fully begin to know God's nature from his revelation in Christ, that is, in the humanity of this man Jesus. Thus, as far as I can see, there is no way we can avoid the implication that God directly participated in Jesus' life and death, not as some kind of outside ordering agent but rather by undergoing personally in some way what was happening to this man, so much so that we must also say that God himself has in some way "changed," "suffered," or even "died" in this person.

Some would say, of course, that it is enough to say that the image of God has changed in him (Jesus). But is it enough? If by *image* we mean only the modern commercial advertising or popular-psychology concept of image, then we say either nothing about God as such (that he has only appeared to change in Christ) or else we are perhaps saying something we didn't intend at all (that God has always been changing, only we have finally awakened to the fact!). If it turns out to have been the latter, so much the better, but if it is that in fact, then we still have not explained what it is in Jesus that has made all the difference—except to alter our perceptions.

This would be in itself a major accomplishment. For the purposes of theodicy alone, a changed image of God from the impassive, aloof, and possibly uncaring God of classical theism, or from the capricious divine monarch of an exaggerated patriarchial monotheism, would be of immense value. The image of an unsuffering God has become altogether insufferable.

However, must not even more be said? This is not the time or place to get involved in the intricacies of Soteriology or in the controversies over the manner of Christ's Atonement. But it is the time and place to insist that a convincing theodicy is more than a question of images, that is, if images are nothing but mere illusions. Of course, this is not true. Images (*eikōnes* in Greek) are the visible manifestations of an invisible reality; platonically speaking, the projection of spiritual ideas into the material world of representations. Or, if we wish to update this line of thought a bit by speaking in the manner of Whitehead (who in some aspects considered himself a Platonist), the image is the actual "concrescence" (or concretization, as we might say) of the eternal possibility (or reality existing in God). In any case, even in the most idealistic philosophies, an image is no mere symbol. To say the very least that can possibly be said about him as an image of God, Jesus, however else he may be explained, reveals to us the fact that God is affected by his creation, for God, who is in some way in Jesus, also in some way suffers through him. For the committed Christian this may be no easier to explain, but still it is a lot easier to say plainly, "God was in Jesus, reconciling the world to himself" (2 Corinthians 5:19). This is no play-acting or pretending; it is not even the case of just another man, no matter how holy, "sympathizing" with God. It is God in him.

Once it is admitted that God could change in this way, the task awaiting a truly renewed Christology would then be how to explain this more convincingly and more effectively. It would begin by coming to grips with a more evolutionary or dynamic understanding of human nature, and it would, from this fresh start, enable us to begin again to confront the problems raised by the Gospels (if we would read them without the blinders imposed by a doctrinaire overfamiliarity). Then, perhaps, we would be able to appreciate the full humanity revealed in their depiction of Jesus—the temptations, the uncertainties, the fears, and not least insignificant, the faith of Christ—yes, like you or me, Jesus had to believe!

From this would come, I think, a new insight into just what is meant when we say that God became man, lived, suffered and died. The picture of a divine Son-Person ghosting a human Jesus person (which is the way we have tended to think despite the careful formulations of doctrine) would be replaced by that of a human who has been formed by the Spirit into the definitive revelation of God. Then we might recognize in him the Christ, the image or Logos that is present in every aspect of creation (for "without him nothing has been made. . .") and yet that has longed from all eternity to express itself in a full, complete, and unrepeatable act of divine, self-emptying, all-fulfilling love.

Clearly, taken quite simply and squarely, Christianity has quite a problem to face, and that problem is not just in theodicy. The problem has only been exacerbated by theodicy, but the problem itself has had its origin in a too-ready assumption that the-

ology had a sure and clear grasp of the basic nature of God.
Confrontation with the mystery of God—that is, to "see" God in
the Hebrew tradition—means death. Certainly it must mean, if
nothing else, the death of our easy theologies, our easy assumptions that we know what God is like. Nietzsche's Zarathustra
proclaimed God's death, and it may well be that, in doing so,
Nietzsche actually meant that our God-consciousness has died,
for, after all, Zarathustra claims that we ourselves have killed him.
If so, there is very little new in this: men have been doing this for
ages. There is blasphemy in that, to be sure, but it is not so much
in God's being declared dead as in man's thinking he can kill him.
The abstract God of the philosophers may well be dead, as well as
the God of the Old Testament, at least when he was pictured too
one-sidedly. But it is not because we succeeded in killing him.
That kind of God is still alive in our theologies; he is still even
somewhat alive in our atheism, haunting modern consciences with
images of theologies once thought to be dead and buried. No, if
God is dead it is because he would have his false images die—the
images of both the impassive unmoved mover and of the Oriental
tyrant. In fact, he put them to death himself when his true image,
his Son, died on the Cross. At that moment, whatever God was, or
whatever man thought God was, died. Any death of God since
then is the death of that "faith" in every man who thought he had
God all explained.

C. Christ and "The Pain of God"

If there is a deep tension, even a contradiction within the
Christian concept of God, even as it is revealed in Christ, how are
we to remedy this state of affairs? Do we deny outright the legacies
of classical philosophy and mystical experience with their exalted
concepts of God as the Ground of Being or the unchanging, unsuffering Godhead that stands behind all changing existence? I, for
one, believe that this too would be folly. Philosophically, such a
God makes sense. Even the dynamic Process Theology drawn
from the thought of A. N. Whitehead would insist on an "antece-
dent" nature of God that shares something of these classical notions of divinity. But, on the other hand, would it do to deny the
truly personal God of Hebrew revelation (and not the distortions
of him) who, for all his majesty, passionately cares for the good of
the human race even when, all too often, he seems to remain silent?

Both concepts, the fruit of human speculation and desire and the fruit of divine revelational initiative in the midst of human history, are valid as far as they go. But for Christians, they do not go far enough.

For Christianity, God must remain God (in the sense of the highest philosophical understanding) while at the same time entering fully and personally into the depths of human tragedy. For us this means that God does indeed suffer, not in the sense that God is afflicted unwillingly by forces beyond his control, but rather that he has allowed himself to become willingly involved, even passionately so, in those sufferings which are part of the process that characterizes the expression of love. This is an active, committed suffering. It is the incarnate passion of a God who is love.

How can we describe this love—this God who is love (1 John 4:16)? The word used most generally in the New Testament is *agapē*. Distinct from the affective *erōs*, which primarily seeks its own fulfillment, *agapē* has more in common with *philos*—the loving friendship that draws like to like. There must, however, be no mistaking such love for something connatural or deserved by humanity. It is shared always as a pure gift, a grace *(charis)* and such love or charity demands self-sacrifice. Hence we are called not only to "love your neighbor as yourself" (Matthew 19:19, repeating Leviticus 19:18), but even to "love your enemies, do good to those who hate you" (Luke 6:27). Surely such love is bound to lead to suffering, to outright tragedy. Did it not do so in the case of Christ?

For all its eloquent vocabulary of love and its sense of the tragic, the Greek mind could not comprehend the self-sacrificing love of God and the pain that such love entails for God, any more than the Hebrew mind, with its concept of God's *hesed* or loving tenderness, could grasp how this kind of love could involve God in a gift of himself in Jesus—the Christ who would die ignominiously for the sake of sinners. Is the human mind capable of wrestling with such an idea?

Kozah Kitamori, a Japanese Protestant theologian, believes that his own people can come to grips with such an idea, thanks to their peculiar sense of the tragic or *tsurasa*, which entails the parental sacrifice of a son for a cause or for a person whose claims transcend all parental love. Kitamori points to the same phenomenon in Abraham's willingness to sacrifice Isaac, but it remains without any one word (in Scripture) to explain it. Neither *faith* nor mere *obedience* can fully account for it (although the word *sacrifice*

might describe it, even though the victim was refused by God).
Neither does *tsurasa,* by Kitamori's own admission, adequately
convey the full sense of pain (by which he translates the word)
when this pain is God's own. This pain of God might be understood as God's wrath transformed by his love, involving not only
the sacrifice of his beloved Son, but also motivated by a divine love
of what is unlovable—humanity in its fallen state. However cultur-
ally (as well as theologically) determined it may be, this concept of
loving pain may bring us closer to probing the heart of a God who
truly grieves and sacrifices himself in his Son, and who makes it
possible for our own pain to be transformed in the sufferings of
Christ.

Writing with insight drawn from both his cultural background and his nation's defeat in World War II, Kitamori saw a
unique opportunity to share with the rest of the world something
of the immense sense of tragedy experienced by his people in their
almost suicidal commitment to a cause they had judged worthy but
that had proved insane.[3]

How much this particularly Japanese sense of tragedy depends on the Buddhist concept of compassionate love is unknown
to me. At first glance it would seem diametrically opposed to the
calm, nonviolent expression of nirvanic bliss that should characterize the realization of the essential oneness of all things. Sacrifice
is the price demanded by divisiveness. If all things are ultimately
one, sacrifice is not only uncalled for, but it would be a prolongation of the violence that characterizes the superficial level of the
phenomenal world. Yet even in the realm of Buddhist thought
there is something that throws additional light on the Christian
attempts to understand the ultimate nature of love. For the Maha-
yana Buddhist, the compassion of the Buddha is best expressed in
the Bodhisattva, the Buddha-to-be. This person, on the threshold
of achieving nirvanic enlightenment, forgoes or postpones the unending enjoyment of the highest state of being in order to reach out
to those who suffer and to endure their agony with them in order
to lead them, along with himself, to ultimate bliss. Thus here we
do find a strong element of self-sacrifice, one for an undoubtedly
worthy cause, and like all sacrifice it involves suffering.

Yet, in the kind of pain that Kitamori is attempting to describe, there is something more than the pains entailed by sacrifice
as we usually understand it. There is the element of tragedy that
goes beyond Kitamori's description even of this pain as a kind of
loving wrath. I suspect that this particularly Japanese sense of pain

may have deeper roots yet—possibly in the Taoist or generally far-Eastern sense of this world, in all its fleetingness, being, or at least revealing, ultimate reality. Hence even Buddhism had to be delivered from its otherworldy Hindu milieu in which all change represented illusion and the only real tragedy was to be duped by this illusion—something that could always be remedied in another life when one presumably would have another go at becoming enlightened.

On the contrary, if according to this transformed Buddhism (considered by its Zen followers as the only authentic Buddhism) nirvana or ultimate reality is *samsara* or the ever-changing world, then sacrifice, particularly unrequited sacrifice, involves an equally ultimate pain.

Here may be the key to a deeper understanding of what we might mean by the pain of God. Here also may be the reason that most critics of Christian theodicy have misinterpreted the seriousness of Christianity when it came to its evaluation of the tragedy involved in the problems of evil. Rather than an ultimate victory over evil being a cause for self-satisfied joy on the part of God, it—more than any other victory—also spells defeat. More than the fragile beauty of the solitary "thusness" of a single flower in a Zen study, even infinitely more tragic than the death of the Kamikaze whose sacrifice turns out to have been in vain, is the loss of a single immortal human soul—a potential "god" who threw away the chance for eternal life and infinite fulfillment.

This sense of the tragic in God, which many Christian mystics saw revealed (rightly or wrongly depending on whether or not one attributes total foreknowledge to Jesus) in the Agony of the Garden of Gethsemane is what we are speaking of when we say that God suffers. Pain (in the ordinary sense of the word) and death are primarily physical phenomena and, in that sense, only relative evils. Suffering, on the other hand, is primarily a psychological phenomenon, and to the extent that God is personal, that is, knowing and loving, makes God, it would seem, equally capable of suffering, even infinitely so if his knowledge and love are infinite. Even sin, which may be the ultimate evil, nevertheless can be forgiven or, unrepented, be given its just deserts, but the suffering it may leave behind can continue forever.

It is in the light of this divine Passion that the Christian sense of *compassion* is given its greatest test, for we are called upon to sacrifice ourselves to an ideal of God-like love that could prove also to be at least partially in vain. We do not believe, as do most

Buddhists, in the essential unity of the universe, except for its common source in the creative act of God. It is rather the essential diversity of the universe and the growing freedom of creatures in the ongoing process of their self-creation that makes it probable that any sacrifice for their sake will meet, at the most, with limited success. It is here that we meet with the distinctively kenotic aspect of the Christian idea of sacrifice, one that has its own peculiar tragic sense. Despite the assurance that the *kenōsis,* or emptying out of the Son's divinity in his act of identification with the human race, will lead to an ultimate victory, it seems true that the refusal of God's invitation would subject God to some eternal diminishment. Again, more traditional theologians may object. Yet, short of a "universialist" restoration, which was ruled out when Origen was condemned, logic will prevail over mercy. God's pain will live on because God will always love. "Can a mother forget the child of her womb? Never shall I forget you, O Israel!" (Isaiah 49:15).

How, then, are we to understand our redemption? How do we see it as having been definitely accomplished in Christ? In the first place, it is something more than Christ's suffering the wrath of God in place of the human race that deserves it. Similarly, it is more than Christ's being the embodiment of God's love seeking our reconciliation. Although both of these Cross-centered insights are correct as far as they go, they are likewise insufficient for a theodicy that must account for suffering that goes beyond the boundaries of sin and guilt. All creation, not just the human race, suffers in the process of its evolution. Thus the importance of seeing the Incarnation as the embodiment, not just of God's plan, but of all creation's "growing pains." Thus it is only when our (and all creation's) pains become God's pain, that Redemption begins to fully take place. It is in this appropriation of suffering by God that the great Irenaean theme that "God becomes man that man might become God" receives its fullest, its cosmic, expression.

From this we might find another possible answer to the apparent excess of human suffering. Might it not be, as Frederick Sontag has suggested, the effect or at least the by-product of God's "excessive love?" We may have reservations about Sontag's judgment that God was neither constrained by necessity (the very nature of the universe) nor by his goodness (which, from Sontag's point of view, would have dictated a less cruel state of affairs). Somewhat differently, we might see this excess as the product of a compromise in which the pain of God is torn between a holy wrath over human misuse of freedom and an all-forgiving love that would, if it could, immediately remove all suffering on the basis of the sufferings of Christ and usher in, without further delay, the kingdom of God's justice, peace, and love. Instead, constrained by the conflicting demands of his wrath and his love, God can only suffer the "pain" of his own internal dialectic, and project, as it were, this conflict on creation. In such a projection we find not only what we misjudge to be the "cruelty" of God, a cruelty intensified in the infliction of a sacrificial death upon his only-begotten Son, but also the expression of an excessive love that refuses to take No for an answer.

No doubt there is something very arresting in this vision of The Hound of Heaven, who is compelled to completely identify himself with every human folly, even every cosmic accident, that his creative love has visited upon the world. But in the end it suffers, I think, from much the same problem as does any theology that attempts to start with theories about God rather than the revelation of Christ and acknowledgment of the world for what it is. It becomes overly speculative and ends up in reveries over other "possible" worlds and scenarios of the *eschaton*. It is not that visions of a better world should not have their part to play, just as they did in the preaching of Christ. The point that we must always remember, however (and this is always the *crucial* point in the most literal sense of the word) is that Jesus lived and suffered fully in the only possible world in his point in time. In him, the Christ, God took on this struggle fully as his own. In our own time we can only attempt to do the same. A better, more just, more loving world may indeed be possible, but it is impossible that it ever be except through the struggle of the Cross. An excess of suffering there may well be, as well as an excess of love, but any excess should not be understood as a surplus, but as that *extra* of both love and suffering (for they are one) that is required for all creation to succeed in reaching its destiny.

Notes

1. With evident reference to Genesis, the Book of Wisdom states that "Death was not God's doing. . . . To be—for this he created all" (1:13–14). Similarly, ". . . God did make man imperishable, . . . it was the devil's envy that brought death into the world . . ." (2:23–24). It is noteworthy that the Wisdom writer also claims that "the world's created things have health in them, in them no fatal poison can be found" (1:14). That the *New American Bible* (Camden, N.J.: Thomas Nelson Inc., 1971) translates the latter phrase as "And there is not a destructive drug among them" does not much help matters, either for theodicy or for literalist theories of biblical inerrancy!

2. I refer to a quotation from William Hamilton's exposition of the subject in the August 1966 *Playboy*. See James L. Christian's excellent textbook, *Philosophy: An Introduction to the Art of Wondering* (San Francisco: Rinehart Press, 1973), p. 461 or in the 2nd ed. (New York: Holt, Rinehart and Winston, 1977), p. 642. For a more selective but in-depth summary discussion of this provocative phrase, the reader is directed to Jürgen Moltmann's *Theology of Hope*, translated by James W. Leitch (New York: Harper & Row, 1967), pp. 168–72.

3. Kitamori's book was published in English under the title *Theology of the Pain of God* (Atlanta, Ga.: John Knox Press, 1965) after having been translated by W. H. H. Norman from the Japanese 5th. revised edition (1958) entitled *Kami no itami no shingaku*. However, this later edition includes a preface written for a 2d edition in 1947.

9

Cosmic Suffering and the Kingdom of God

> Now the earth can certainly clasp me in her giant arms. She can swell me with her life, or draw me back into her dust. She can deck herself with every charm, with every horror, with every mystery. She can intoxicate me with her perfume of tangibility and unity. She can cast me to my knees in expectation of what is maturing in her breast.
>
> But her enchantments can no longer do me harm, since she has become for me, over and above herself, the body of Him who is and of Him who is coming.
>
> —Pierre Teilhard de Chardin
> *The Divine Milieu*

God's response to the problem of evil is to be found in the mystery of his own suffering in Christ. Yet this Christ, who embodied in himself "the pain of God," had to experience the seeming "godforsakenness" of the human race on the Cross. If the Christ, as God's definitive answer to the evils of this world, had to so suffer, what real hope is there for us?

What hope is there for our joys and our sorrowing, for all our human efforts to make this a better, more just, or more beautiful world? Does not anything really count in the end, except to have saved our "souls"?

The total Christian answer, however, has never been that. It has been a great deal more. It has been capsulized in the concept of Resurrection, and this not just of Christ, but also of the universe

159

with and in Christ. Obviously this answer is not a simple one, for concealed within this faith can be a wide variety of attitudes. They can range from a deep pessimism regarding the future of the created world to a boundless optimism regarding its final outcome, or, again, from stoical resignation to the sufferings life entails to a dogged determination that life, even this side of eternity, can be made not just tolerable but even enjoyable. If Christianity has, in the popular estimation, persisted in seeing this life as a vale of tears, it has for some others held the promise contained in Irenaeus's vision of God's glory seen as "man, fully alive."

Who, then, is right? Has the Christian optimist any more claim to authentic hope for the future than the Christian pessimist has to his claim to being realistic about the present life, especially when both ultimately lay claim to a hope that transcends all purely earthly concern?

To formulate an answer to such a question is not easy, yet must be attempted. Our answer will to a great extent determine the mode of our presence in and toward life on this earth. More important, it will determine to what extent we assume responsibility for the world and the attitude we take toward the suffering that life entails. Nor will the answer always be clear; it more often may be ambiguous, demanding accommodation to suffering as well as resistance to it, acceptance as well as struggle. If this should turn out to be true, then we must know the proper time for each, neither deserting our battle stations before the ship has sunk nor claiming victory if the hulk alone remains afloat. Mere survival, either as individuals or even as a crew, is not enough. Evolution, we must hope, is more than just a "ship of fools." Certainly God expected more. May we not also?

A. Suffering and The Cosmic Christ

I have repeatedly alluded to the concept of a cosmic suffering, a process within which, to borrow St. Paul's words, "all creation groans and is in travail." The late monk-poet Thomas Merton wrote of Origen, the controversial theologian of early Christianity,

> Who thought he heard all beings
> From stars to stones, Angels to elements, alive
> Crying for the Redeemer with a live grief.[1]

What are we to think of this ancient theme? Is it merely poetic hyperbole, or is it to be taken seriously as an integral part of the Christian faith? And if so, what are its real implications for theodicy and for the problem of human suffering in particular?

Christ, it is true, did suffer in our place. He died, not only "for us and our salvation," but also in our "stead," taking upon himself the sufferings that we deserve. In this he can be said to have been the one "sacrifice" who is the cause of our redemption and our reconciliation with God. These salvational themes are familiar to all who have read or have been exposed to the New Testament, especially the Pauline writings. But this great work of "At-one-ment" is more than a legalistic justification or even a superimposition of God-life (grace) upon human nature. It is rooted in the Incarnation of God in his Son who has, in the language of the early Church Fathers, "become man that man might become God." No matter how often repeated, this seems too bold a statement, even taken metaphorically. Are we then to conclude that this great theme, drawn from the second-century Bishop Irenaeus (and also strongly favored by Origen a century or so later), is likewise too dangerous to be taken seriously?

If so, then we must back up a bit and take a serious look at some of the other related themes in Scripture, particularly those dealing with the sufferings of Christ. In the Epistle to the Colossians, for example, we are told that St. Paul is happy to "make up all that is lacking from the sufferings of Christ for the sake of his body, the Church" (Colossians 1:24; see footnote *m.* in *The Jerusalem Bible*). Does it not appear that it is no longer Jesus of Nazareth who died on the Cross who suffers but the Christ who was raised and glorified by the Father who now suffers in his followers? Had not Paul (the onetime Saul) been told that it was Jesus whom he had lately persecuted when he had delivered Christians over to be flogged and expelled from the Synagogues (Acts 9:4; compare with Galatians 1:13)? The identification is more than metaphorical: it is the same Jesus Christ who is now "the head of his Church; which is his body, the fullness of him who fills the whole creation" (Ephesians 1:23). Again, it is Christ as "Head" who both "holds the whole body together . . . the only way that it can reach its full growth in God" (Colossians 2:19), and yet does so in such a way that "the body grows until it has built itself up in love." The result of this is a growth that takes place "until we become the perfect Man, fully mature with the fullness of Christ himself" (Ephesians 4:16b and 13).

Two basic themes capture our attention in these passages. The first of these themes is the concept of Christ's Body, which is primarily identified with his Church and which displays a growth that is the result of a double movement: one the action of Christ, its head, and the other the action of the members, "every joint adding its own strength," and "each separate part working according to its function" (Ephesians 4:16a). The building up of this Body of Christ is thus a cooperative effort which, although always dependent on the life-giving presence of Christ in his members, is nevertheless also a function of the members. Each member contributes his or her own gifts, efforts, and suffering to the great work of bringing the whole body to its maturity as the New Man—the human race reconstituted in the image of Christ. It would appear that, for St. Paul, the image of Christ's Church as his Body is no mere metaphor, for the risen Christ is truly present in his members, who have sacramentally died and risen with him in Baptism and who are one body with him in the unity of the Eucharist (1 Corinthians 12:13; 10:17). This is the reason Paul was told it was "Jesus," not just Christians, that he had persecuted.

The second of these major themes follows from and expands the scope of the first. This combined divine-human effort, while unfinished, both looks forward to and is even now drawn by that fullness, that *plērōma* (to use the exact Pauline word here)[2] which designates both the source and the ultimate end of this great process. Thus it is that the formation of the complete Body of Christ is destined to reach its fulfillment in an even more comprehensive reality—the union of the whole universe with God. Yet a certain tension remains. If we read the texts very closely, we find that although in Christ's body "lies the *fullness* of divinity" (Colossians 2:9), and in his body-Church is to be found "the *fullness* of him who fills [*plēroumenou*] the whole universe" (Ephesians 1:23), there is nevertheless a certain incompleteness about all this until we "are filled with the utter *fullness* of God" (Ephesians 3:19), fully mature with *fullness* of Christ himself" (Ephesians 4:13).

It is in the context of the repetition of this highly charged word and the tension it displays between what is complete and what yet remains to be completed that we must turn again to the statement made in Colossians that the apostle is "happy to *make up*" (*antanaplērō*, a combination word that is unique in all the Scriptures) all that has still to be undergone by Christ for the sake of his body, the Church" (Colossians 1:24). We have to see that it is not simply a case of Christians suffering in imitation of Christ or in the footsteps of Jesus, as it is with one who patterns himself after a model. It is much more than that. We are people who actually find ourselves in a relationship of intensive and intimate sharing of these same sufferings. The Christian actually fills up what is still lacking in Christ's sufferings; he completes that which is otherwise incomplete. No doubt the historical Christ, Jesus of Nazareth, has suffered all he was to suffer, yet the glorified Christ, who is one with his Church-Body on earth, still suffers in that body and will continue to do so until God's purpose has been achieved when time has "run its course to the end [literally, for a dispensation of time's fullness] that he would bring everything together under Christ . . ." (Ephesians 1:10).

Obviously this multifaceted Pleroma of Christ, the fullness of God in him, the fullness of Christ to be accomplished in his body, the Church, the fullness of God's plan for creation—all this displays a variety of meaning and nuances that one word, no matter how versatile, can scarcely contain. Yet through all this, running like a golden thread through a variegated tapestry, this one word displays a general consistency. We are given a repeated glimpse of a wondrous reality that both exists in God and yet still seeks fulfillment in his universe, something that transcends time and yet speaks of its completion in time. It is active, in that the Pleroma is that which fills Christ and through him the Church and the universe, and yet it contains a certain "passive" quality, in that the Pleroma is in some manner still to be completed not only in but also through the universe, which as yet remains unfinished. This completion, however, cannot take place without the sum of sufferings that still remain to be undergone by and in the body of Christ in his Church.

There can be no question about the fact that this great process is both initiated and completed by God. In terms of the suffering involved, there is a repeated emphasis on the element of subjection. We can see this clearly in the remarkably pleromic passage of 1 Corinthians 15:28, where the final victory over evil and death is foretold "when everything is subjected to him," and "then the Son himself will be subject in his turn to the One who subjected all things to him, so that God may be all in all." There can be no doubt here of the fact that this subjection must be related to and seen as a remedial countermovement to that situation in which "all creation has been made subject to futility, not for any fault on the part of creation," but having been "made so by the work of him [God] who so subjected it" (Romans 8:20). From the Pauline perspective, of course, this whole movement of subjection was occasioned by original sin and the divine compassion that seeks to undo its effects.

Yet, we must ask, is not this subjection simply part of an even broader movement of co-creative love and unitive fulfillment? "From the beginning till now the entire creation . . . has been groaning in one great act of giving birth . . ." (Romans 8:22). Birth to what?

Here, at the risk of complicating even further an already difficult subject, it seems necessary to call attention to the fact that the Church has never made up its mind, officially, as to just how essential the Original Sin concept really is to our understanding of the Redemption. That it forms an essential part of the situation that needs remedy there can be no doubt. But is mankind's sinfulness the only reason that God became man? The whole Irenaean approach, that the Incarnation took place "so that man might become [as] God," implies that there is a higher reason to the Incarnation than just the remedying of sin. This broader approach seems to have become more and more forgotten as the ages passed, until John Duns Scotus, great thirteenth-century theologian, revived interest in the idea that the Incarnation would have taken place even without the need to atone for mankind's sinfulness. Thomas Aquinas opposed this view, but, interestingly, he seems finally to have admitted its validity in his "Compendium of Theology," written shortly before his death. In it he admits that even if sin had not occurred, it would seem fitting that God would become man so as to complete the great work of his creation by a kind of "circular movement" in which the Incarnation would enable all creation to be rejoined to its Maker.[3]

If such an opinion is admissible (and we could hardly ask for more traditional authorities to consider it so), then those who, like Teilhard, today insist that we expand our vision of the Incarnation and Redemption into a broader concept of Pleromization stand in very good company. From this broadened, more cosmic standpoint, our subjection to the law of sin is, as it were, only an unfortunate and perhaps unavoidable concomitant to this all-embracing state of subjection to the painful process involved in the growth and liberation of the universe. We suffer, not just because we deserve to, but as an essential part of our creatureliness. Our "passivity" (to take suffering in its root meaning) is also an activity, in that from it is wrought the material in which the fullness of creation is incorporated (made one body with) in the Pleroma of God.

In view of all this, however, need our outlook on suffering be passive? Must we not also, like Teilhard, eagerly seize upon the oft-repeated words that resound through the Pauline epistles? For not only do we "suffer with" and "die with" Christ, but we also "work with" and "rise with" him into the glory and freedom of "the children of God" in the "New Creation," the pleromic Kingdom of God.

B. Parousia and Transfiguration

From this cosmic or pleromic view of the Incarnation and Redemption, it should become clear that the experience of suffering must be lifted out of the realm of the isolated and purely subjective. A major part of the tragedy of suffering is the sense of isolation and alienation it produces, but Christians must understand that their sufferings are not undergone alone, but that "if one part [of the body] is hurt, all parts are hurt with it . . ." (1 Corinthians 12:26). Or if this seems too negative, then we must understand that if through our suffering some good results, then too we "make a unity in the work of service, building up the body of Christ" (Ephesians 4:12). From this point of view, no one's suffering or effort need be in vain. Even that suffering which appears to be useless is somehow caught up in the great movement in which, despite its seeming futility, all pain is transformed in the victory of Christ. No mere moral unanimity is expounded here, excellent as such spiritual solidarity may be. We become not merely imitators of Christ in his sufferings, but participants with him in his full coming-to-be.

Any such view, particularly one of such sweeping grandeur, is liable to distortion or misinterpretation. Because of its ability to view suffering from a positive standpoint, Christianity has been often thought of as a religion of suffering, and accused of reveling in it, glorifying it, or at least excusing it. The Cross continues to scandalize many sensitive persons and to affront many who would seek an escape from the tragedies of life. Others would object that it is precisely in its acceptance of suffering, both in imitation of and in union with Christ, that Christianity has failed to do all it could to alleviate suffering when it is possible to do so.

The belief in the *Parousia*, the Second Coming of Christ, is the theological and psychological touchstone that has, down through the ages, both determined the Christian view of the worth of this world and the struggle to live within its limitations. Strange as this assertion may seem, the evidence of history is inescapable. As long as infant Christianity clung to its expectation of an imminent return of the Savior, "the Son of Man seated at the right hand of the Power and coming on the clouds of heaven" (Matthew 26:64), the temptation was to consider this world as a passing phenomenon of little importance. Suffering remained only as a temporary prelude to a timeless *Eschaton* or end-state of eternal glory. As time passed, however, and nothing happened, the Kingdom of God that the Synoptic Gospels constantly proclaim as being "close at hand" came to be almost entirely misunderstood, partly by a preferential misuse of the formula, "Kingdom of Heaven" (used in Matthew in accordance with the Jewish preference of avoiding overuse of the divine name) and partly by an almost constant mistranslation of "is among you" as "within you" in Luke 17:21.

True, there was a gradual evolution, even within the New Testament, toward a more realized eschatology, one in which the Kingdom was seen to already exist, both in the glorified Christ and in his Church. This reversal of outlook reached a culmination first in the Constantinian Era and again in the High Middle Ages, when Christianity found itself in a most-favored position as heir to the classical cultures of the past, the bedrock of political and social stability, and the patron of all that was new in the arts and sciences.

However, when times became difficult, when the Church itself became corrupt, or when life itself became oppressive, there would be a revival either of apocalyptic imminence, with prophecies of a soon-to-be accomplished return of Christ, or else—or even sometimes in conjunction with it—there would be a new emphasis on the essential interiority of the Kingdom within souls, leading to an otherworldly fulfillment in heaven.

There can be no doubt that the tension between these two views of eschatology has been in many ways beneficial, despite the conflict, even bloodshed, it has occasioned. It fueled the demands for reform and lit the fires of a fervent mysticism. Without the conflict between the "already" and the "not yet," Christianity might long ago have settled down to one or the other extreme—smug, worldly triumphalism or an unworldly disdain of all human progress. Yet even while avoiding the more extreme positions, widely varying interpretations can be placed on the ultimate significance of our lives in this world and on the worth of creation itself.

I am reminded here of an experience that struck me most

forcibly in this regard. Years ago, touring the great Cathedral of Salisbury, I moved with awed admiration among the tombs of bishops, abbots, and noble men and women of many centuries past, whose serene and stylized effigies depicted them in peaceful sleep awaiting the great resurrection at the end of time. But then I was brusquely jolted by the gruesome tomb lids depicting the cadaverous and decaying remains of those who were buried later, during the height of the Renaissance. It was as if the plagues and other disasters of the later Middle Ages were a watershed separating the earlier period, when life, for all its violence, was inspired by a vision of a great and glorious beyond, from the more recent period, which, despite all its opulence and the revival of classical culture, had nothing to offer for the future except corruption. The joyful hope of resurrection seemed to have been dashed on the infernal brimstones of despair. Transfiguration had given way to decomposition, eternal life to eternal death.

Perhaps I have taken this experience too seriously, or am guilty of a literalism that has misread the artisan's intent. All those who were buried there and those who were commissioned to adorn their tombs were, presumably, fairly orthodox Christians. Both the sculptors and the deceased believed, we might suppose, in the resurrection of the dead. But how did they envision it?

Traditionally, including both eras in my illustration, eschatology, as it has come to be termed, has dwelt on the "Four Last Things": Death, Judgment, Heaven, and Hell, with Purgatory and Resurrection dealt with as corollaries. However, what is most significant is that almost without exception, these beliefs were visualized primarily in individualistic terms, without any thought of the possible incorporation of the physical universe. Even in Dante's great trilogy, which manifests a striking awareness of the Communion of Saints, the shared glory of Paradise, the beseeching state of the souls in Purgatory, and the contrasting total alienation from all that is human and divine of those who languish in the Inferno, the vivid imagery gives little indication of any need to be taken literally. There seems to be no indication that resurrection, either for glory or punishment, was to be understood as anything actually fulfilling, much less involving, the restoration of the universe in Christ. Others may interpret this quite differently and prove me wrong, but I suspect that there has been little attempt or even motivation to do otherwise.

If so, there should not be much surprise. The doctrine of the Resurrection, not only of "the Dead," but even of Christ, has occasioned not only quite an amount of debate but even more silence through the centuries. Even in the New Testament we find some diversity if not outright difficulty in expression. The empty tomb stories seem to have been, at least at first, a separate and quite different approach as contrasted to the accounts of the mysterious post-resurrection appearances of Christ, depicting him as physically present, eating and drinking with his apostles and disciples. Yet both approaches, particularly in the latter, with Jesus instantaneously passing from their sight, seem to hint at a kind of experience that defies description and can only resort to confused stories as a way of proclaiming that Jesus is no longer dead. Even as early as the Pauline Epistles, however, we find yet another approach, in which the risen body of Christ seems to be identified entirely with the Eucharistic Body of Christ and his sacramental presence in the Church. "You," Paul writes the Corinthians, "together are Christ's body" (1 Corinthians 12:27), or again, the Church "is his body—and we are its living parts" (Ephesians 5:30).

Yet this identification of living Christians as the living Body of Christ does not, for Paul, eliminate the need of or the promise of future resurrection for those Christians who have died. Long passages, particularly as found in 1 Corinthians 15, wrestle with the problem of expressing the nature of resurrected life, and particularly the relationship of the resurrected body to the body as it once existed in this life. "Everything that is flesh is not the same [kind of] flesh: . . . there are heavenly bodies and there are earthly bodies . . ." (1 Corinthians 15:39, 40). "It is the same with the resurrection of the dead: the thing that is sown is perishable but what is raised is imperishable . . ." (1 Corinthians 15:42).

The key to understanding Paul's attempt to express what seems inexpressible is to be found in verse 44 of the same chapter. "When it [the earthly body] is sown it embodies the soul, when it is raised it embodies the spirit." We must remember that, while Paul based his ideas in a Hebrew anthropology, his use of the Greek word for soul *(psychē)* has no corresponding concept in Hebrew. There is for him no natural, immortal, immaterial self that guarantees life after death. Hence it is only by virtue of the "spirit" *(pneuma)* given by God that life after death becomes possible. Yet it is, at the same time, a life in a body—the only kind of life that there can be for a human creature. This is possible only because the Christian's natural life, the combination of body *(soma)* and soul *(psychē)*, has been transformed by God's Holy Spirit and has, already in this life, been incorporated into the risen body of Christ. Without this action of the Spirit the natural body remains dominated by sin and is destined to the destruction awaiting all mere flesh *(sarx)*.

These distinctions are important, for only with their help can we begin to make any sense of the seeming contradictions regarding the fate of the physical universe in terms of a wider, more universal *Eschaton*, one that must include St. Paul's vision of "all creation" destined to share "in the freedom of the children of God" (Romans 8:21). How otherwise can we even begin to account for the juxtaposition of such phrases as those found in 2 Peter 3:10–13, where we are told that "with a roar the sky will vanish, the elements will catch fire and fall apart, the earth and all it contains will be burnt up. . ." and yet "what we are waiting for is what he promised: the new heavens and new earth. . ."? Even allowing for this much later author's change of perspective and for his penchant for quoting the Old Testament prophets, how do we explain this double insistence on both the destruction *and* the reconstitution of the material universe? Again, even when we make allowances for the overwhelmingly apocalyptic style of The Book of Revelation, we find this same dramatic contrast between themes of total destruction and total renovation of the physical universe, including again the use of the same Isaian passage prophesying "a new heaven and a new earth" (Revelation 21:1; cf. Isaiah 65:17).

True, for many these themes of cosmic upheaval and recreation are to be explained "spiritually" as fantasies of apocalyptic imagery, eminently suited to a period when the traditional motifs of "classical" Old Testament prophecy had given way to the more visionary expressions of "the last days." Quite the opposite from what we might expect, when the literary style had turned so highly imaginative (who could take literally the ideas of beasts with ten horns or creatures with "eyes" all over?), literal belief in the resurrection of the body became strongest. Hence Jesus himself took a very strong stand on this issue against the skeptical Sadducees, even agreeing with the Pharisees—something he did not often do. Yet, at the same time, Jesus undercut the skeptics' crude arguments against resurrection (when they brought up the "case" of successive marriages—"whose wife will she be?") by roundly denouncing his critics for their crude materialism. But as for the supposed "dead," they are not dead, said Jesus, for their God "is the God of the living" (see Luke 21:27–38).

For those who have taken the doctrine of the Resurrection seriously (which includes most Jews who have taken the idea of eternal life seriously), the future life after the great Parousia at the end of all time has never been envisioned as a world of disembodied souls. Even during the periods when hopes concerning the transformation of the universe became clouded, traditional theologians such as St. Thomas Aquinas stoutly maintained that the full realization of beatific life must include that of a resurrected physical existence. One medieval pope even expressed to his dying day—much to the alarm of his theological advisers—his firm conviction that the souls in heaven could not be completely happy until such an event had occurred!

How can we envision such a resurrection except in terms of a relationship to and an existence within a resurrected universe? If a permanent state of disembodied existence, conceived in terms more suitable to Platonic idealism than biblical realism, seems out of kilter with traditional Christian belief, can a paradise of physically resurrected human beings existing without any contact with a transformed universe make any more sense? If one begins by denying the latter possibility, then belief in the resurrection of the individual seems entirely pointless, and one may well end up, as have many modern Christians, denying the Resurrection of Christ, in any physical or "real" sense. St. Paul's incisive polemic against such spiritualistic interpretations proves that the tendency is hardly "modern." "If there is no resurrection from the dead, Christ himself cannot have been raised . . . and if Christ has not been raised, you are still in your sins. And what is more serious, all who have died in Christ have perished" (1 Corinthians 15:13, 17–18).

St. Paul's argument may appear a bit strident to some, and curious in its reverse logic (the latter trait common to the style of rabbinic discourse), but it may be also very much to the point for the modern mind. In this day when Whiteheadian metaphysics or Teilhardian hyperphysics have contributed a plausible explanation of the facts of evolutionary process, it is even more curious to find Christians whose major problems with basic Christian doctrines (like the Resurrection and the Eucharist, to take two very appropriate examples in this matter) seem to arise principally from outmoded concepts of matter/spirit or body/soul dualism than from any other logically traceable reason.

By this I am not trying to say that one can "prove" the Resurrection of Christ or of anyone else by means of modern metaphysics, much less by the physics that they seek to explain. What I am saying is, that while the classic philosophies of ancient Greece may have given us useful conceptual tools to wrestle with the problems of faith, as often as not they again produced almost as many problems as solutions. The earthy, and very often crude, realism of the Hebrews, especially when it comes to anthropology, has turned out to be a lot closer to the facts than the rarefied, but often thoroughly dualistic, thinking behind much of Greek idealism.

It may be just because the Church recognized the clash between the biblical approach to these matters and that of the Greeks, that Christians have always had the freedom to reinterpret these ideas, while preserving the essential actuality of Christ's Resurrection and a similar belief in the destiny of us all. Even St. Paul seemed ill at ease with a gross literalism that thought of resurrection in terms of a future reconstitution of our present physical existence. There is clearly in his thought, as well as in the Gospels, a distinct discontinuity between earthy preresurrectional and spiritual (perhaps better rendered "spiritualized") postresurrected life. They exist on two different planes. Life after death, even in a resurrected physical existence, is not merely a prolongation of the present life. It is something else entirely. But it is still our life, that of a personality formed in the flesh and continuing to exist in relationship to that "embodiedness" which is the root of our individuality. Beyond this nothing can be said for sure.

Even this much can throw a great deal of light on the meaning of suffering, especially physical pain and death. Although ideally all suffering in the body can be seen as contributing to "the making of souls," as theologians such as John Hick would have it, nevertheless we know from sad experience that this does not always prove to be so. Some persons collapse or become entirely embittered by their sufferings. To hint that if they had been of higher moral stamina they would have benefited rather than succumbed is a gratuitous assertion implying that we, in their place, would have proved more resolute. The plain facts are otherwise. All too often suffering is, as Hick admits, entirely excessive and, in effect, unredeemed. How do we explain this in a universe ordered entirely, on the physical plane, toward the production of immortal souls destined for a completely spiritual existence? As a miscalculation or even a "mean streak" in God? That would seem too much, even for someone who would modify his beliefs about the power of God, limiting it to the possession of "all the power necessary to achieve his ends" (Schilling, in *God and Human Anguish*, p. 189).

On the contrary, if we assume that this creative process is an evolutionary one in which matter and spirit form a single con-

tinuum of existence, then suffering, both physical and psychological (which cannot really be separated in such a world view), is
unavoidable. Rather than being ordered by God in hopes that
suffering will prove beneficial (implying that God might have ordered things in some alternative manner to the same end), suffering
remains the basic law of all existence that seeks greater being. This
is not to say that some suffering does not appear to be altogether
excessive in terms of not having been deserved by its victims, nor is
it to deny that the human race itself has often been guilty of increasing the amount of suffering far beyond what was necessary.
But it is also to say that, generally speaking, suffering occurs where
there is growth taking place.

The implications of this, if we can admit it, are immense. If
suffering, even only in the sense of physical pain, occurs in the
universe, it is not just because God commands it as a trial, or even
just permits it as an unavoidable by-product in the evolutionary
process. It is more than these. It is the catalyst of the process itself,
and this on *all* levels. This means that suffering or its equivalent,
whatever it may be, is part of a cosmic process. Because this activity occurs on all levels of existence, from the rending of the earth's
crust and the pain of the smallest sensitive creatures, to the psychological agonies suffered by humans, it also must mean that all these
levels of the universe are also in some way destined for and ordered
toward a higher, transfigured, or even resurrected existence! Thus
if all creation, as St. Paul has told us, has been "groaning" and "in
travail," it may not just be for the sake of the appearance of the
human race or for its redemption. It has also been so that all
creatures too might in some way share "the freedom of the sons of
God."

This is why, although one might speak of a certain recalci-
trance in the structure of things that resists transformation and in
so doing occasions further pain or suffering, we might also speak
of a kind of unbounded exuberance within nature. Thus nature
unceasingly attempts new combinations and recombinations of existence, with the whole mass of evolving energies, ranging from the
most basic building blocks of material existence to the highest
psychic forces, engaged in a relentless drive toward more and fuller
being. It is almost as if there is an inborn pleromic tendency within
creation itself. Although limited by the particular patterns of nature that this world has assumed out of a host of other theoretical
possibilities, nature nevertheless tries every avenue of development
that remains open within the limits imposed by chance, whether it

turns out to be a dead end or not. Evolution will not cease, Teilhard once wrote, until "everything possible has been tried." "Boundless, abstract possibility," according to Whitehead, is part of that creativity which has its origin in God. Creativity is perhaps the key idea here when we speak of *Resurrection, transformation,* or *transfiguration.* All these words, each in their own context, speak of an ongoing creation, a divine-human partnership that cannot be ultimately thwarted by sin or death, even if it be the natural death of the universe. Despite the centrality of the Cross, Christians have always known their belief to be a resurrection-Faith, an unshakable confidence in an unending future. On this transcendental dimension everything depends.

Ernst Bloch, the Marxist philosopher who was exiled to the West because of his unorthodox stance, has understood the problem thus: Communism has attracted followers and held their allegiance as long as a better future was far off enough to give the illusion of a paradise ahead. Once the worker's paradise begins to materialize, it soon displays all the emptiness of any crass materialism with its wholesale betrayal of the spirit of man. It is a philosophy of evolution, but of an evolutionary dead-end. Christianity will survive long after Marxism has died, because Christianity, despite all its failings, has nevertheless kept a transcendental image before mankind. Sometimes a distorted image, or a tarnished one, but it has been this image of a future of endless possibility that has been and will continue to be its eternal strength. If Bloch's analysis is correct, then what has to be said is that while Communism has lacked a transforming faith to see beyond the limitations of this present world, what Christianity has so often lacked is enough imagination to see what its faith would mean for this world if it were ever put fully into practice. Rather than an "opium of the people" stultifying with promises of "pie in the sky" in the face of suffering, a fully Christian world vision would be the great energizer mobilizing the totality of human resources in an onslaught against human misery.

Indeed, if a so-called "liberation theology" is viewed with some alarm by many Christians today, the real reason is not because it shares any theoretically materialistic basis with Communiusm. It is rather becaues it refuses to go along with the practical materialism of Christians who are content with the status quo, with the piece of pie they have already! The battle today is really not between East and West, Capitalist and Communist. The battle line cuts almost evenly across all national allegiances, religious confessions, and even political ideologies. It is a battle of quality versus quantity, over whether there is to be a better future for the human race or simply more of the same.

C. *The Accomplishment of the Kingdom*

The destiny of the universe is both in and out of our hands. In reality three factors—the divine, the human, and the cosmic—all have a part to play. Too often this last element is forgotten. Despite the whimsical musings of philosophers and science fiction writers, time is irreversible. The entropic consummation of energy shows little sign of abatement, and while astrophysicists may speculate on the hypothetical possibilities of a universe of "reciprocating" eons or even a yet-to-be-discovered "steady state," all substantiated evidence points to a single "big bang" that is slowly but inexorably leading toward a final cosmic death of all creation. Even apart from the remotely possible accident that could bring a sudden, premature end to this planet, we must face the fact that, by all accepted calculations, our own life-supporting star, the sun, is near the mid-point of its ten-billion-year life span, and for only a portion of that span is the sun capable of supporting life on earth. Barring the unlikely possibility of human colonization of another planet in another solar system, the future of the human race is already clearly limited, and schemes to extend these limits do not change the basic dilemma. Dreams of natural infinitude are dashed on the crumbling rocks of reality. The final hour for the human race might be postponed but not ultimately avoided.

Given this cosmic timetable, what other possibilities remain? Here the other two factors come most clearly into play. Apart from the cosmic limits of existence, both God and humanity may very well place further limits on the future. The human race already has reached the point where it can self-destruct, bringing not only all its civilizations but even its existence to a screeching, flaming halt. Or God, in his wisdom or even in his rage, could intervene at any time. Yet all indications are that God would not do so. God's ancient pledge, given in the story of Noah, was that God would never again destroy all life. Mankind may well save God the trouble; any sudden end to human history will most likely be our doing, not God's.

Instead, what God, in his redeeming love, seems intent on is transforming the best of the human effort into his Kingdom and transfiguring the sufferings of all creation into the substance of the "new heavens and new earth." It is God alone who will place the capstone on all history and who alone is capable of making it into the edifice of his Kingdom. Otherwise all human effort remains as surely doomed as the universe that gave it birth.

Yet, for all this, the human effort remains critical, for what can be transformed by God except that which has been made subject to him through his Son? Yet what will be made subject to the Son except that which has already been subjected by the human race for God's own purposes? This is the great pleromic "chain of being," of all things, and of all the sufferings that it took to produce them, that can be incorporated into the fullness of God's existence, "that God may be all in all."

The implications of this pleromic view are immense. For too long we have neatly divided the world between the secular and the sacred. For too long the humble efforts of ordinary men and women have been put down as inconsequential compared to the divine work of "saving souls." For too long people have been counselled to bear their sufferings patiently, no matter how destructive to self or society. We are surely called to suffer, but this suffering must be for the sake of building up the structure of God's Kingdom and not the destruction of the human, earthly foundations on which it will stand. True, these foundations must be made on the rock of faith and not on the shifting sands of merely human hopes. But the whole structure, from bottom to top, can be achieved only in a combined effort of human work and divine grace.

Similarly, on the human level, the work of building the earth into a structure worthy of God's plans for creation must be seen as a cooperative venture involving all races, all nations, and all individuals. Every task, if it helps the total edifice to take shape, must be considered as a vital component in the overall scheme of things. Like St. Paul's description of the Body-Church of Christ, in which each member has its proper function with no one part replaceable by another, this pleromic view of the universe demands that the distinctive contribution of each individual's vocation be acknowledged precisely in terms of its complementary relationship to the whole. Rather than reducing humanity to an amorphous category of "the masses," as opposed to a fragmented collection of isolated individuals, the true Kingdom of God must be seen as personalistic in the highest sense of the word, a higher union that leads to greater differentiation. We must not obscure the paramount importance of certain callings, especially those dedicated to the greatest needs and highest aspirations of the human race. Nor should we overlook the wide variations in talents that persons can bring to this service. But, most of all, we must accord deep respect to the unique contribution that each one is capable of making, if for no other reason than that each person is truly unique.

As a result, the sufferings of each person must also be seen as unique but not isolated. The struggles that each one undergoes in achieving his or her destiny may be, in many ways, not unlike those of the next person, yet at the same time they are this person's unique payment of the price demanded of the whole human race in its quest for fulfillment and greater being. More important, we must understand that even senseless evils—apparently useless suffering, tragic accidents, natural catastrophes, even outrageous crimes against innocents—are in some sense redeemable if they are considered in this light. None of them cease to be tragic, particularly when they could have been avoided; nevertheless, the pains that are caused need not be entirely wasted. Even more than the seeming dead ends that have occurred in the course of evolution and yet paved the way for other eventualities, the apparently senseless sufferings undergone by the human race have often proved to be the springboards from which new leaps of human achievement have taken place.

This is not to say that all evil is necessarily turned into good or that every tragedy leads eventually to a happy ending. Even the optimistic message of St. Paul that "everything turns out for the good" is modified by the specification "for those who love God," and even that is seen only as a result of God's cooperation (Romans 8:28). This seems only possible, in many cases, in terms of a future life. In terms of life in this world, God cooperates with us as our "fellow sufferer," much as Whitehead has told us. For the Christian, especially, as God "goes on working," so does his Son (John 5:17). But just as God can be said to be our fellow worker, so too he is in some way our fellow gambler, "hoping against hope" and trusting that all will not have proved to have been in vain. In this sense the great Blondelian theme of the essence of being in this world as "Action" is manifested, not only as the activity of building the earth but also in the passivity of suffering, which is transformed in the struggle of evolution.

It is here, much in terms of "la grande option" that so preoccupied Teilhard de Chardin in his waning years, that faith finds its greatest challenge. For those who, as Bertrand Russell told us, see the universe only as an accidental collection of atoms doomed, just as accidentally, to a final dissolution, the only rational attitude is indeed one of "unyielding despair." That the human race has become, in Julian Huxley's apt phrase, "evolution become conscious of itself" only makes matters worse, for if we are destined to total extinction just as surely as the lowliest microorganism, then nothing, not even the greatest joys or achievements of the human race, much less the sufferings and struggles of human and brute creatures alike, amounts to the slightest cause for self-congratulation or even, for that matter, a rational cause for regret. What is simply is, and what has been or will be is of no real concern nor should it be. Nihilism will have won its way and evolution, rather than being "open-ended," will have proved only to have been a long passage leading to a final, irrevocably closed door.

Little wonder that our ancestors in the faith, although living in a very different age with its own world views, nevertheless saw the future of the world and the meaning of their sufferings in terms that ultimately pointed to eternity for their justification and the grounds for any possible hope. The origin and the future of evolution remain, just as much as a simple creation coming directly from the hands of God, a mystery encompassed by a fathomless doubt. Only faith can lift the veil that enshrouds the void before time, and only a faith-founded hope can assure us that there will be any future. For Christians today God has not so much made man as "God makes man make himself." But this does not so much change the dilemma of suffering or the conditions of the human struggle as it modifies the choice of how we seek to fight. As our ancestors had realized, so we must also realize that any lasting victory can come only when, after we have done our utmost to defeat evil in all its many forms, God himself will return in the person of his Son, the "Firstborn of all creation . . . the Firstborn from the dead" (Colossians 1:15, 18).

It is this expectation of the Kingdom, this longing for the Parousia, that has been the core of all hope and the touchstone of all renewed vitality in Christian life. Understood in many ways, sometimes naively, impatiently, and unrealistically, or sometimes lethargically, even cynically, the first recorded liturgical prayer of Christians beyond the one given to them by the Master himself resounds with this undying hope for the future and the faith that nothing need have been in vain. "Maranatha!" "Come Lord!"

Only then, when he will have come, will all the problems of evil, as lived within the course of evolution, be resolved in the mystery of God.

Notes

1. The above quote is taken from Thomas Merton's poem, "Origen," which first appeared in *New Directions in Prose and Poetry* 19; edited by James Laughlin (New York: New Directions, 1966), pp. 288–89. It appeared again in *The Collected Poems of Thomas Merton* (New York: New Directions, 1977) pp. 640–41. While one might question the introduction of poetic musings at this point, I have submitted the above passage as a kind of counterbalance and leitmotif to the rather involved discussion which follows. Merton's point here seems to have been to concretely represent the spirit of Origen's theory of *apokatastasis* or "restoration" of creation in Christ, a popular theme of early patristic theology paralleling and complementing the even earlier Irenaean theme of *anakephalaiōsis* or "recapitulation" of the universe in Christ. As George A. Maloney, S.J., has eloquently proved in *The Cosmic Christ: From Paul to Teilhard* (New York: Sheed & Ward, 1968), Teilhard's theme of "Pleromization" directly continues this same theological tradition.

2. The Greek word *plērōma*, which I have rendered as "fullness" in the passages that follow, has also been translated as "completion," "complement," or "plenitude." Probably drawn from Stoic or even Gnostic sources (as seems to be the case with the Pauline body-head theme), the word becomes a prominent part of the Pauline vocabulary in the later pastoral epistles (most notably in Colossians and Ephesians) to which many exegetes assign authorship other than Paul himself. However, the appearance of this word *plērōma* in these later epistles is in continuity with a similar theme, that of 1 Corinthians 15:28, where Paul speaks of God, through the subjection of the universe in Christ, as becoming "All in all" (*pantos en pasin*). For a more detailed discussion of the various sense of this word as it appears in the Pauline Epistles, the reader is referred to my earlier study of this question: Richard W. Kropf, *Teilhard, Scripture, and Revelation: A Study of Teilhard de Chardin's Reinterpretation of Pauline Themes* (Rutherford, Madison, Teaneck, N.J.: Fairleigh Dickinson University Press, 1980), especially Chapter 5.

3. Cf. especially Chapter 201 on "Other Reasons for the Incarnation," Thomas Aquinas, *Compendium of Theology*, translated by Cyril Vollert (St. Louis: B. Herder Book Co., 1947), p. 216. For citations from John Duns Scotus as well as references to Karl Rahner and others backing this point of view, the reader is directed to Gabriel M. Allegra, O.F.M., *My Conversations with Teilhard de Chardin on the Primacy of Christ: Peking, 1942–1945* (Chicago: Franciscan Herald Press, 1971).

Epilogue
From Denial to Acceptance:
A Personal Reflection

Over the years it has struck me more and more how people not only manage to survive but even to prosper, in spite of the most perilous circumstances. Listening to survivors of war experiences, reading the stories of those who have lived through great disasters, or talking to those who have undergone many months or even years of seemingly fruitless medical treatment, I am continually confronted by one question: had they known what was in store for them, would they (or would I) have had the courage to go on? The answer that I am continually tempted to arrive at is: no; the reason that they managed to live through the experience was that they did not realize at the time that they were in such danger or that the odds against their survival were so great.

This may be a rather cynical view, gratuitously given by one who has never had to endure such hardship or uncertainty. Perhaps I have failed to reckon with the fears they may have had before the event happened, fears that may have been harder to conquer than the experience itself. Similarly, I have left faith too much out of the picture, a faith that may have been all the greater for the fear it had to contend with. My tendency to overlook these other factors may indicate a hidden preference for not anticipating things, a covert belief that the blissfully ignorant are in some way better off than those whose realism may be overwrought.

If so, why attempt to write such a book as this? Would it not be better to simply leave people alone and not ask them to think about such things, lest in anticipating too much they fear and lose

179

heart? Or, if people suddenly find themselves in the midst of some catastrophe, would it not be better to let them muster whatever faith they have and cope with the situation on that basis, no matter how poorly thought out or even distorted that faith may be? After all, if one way or another, they actually do survive, why quibble? Is not survival the whole point of evolution in the end?

Perhaps so, but I am not entirely convinced of that. It seems that there is something more, something more significant that would argue for the superiority of humans over houseflies, some consciousness and freedom that make a few years of intelligent awareness infinitely more valuable than eons of unconscious tenacity.

In any case, after this comprehensive sweep of the whole matter of evil and its existence in God's universe, it is questions like these that bring me back full circle to the place we started—our insistence on the problematic quality of evil in the face of divine mystery. Certainly the distinction invites reconsideration, especially when one is forced to admit the difference between thoughts about living and the actual living of life.

Marcel's rather loose distinction between *problem* as amenable to intellectual solution and *mystery* as demanding lived participation was invoked. Yet almost immediately Marcel's insistence on evil as mystery was rejected, at least on the basis of his contention that "all explanations fail." I do not admit that they do, at least as far as they go. To the contrary, I think that I have made a comprehensible case as to why there is and must be evil in the universe, a great deal of which is experienced as unfair. Likewise, I think I have shown that there is a very logical coherence in the connection between this interplay of chance and the accidents it brings in its wake and the kind of universe God seems to have intended when wished to share his creation with beings who would share in his own freedom and love. If there is any mystery here, beyond the strictly theological sense of a truth that cannot nor ever will be penetrated completely by human reason, it must be in this creative expression of God's own nature as it is found in humans themselves.

Yet as soon as we begin to talk about such an expression of God's design in human life, we have to admit with Marcel that to some degree there is something mysterious about human life and the part that evil plays in it. In this sense the problems posed by the existence of evil have to be more than abstractly analyzed; they have to be lived through and contended with as part of the even more positively mysterious process of human life.

It is at this point, however, that the beginning of this book and the observation made at the beginning of this postscript coincide, or maybe collide. If people seem to survive better on the basis of not realizing or fully understanding what they are going through, would this not suggest that the problem of evil should be left to the speculations of intellectuals and that most people are better off when left in a "mysterious" state of confusion? Might they not, in knowing the whole state of affairs, especially the mystery of a God who may in some way suffer with us, lose their trusting faith altogether?

Again, I must disagree. The reason for this disagreement is not some conviction of the intellectual superiority of my position. It is based on my own appreciation of the truth that is experienced as part of the process of living. In the twenty some years since I began pastoral work, as well as in the more recent years when study and teaching brought the opportunities for friendships intermixed with pastoral concerns that were often much more sustained than most of those I experienced in parish work, I have learned a great deal. More vital still, however, has been my own life experience in the four years between the inception of the actual writing of this book and its completion—the death of both of my parents, the death, after a long battle with cancer, of the aunt to whom I dedicated this book, and the deaths of others too numerous to name here.

Nor was it just the experience of living with the dying. There were the survivors to deal with: my father who agonized over my mother's long paralysis; my cousins and uncle who were daily faced with the task of groping for the proper words and, after their loss, with the apparent senselessness of it all. Finally, there was myself. Perhaps it was the hardest for me, for trying to respond to their assumption that I somehow had all the answers, or that I should be expected to have them, there was also the camouflaging of my need to understand my own suffering. It almost seems that thought was out of touch with life; that the shoemaker himself was barefoot and, what is worse, did not even realize it!

Most of all, it has been in the process of sharing a close friend's loss that I began to understand my own. In so doing I also began to experience in a much more personal way the stages described by Dr. Elizabeth Kübler-Ross in her studies of dying patients. What I had observed in people who actually faced certain death, and had sensed too in the living who had to repeat the process in themselves as survivors, I now felt most fully in myself the denial, the bargaining, the anger, and finally, but never totally, the acceptance.

"Time heals." So I was told (as I had so often told others). And yet, I know that that is not entirely true. Perhaps the keenness of the reactions dulls in time, yet the pain is still there. Time in itself accomplishes very little except forgetfulness, and very often does an imperfect job at that. Bargaining usually must give way to anger when there is no longer any possible deal to be won. Open anger is just as often replaced by depression as by acceptance, and I have frequently seen where lifelong denial seems to have been the only way out. In such cases deliberate oblivion replaces any catharsis that time might have allowed. When such a "solution" has been achieved, we must persist in asking: "at what price?"

Could it be that the acceptance wrought by time is only apparent, not unlike (in fact often accompanied by) anger that has been repressed and turned within? If so, I would in both instances judge that the last state may be no better than the first. The denial of the full reality of the tragic in our lives amounts to an attempt to live in a blissful ignorance that would avoid the hard questions of theodicy. To passively wish for time to cure all ills is not too different from a wish to lobotomize our memories or to rewrite our personal history in the fashion that has so appealed to families, institutions, and nations that would prefer, if they could, to forget the past. As individuals we are nevertheless part of these structures, and so we reproduce their reactions to evil.

Kübler-Ross's stages of dying or confronting loss seem particularly fruitful here. If the old evolutionary law of "recapitulation"—that ontogeny imitates phylogeny—is applicable in a psychological and sociological sense, the reverse is probably even more true. Whole societies, as Ernest Becker eloquently pointed out, engage in a systematic denial of death. Whole industries are built upon it. Some would single out the typical American funeral home as a prime example, although Kübler-Ross thinks that the medical profession as a whole is even less able to cope with death. If denial is so widespread, then there should be no surprise that bargaining plays the next most prevalent role. Here is where the medical care industry surely plays the lead, transforming the denial of death into a less preposterous but nevertheless just as futile attempt to ward off the inevitable with prospects of cures or remissions of often very dubious quality.

But I would be very much less than honest to point my finger at these professions while ignoring my own. When it comes to denial and bargaining, the martyred theologian Bonhoeffer most cannily summed up the situation when he accused Christianity of having turned itself into just another religion—*religion* in the sense of an emotional and ritualized escape hatch from reality. In so doing Christianity has vitiated the central meaning of the Incarnation as well as its central symbol, the Cross. It is only in dying to ourselves (which includes facing the whole truth) that we will live. It has been this challenge of Bonhoeffer's "worldly Christianity" that has rightly been identified by the conservative reaction as the cause of much of the upset in the Church today. Theologically speaking, much of the New Theology that led to Vatican II, dominated it, and kept its effects alive has been of this tone. To the extent that we can talk of theology as psychologically motivated, there has been a new determination to purge religion, or at least the Christian religion, of its regression to the functions of denial and bargaining. We can hardly be surprised at the bitter reaction to this movement, for anger forms the next step in the normal course of things.

Unlike denial and bargaining, phases that may be very brief or absent entirely in more mature personalities, I have found that *anger* is almost bound to be present in one form or another, even though it may be very much disguised. This is partly because the targets of the anger also can vary a great deal, ranging all the way from God to oneself. Very often, however, the anger may be directed toward the deceased (for having abandoned the living) or may be projected on an innocent third party. In any case, I believe that some expression of anger is entirely normal and to be expected. Perhaps it should even be encouraged in some way, lest reversion to a less realistic state, such as perpetual denial, occur. In this regard, however, some interesting dimensions of faith (or its lack) are revealed.

If denial and bargaining seem to be the weaknesses of misunderstood and misused religion, atheism may very often be the result of unresolved anger over the seeming unfairness of life. Belief in God, even an unjust God, provides a focus for this anger. I have known people, even firm believers, who were outraged at God and yet, finding their outrage not returned in kind, eventually found also forgiveness and acceptance. The doctrinaire atheist, of course, cannot allow himself this failing of faith, and thus, paradoxically, atheism of this sort would seem to defeat its own purpose. However, it would seem that the very act of denying God as such may serve as an expression of anger that brings with it a certain catharsis. Although the agnostic can perhaps feel all this emotionally, but not being able to identify the objects of feeling with any sureness, he or she becomes the more susceptible to repression of anger and the depression that is almost certain to ensure. In fact, Kübler-Ross has something very interesting to say on this matter: she and her team of counsellors had generally found that when patients were told of their impending deaths, the two types who seemed to achieve acceptance most readily were either strong, even simple, believers on the one hand, or else outright unbelievers, on the other. It seems that those who were weak believers (which implies weak unbelievers as well) had the greatest difficulty in facing the truth. Hate cannot be translated into denial where there is not some residue of affirmation or at least rejected love. One cannot help wondering whether the final "acceptance" offered by a truly rigorous, thoroughgoing atheism would not also have to imply a total nihilism, the denial of a value to life or of the evolutionary process itself.

It is most likely for this same or similar reasons that some would protest that the "process" concept of a "suffering God" elicits some alarm, for such a God does not fit the description of the supremely "simple" God of traditional theism, nor does it, on the other hand, provide the easy scapegoat for the atheists' rage.

Aside from these extremes of either total, unquestioning belief or of total rejection of all unseen, hence "unproved" values, the problem of anger becomes even more complex. Rumination over the past can always turn up a multitude of shortcomings, of failed commitments or irresponsible decisions or occasionally of outright stupidity. No one has a corner on the market for these. Thus for almost every tragedy, even the unpreventable "acts of God," a host of "could have beens" can be conjured up to haunt and taunt us. "If only I had done thus or so. . . ." "If only I had foreseen. . . ." One can torture oneself for life with thoughts like these or die in a state of self-inflicted martyrdom to what needs no proof—our common humanity. Many apparently choose to do so, living their lives in a prolonged state of depression that amounts to a living suicide. Almost all cases of depression are simply of rage turned against oneself, of anger turned outside in.

Acceptance can be understood according to a wide variety of contexts, ranging from that of the terminal patient who knows death is imminent to the bereaved who knows that life must go on. Acceptance also has to cover a wide range of other life possibilities as well, from the very personal but common middle-aged crisis of the possible limits of one's realizable ambitions to the very impersonal but nevertheless very real restrictions placed upon us by economic, political, and social factors that are largely beyond our control. Finally, acceptance can cover a whole spectrum of emotional attitudes, ranging from a mild state of depression accompanied by a perpetual attitude of pessimism to a rather bouyant optimism. Within such a wide range of possibilities most people seem to find a fairly comfortable niche; some are never quite happy unless they are constantly anticipating some improvement of their situation, no matter how slight, while others, anticipating very little, thrive on being happy with the little they already have. Who is to say what is best?

I suspect that a lot has to do with how we understand human nature. Most ancient philosophical systems, as well as modern psychological models, understand the human being as basically "homeostatic," that is, finding its well-being to consist in a balanced state of physical and psychological needs and their fulfillment. Thus, the classical Freudian and Adlerian systems of psychiatry held that the pleasure and power drives, respectively, and their proper satisfaction in terms of either gratification or self-actualization, were the key to human happiness and contentment. There can be no doubt that there is a great deal of basic truth in this, which can be ignored only at the risk of great possibility of human psychological distress. Yet I wonder if it can be the whole truth? Most of all, I wonder what conclusions such a view would lead to when it comes to the matter of accepting loss, suffering, and death?

Would not a "homeostatic" view of life necessarily entail a totally passive view of acceptance? Once the hope of personal fulfillment, understood in terms of the enjoyment of power or pleasure, seems no longer possible, at that point the logical thing to do would seem to be to simply "call it quits," to no longer try to accomplish anything, to resign oneself to being useless or even to rebel at being a burden on others. If any decisive act could be contemplated in such a situation as viewed from this sort of understanding of life, suicide would appear to be the most logical step. Fortunately, most of us are not too logical in the midst of such crises, or we sense our confusion enough to wisely postpone major decisions. In terms of our prevailing culture, this limited view of life's meaning and possibilities looms large when we are faced with such grimly curtailed possibilities. Usually, if given a chance and proper encouragement, the breakdown of such a homeostatic view may very well serve to spur us on to a new, more dynamic view of life and the reasons for living.

How describe such an expanded and dynamic view of life? There seems to be no single word for it. *Heterostatic* might be a step in that direction, except that *stasis* or state implies something much more fixed than the dynamic that I am attempting to describe. Besides, appeals to another, better state, especially when conceived in terms of another life beyond, can all too easily degenerate into just another state of passivity in the face of evil. On the contrary, what I have in mind is more along the lines of Viktor Frankl's dynamic view of human nature as seeking meaning beyond itself and its selfish concerns—a view that, in theological terms, one might aptly designate as *transcendental*. Whatever we wish to call it, it is a view that is definitely not homeostatic, and as such refuses to see the meaning of life in terms of egocentric "self-fulfillment," "self-actualization," or "happiness." It is not that it sees anything wrong in these, but on the contrary would promote them just as much as any "homeostatic" view only (and this is the major difference) by the paradoxical forgetting of or renunciation of these goals as ends in themselves! As Frankl is fond of pointing out again and again, happiness and fulfillment, if pursued, will never be found; instead, they can only "ensue," that is, occur as by-products of living our lives in pursuit of a meaning that transcends our own concerns for fulfillment or happiness. From this point of view, I think, *acceptance* becomes a very different thing from the passive concept that the word seems to imply or the negative thing that many take it to be.

Acceptance, understood in this way, is highly dynamic, even, up to a point, aggressive, for it is made up, in almost equal proportions, of humility and ambition! It is humble, first of all, in the root sense of the word, that is, of being "down-to-earth" or completely realistic. This view of acceptance acknowledges that we are limited beings, hemmed in by time, completely finite in our capacities. But its meaning is also ambitious in the sense that it includes longing for the absolute, for immortality, for infinity, and is brash enough to believe their achievement possible because it also believes that, while much depends on us, not everything depends on us alone. Hence what may seem, in naturalistic terms, an impossible conflict of principles, becomes transformed, in the eyes of faith, into a dynamic source of energy. *Acceptance* from this point of view is, in effect, an acceptance of the status quo only insofar as it serves to take us beyond it. And to this extent, it is an acceptance of ultimate risk.

Many find this hard to believe. Even for unbelievers, *faith* would represent a state of absolute security. Is it not "the substance of things hoped for," the certainty on which we can depend? Perhaps, but I think that this is true only in a very pardoxical way. Years ago, during my first assignment in pastoral work, I stopped one day in a hospital room to meet a young man, not because he was on my list of sick parishioners (which he wasn't) but because someone told me that I should if I wanted to meet someone of extraordinary faith. I had been told that the patient was dying of cystic fibrosis, a childhood disease that kills most of its victims well before adulthood. Having run into this depressing condition in the past, I was expecting the worst—or at best, an atmosphere of unworldly piety. On the contrary, I was surprised to meet a young man in his early twenties who, despite his weakened condition, was very much alive in the face of it all. Despite his chronic condition, with frequent stays in the hospital, he was, I was surprised to learn, a pre-med student at a local branch of one of our major state universities and he was very well versed on the statistics of his unlikely survival to earn his basic college degree. It was as if he had singlemindedly determined that he was going to do all he could possibly do to defeat this disease that had doomed him and so many others. There was little or no pious lugubriousness over his impending death (which he was very much aware of). Instead, he had determined to be a fighter till the last.

But at the same time there was an absolutely astounding sense of faith. It was as if the medical school plans were really but a symbol of something much deeper, a kind of risking of himself in an "impossible dream" that encapsulated a zest for life; but one sensed, almost immediately, that the zest was for something more than this life could ever offer him, something that could only be his if he lived his life to its very fullest. I came away feeling that here indeed was a young man of faith, not a faith that rested in a security of pious platitudes but a faith that risked itself reaching for an unknown beyond. In this faith there was manifested not so much a difference of quantity, such as between one of little faith and much faith, but of quality—between the fearfulness of the timid believer and the courage of the saint. The young man died not too many weeks later, but few who knew him will ever forget him.

Perhaps it was just a coincidence, but it proved to be one that also displayed an almost Telhardian note of "convergence," for about this time I first read Teilhard's *Divine Milieu* after having struggled, half-comprehending, through *The Phenomenon of Man.* Now that I look back on it, it was the experience of meeting this extraordinary young man in the hospital that exemplified and brought alive the very thing that Teilhard was insisting upon—that it is only after the activities of a life fully lived that the passivities of suffering can be made to yield their greatest fruit. It is not in any premature capitulation to defeat that a victory can be won. Rather, it is only when there has been a struggle against evil in all its forms up to the last possible moment, that acceptance of the inevitable becomes the moment of true sacrifice, the flames of which alone can transform our lives into a holocaust worthy of God. Only with this dynamic acceptance and self-giving can our lives and our work be transfigured into a lasting contribution to the Kingdom of God, an enduring part of the Body of Christ—our fullest contribution to the Pleroma, the fullness of God.

Bibliography

Ahern, M. B. *The Problem of Evil.* London: Routledge & Kegan Paul, 1971.

Allegra, Gabriel M., O. F. M. *My Conversations with Teilhard de Chardin on the Primacy of Christ: Peking, 1942–1945.* Chicago: Franciscan Herald Press, 1971.

Angeles, Peter, ed. *Critiques of God.* Buffalo, N.Y.: Prometheus Press, 1976.

Aquinas, Thomas. *Compendium of Theology.* Translated by Cyril Vollert. St. Louis: B. Herder Book Co., 1947.

——. *The Disputed Questions on Truth.* Translated from the definitive Leonine text by R. W. Mulligan (I–IX), J. V. McGlynn (X–XX), and R. W. Schmidt (XXI–XXIX). Chicago: H. Regnery, 1964.

——. *On the Truth of the Catholic Faith (Summa Contra Gentiles).* Translated with introduction and notes by Anton C. Pegis. Garden City, N.Y.: Doubleday, 1955. (Cf. esp. III, 71.)

——. *Summa Theologica.* Translated by the Fathers of the English Dominican Province. New York: Benzinger Brothers, 1947–1948. (Cf. esp. I, Q.25. a.6; Q.49).

Augustine, St. *The City of God.* (Cf. esp. Book XI, Sections 20–23; Book XII, Sections 3–7.) Translated by Marcus Dods. New York: Modern Library, 1950.

Austin, Bill. *The Back Side of God.* Wheaton, Ill.: Tyndale Press, n.d.

Austin, William H. *The Relevance of Natural Science to Theology.* New York: Barnes and Noble, 1976.

Baum, Gregory. *Man Becoming.* New York: Herder & Herder, 1970.

Becker, Ernest. *Escape from Evil.* New York: Free Press, 1975.

——. *The Denial of Death.* New York: Macmillan, 1973.

——. *The Structure of Evil.* New York: Brazilier, 1968.

Berdyaev, Nikolai. *The Destiny of Man.* Translated by Natalie Dudding-ton. New York: Harper & Row, 1960.

———. *Freedom and the Spirit.* Translated by Oliver Fielding Clarke. Freeport, N.Y.: Books for Libraries Press, 1972.

———. *Truth and Revelation.* Translated from the Russian by R. M. France. New York: Collier, 1962.

Berkhof, Hendrik. *Christ and the Powers.* Translated from the Dutch by John Howard Yoder. Scottsdale, Penna: Herald Press, 1962.

Bloch, Ernst. *Man on His Own: Essays in the Philosophy of Religion.* Translated by E. B. Ashton. New York: Herder & Herder, 1970.

Bonhoeffer, Dietrich. *The Cost of Discipleship.* Translated by R. H. Fuller with revisions by Irmgard Booth. New York: Macmillan, 1963.

Boyle, Joseph M. Jr., German Grisez, and Olaf Tollefsen. *Free Choice: A Self-Referential Argument.* Notre Dame, Ind.: Notre Dame University Press, 1976.

Buber, Martin. *Good and Evil.* Translated by Ronald Gregory Smith (Part I) and Michael Bullock (Part II). New York: Charles Scribner's Sons, 1953.

Camus, Albert. *The Fall.* Translated by Justin O'Brien. London: H. Hamilton, 1957.

———. *The Myth of Sisyphus and Other Essays.* Translated by Justin O'Brien. New York: Vintage Books, 1959.

Choron, Jacques. *Death and Western Thought.* New York: Collier, 1963.

Conlin, Connellan. *Why Does Evil Exist?* Hicksville, N.Y.: Exposition Press, 1974.

Danto, Arthur C. *Mysticism and Morality.* New York: Harper & Row, 1972.

DeCoursey, Mary Edwin, S. C. L. *The Theory of Evil in the Metaphysics of St. Thomas.* Washington, D.C.: Catholic University Press, 1948.

Deutsch, Eliot. *Advaita Vedānta: A Philosophical Reconstruction.* Honolulu: University Press of Hawaii, 1973.

Dillard, Annie. *Holy the Firm.* New York: Harper & Row, 1977.

Dobzhansky, Theodosius. *The Biology of Ultimate Concern.* London: Rapp Whitings, 1967.

Dostoyevsky, Feodor. *The Brothers Karamazov.* Translated by Constance Garnett. New York: Heritage Press, 1960.

———. *The Possessed.* Translated by Constance Garnett. New York: New American Library, 1962.

Eiseley, Loren. *The Invisible Pyramid.* New York: Random House, 1972.

————. *The Unexpected Universe.* New York: Harcourt Brace & World, 1966.

Frankl, Viktor. *Man's Search for Meaning.* Boston: Beacon Press, 1959.

————. *The Will to Meaning: Foundations and Applications of Logotherapy.* New York: New American Library, 1970.

Fromm, Erich. *Escape From Freedom.* New York: Discus/Avon, 1965.

————. *You Shall Be As Gods; A Radical Interpretation of the Old Testament and Its Traditions.* New York: Harcourt Brace & World, 1966.

Galligan, Michael. *God and Evil.* New York: Paulist Press, 1976.

Goudge, T. A. *The Ascent of Life: A Philosophical Study of the Theory of Evolution.* Toronto: University of Toronto Press, 1961.

Greenfield, Stephen A. "A Whiteheadian Perspective of the Problem of Evil: Whitehead's Understanding of Evil and Christian Theodicy." Ph.D. diss., Fordham University, New York, 1973.

Griffin, David Ray. *God, Power, and Evil: A Process Theodicy.* Philadelphia: Westminster Press, 1976.

————. *A Process Christology.* Philadelphia: Westminster Press, 1973.

Halle, Louis J. *Out of Chaos.* Boston: Houghton Mifflin, 1977.

Hartshorne, Charles. *Man's Vision of God.* New York: Harper & Row, 1965.

Hebblethwaite, Brian. *Evil, Suffering, and Religion.* New York: Hawthorne Books, 1976.

Heisenberg, Werner. *Physics and Beyond: Encounters and Conversations.* Translated from the German by Arnold J. Pomerans. New York: Harper & Row, 1971.

————. *Physics and Philosophy: The Revolution in Modern Science.* New York: Harper & Row, 1958.

Hick, John. *Evil and the God of Love.* London: Macmillan: New York: Harper & Row, 1966.

Huxley, Julian. *Evolution in Action.* New York: Harper & Row, 1957.

————. *Knowledge, Morality, & Destiny.* (Original Title: New Bottles for New Wine.) New York: New American Library, 1960.

Jones, Alexander, ed. *The Jerusalem Bible.* Garden City, N.Y.: Doubleday, 1966.

Kazantzakis, Nikos. *The Saviors of God.* Translated with introduction by Kimor Friar. New York: Simon & Schuster, 1960.

Kitamori, Kozah. *Theology of the Pain of God.* Translated by W. H. H. Norman from the Japanese original *Kami no itami no shingaku* (1958). Atlanta: John Knox Press, 1965.

Kropf, Richard W. *Teilhard, Scripture, and Revelation: A Study of Teilhard de Chardin's Reinterpretation of Pauline Themes.* Rutherford, Madison, Teaneck: Fairleigh Dickinson University Press, 1980.

Kübler-Ross, Elizabeth. *Questions and Answers on Death and Dying.* New York: Macmillan, 1962.

Kushner, Harold. *When Bad Things Happen to Good People.* New York: Schocken Books, 1982.

Lewis, C. S. *The Problem of Pain.* New York: Macmillan, 1962.

Madden, Edward H. and Peter H. Hare. *Evil and the Concept of God.* Springfield, Ill.: Chas. C. Thomas, Publisher, 1968.

Maloney, George A. S.J. *The Cosmic Christ: From Paul to Teilhard.* New York: Sheed & Ward, 1968.

Marcel, Gabriel. *Creative Fidelity.* Translated from the French by with introduction by Robert Rosthal. New York: Farrar Straus, 1964.

———. *Problematic Man.* Translated by Brian Thompson. New York: Herder & Herder, 1967.

———. *Tragic Wisdom and Beyond.* Translated by Stephen Jolin and Peter McCormick. Evanston, Ill.: Northwestern University Press, 1973.

Maritain, Jacques. *God and the Permission of Evil.* Translated by Joseph W. Evans. Milwaukee: Bruce Publishing Co., 1966.

Medawar, Peter B. & J. S. Medawar. *The Life Science.* New York: Harper & Row, 1977.

Merton, Thomas. *The Collected Poems of Thomas Merton.* New York: New Directions, 1977.

McCloskey, H. J. "God and Evil." *Philosophical Quarterly* 10, no. 39 (April, 1960), 97–114 (reprinted in Angeles, Peter, *Critiques of God,* cf. above).

Moltmann, Jürgen. *The Crucified God: The Cross of Christ as the Foundation and Criticism of Christian Theology.* Translated by R. A. Wilson and John Bowden. New York: Harper & Row, 1974.

———. *Theology of Hope: On the Ground and Implications of a Christian Eschatology.* Translated by James W. Leitch. New York: Harper & Row, 1967.

Monod, Jacques. *Chance and Necessity: An Essay on the Natural Philosophy of Modern Biology.* Translated from the French by Austryn Wainhouse. New York: Knopf, 1971.

Nogar, Raymond. *The Lord of the Absurd.* New York: Herder & Herder, 1967.

———. *The Wisdom of Evolution.* New York: Doubleday & Co., 1963.

Pannikar, Raimundo. *Myth, Faith, and Hermeneutics: Toward Cross-Cultural Religious Understanding.* New York: Paulist Press, 1980.

Petit, François. *The Problem of Evil.* Translated from the French by Christopher Williams. New York: Hawthorne Books, 1959.

Pieper, Josef. *Hope and History.* Translated by Richard and Clara Winston. New York: Herder & Herder, 1969.

Pike, Nelson, ed. *God and Evil.* Englewood Cliffs, N.J.: Prentice-Hall, 1964.

Plantinga, Alvin. *God, Freedom, and Evil.* New York: Harper & Row, 1974.

Rahner, Karl, ed. *The Encyclopedia of Theology: The Concise Sacramentum Mundi.* New York: Seabury Press, 1975.

Puligandla, R. *Fundamentals of Indian Philosophy* Nashville, New York: Abington Press, 1975.

Rahner, Karl. *Hominization: The Evolutionary Origin of Man as a Theological Problem.* Translated by William O'Hara. New York: Herder & Herder, 1966.

―――. *On the Theology of Death.* Translated by Charles H. Henkey. New York: Herder & Herder, 1961.

Ricoeur, Paul. *The Symbolism of Evil.* Translated from the French by Emerson Buchanan. Boston: Beacon Press, 1969.

Russell, Bertrand. *Mysticism and Logic.* New York: Doubleday/Anchor, 1957.

Sanford, John A. *Evil: The Shadow Side of Reality.* New York: Crossroad Publishing, 1981.

Sarano, J. *The Hidden Face of Pain.* Valley Forge, Penna.: Judson Press, 1970.

Schillebeeckx, Edward. *Jesus: An Experiment in Christology.* Translated by Hubert Hoskins. New York: The Seabury Press, 1979. Cf. esp. Part 4, Section 2, Chapter 2.

Schneidau, Herbert N. *Sacred Discontent: The Bible and Western Tradition.* Baton Rouge, La.: Louisiana State University Press, 1976.

Schilling, S. Paul. *God and Human Anguish.* Nashville, Tenn.: Abingdon Press, 1977.

Schoonenberg, Piet. *Man and Sin: A Theological View.* Translated by Joseph Donceel. Notre Dame, Ind.: Notre Dame University Press, 1965. See "Sin" in *Encyclopedia of Theology.* Cf. Rahner above.

Simpson, George Gaylord. *This View of Life.* New York: Harcourt Brace & World, 1964.

Siwek, Paul. *Le Problème du mal.* Rio de Janerio; Desclees de Brouwer et cie., 1942. (English version: *The Philosophy of Evil.* New York: Ronald Press, 1965.)

Skinner, B. F. *Beyond Freedom and Dignity.* New York: Bantam/Vintage, 1972.

Sontag, Frederick. *God, Why Did You Do That?.* Philadelphia: Westminster Press, 1970.

Taylor, Michael J., ed. *The Mystery of Suffering and Death.* New York: Doubleday, 1974.

Teilhard de Chardin, Pierre. *The Activation of Energy.* Translated by René Hague. London: Collins, 1970.

————. *Christianity and Evolution.* Translated by René Hague. London: Collins, 1971.

————. *The Divine Milieu.* Translated by Bernard Wall. New York: Harper & Brothers, 1960.

————. *The Future of Man.* Translated by Norman Denny. New York: Harper & Row, 1964.

————. *Human Energy.* Translated by J. M. Cohen, London: Collins, 1969.

————. *The Phenomenon of Man.* Translated by Bernard Wall. New York: Harper & Row, 1961.

————. *Science and Christ.* Translated by René Hague. New York: Harper & Row, 1965.

Towner, W. Sibley. *How God Deals With Evil.* Philadelphia: Westminster, 1976.

Tsanoff, Radoslav Andrean. *The Nature of Evil.* New York: Macmillan, 1931.

Ward, James. *The Realms of Ends: Or Pluralism and Theism.* Garden City, N.Y.: AMS (Natural History Press, division of Doubleday Press), 1978.

Weil, Simone. *A Simone Weil Reader.* Edited by George A. Panichas. New York: David McKay Co., Inc., 1977.

Whitehead, Alfred N. *Process and Reality.* New York: Harper & Row, 1961.

Wiesel, Eliezer. *Night.* Translated from the French by Stella Rodway. New York: Avon Press, 1972.

Wild, Robert. *Who I Will Be: Is There Joy and Suffering in God?.* Danville, N.J.: Dimension Books, 1976.

Index